Mr Todiwala's
SPICE BOX

Cyrus todiwala

Mr Todiwala's
SPICE BOX

120 recipes from just 10 spices

CYRUS TODIWALA

MITCHELL BEAZLEY

An Hachette UK Company
www.hachette.co.uk

First published in Great Britain in 2016 by Mitchell Beazley,
a division of Octopus Publishing Group Ltd,
Carmelite House, 50 Victoria Embankment,
London EC4Y 0DZ
www.octopusbooks.co.uk

Design & layout copyright © Octopus Publishing Group Ltd 2016
Text copyright © Cyrus Todiwala 2016
Photography copyright © Yuki Sugiura 2016

ISBN 978-1-78472-128-2

A CIP catalogue record for this book is available from the British Library.

Printed and bound in China.

10 9 8 7 6 5 4 3 2 1

Publisher's note
Standard level spoon measurements are used in all recipes.
1 tablespoon = one 15 ml spoon
1 teaspoon = one 5 ml spoon

Both imperial and metric measurements have been given in all recipes.
Use one set of measurements only and not a mixture of both.

Eggs should be medium unless otherwise stated.

Art Director and Designer: Yasia Williams-Leedham
Senior Editor: Leanne Bryan
Copy Editor: Trish Burgess
Photographer: Yuki Sugiura
Home Economist: Marina Filippelli
Prop Stylist: Alexander Breeze
Production Controller: Sarah Kramer

CONTENTS

Introduction

Professional chefs often make the mistake of assuming knowledge in their audience, and I must admit that I've been guilty of that myself. I've demonstrated recipes to audiences and students as though they will know exactly what I'm talking about, and forgotten that I have accumulated my knowledge and experience over many years. This book, a distillation of my collaborations with both great chefs and domestic cooks, aims to put that right. It offers simplified recipes and techniques for making many classic recipes, but it goes one step further than that and bases them around a selection of ten well-known spices – hence the *Spice Box* title of this book.

The criteria for including each spice in this book were versatility – the ways it could be used to cook a wide range of dishes – and accessibility – the ease of buying it. You don't need a vast array of seldom-used ingredients cluttering up your cupboard; just ten inexpensive and readily available spices will allow you to cook fantastic food whenever you like. A recipe for garam masala – made from ingredients in the Spice Box – can be found on page 58. And I am assuming that you will already have black peppercorns and white pepper in your larder.

You will notice that some traditional spices, such as fenugreek and nutmeg, are missing, but go ahead and add these or any other extras as you wish. My recipes are intended to get you started: they are not formulae set in stone. I want you to be inventive and bold, creating your own dish that shows off your personality.

The vital ten spices in my Spice Box are:

1. BLACK MUSTARD SEEDS

2. RED CHILLI

3. CUMIN

4. CORIANDER

5. TURMERIC

6. CARDAMOM

7. CLOVES

8. SAFFRON

9. CINNAMON

10. MACE

Some of my recipes include additional ingredients, such as curry leaves, that may occasionally be a bit difficult to track down. Don't let that worry you – simply try the dish without them, and when you do manage to find them, try the recipe again and notice the difference. Both versions will taste good, but the latter will be even better.

Herbs and other key fresh ingredients include:

FRESH CORIANDER

CURRY LEAVES (PREFERABLY FRESH)

GARLIC

FRESH ROOT GINGER

LIMES OR LEMONS

MINT LEAVES

ONIONS (ALL TYPES, INCLUDING SHALLOTS)

FRESH RED & GREEN CHILLIES

Most of the above are widely available these days and will be a great help when making your first foray into creating delicious Indian food.

Some of my recipes might look long at first glance, especially if they have separate marinades or sauces, but please don't be put off. They are really not complicated or daunting. My advice is to set out everything you require before you start and that will make the process much easier.

In many cases, the core ingredients – meat, poultry, fish, seafood or vegetables – can be substituted as you wish. Indeed, I want you to feel free to mix and match and try different ingredients. Apart from baking recipes, which do need to be precisely followed, most great dishes have been created through experimentation. At the very worst you might produce something rather different from the original recipe, but if it tastes good, what's the problem? Where I know for a fact that something, such as a marinade, works only with a particular ingredient, I have pointed it out so that you won't waste time and money.

Most recipes are a translation of the author's imagination, knowledge, experience and taste preferences, so they are highly personal. I hope you will enjoy my ideas, but most of all I want you to make them your own. That's the secret of great food.

Have fun!

SOUPS & STARTERS

BEETROOT ANI NAARL RASAM

Beetroot & coconut rasam

RASAM (PRONOUNCED 'RUSSUM'), AS THIS DISH IS COMMONLY KNOWN IN SOUTH INDIA, IS A VERY VERSATILE AND HEALTHY SOUP. IT IS GENERALLY SIPPED WITH THE MEAL TO ADD FLAVOUR, AND ACTS RATHER LIKE A DIGESTIVE. ALTHOUGH USUALLY MADE WITH LENTILS, THERE ARE MANY VARIATIONS WITHOUT, AND THE FLAVOURINGS ARE SIMILARLY VARIOUS. THE RECIPE BELOW IS A FAIRLY STANDARD VERSION, WITH MY OWN PARTICULAR TOUCHES.

SERVES 6

YELLOW OR PINK LENTILS (TOOR OR MASOOR DAAL) 150g (5½oz)

BEETROOT 400g (14oz), topped, tailed and thinly sliced

ONION 1 small, finely chopped

WATER 1–1.5 litres (1¾–2¾ pints)

GROUND TURMERIC ¼ teaspoon

SUNFLOWER OR EXTRA VIRGIN RAPESEED OIL 1 tablespoon

BLACK MUSTARD SEEDS ¼ teaspoon

CURRY LEAVES 10–12, preferably fresh, shredded; if using dried, soak in water for 10–12 minutes, and dry thoroughly before shredding

CORIANDER SEEDS 1 tablespoon, finely crushed

DRIED RED CHILLIES 2–3 large, whole

CUMIN SEEDS ¼ teaspoon

BLACK PEPPERCORNS 5–6

GARLIC 1 clove, crushed

TAMARIND PULP 2 tablespoons, or to taste, as some tamarind preparations are very strong

COCONUT MILK 1 × 400ml (14fl oz) can, well shaken

SALT

Wash the lentils well until the liquid clears. Transfer to a bowl, add enough water to cover by 2.5cm (1in) and leave to soak for a few hours.

Drain the lentils and place in a flameproof casserole dish. Add the beetroot, onion and measured water, followed by the turmeric and some salt. Bring to the boil, then partially cover and simmer until soft. Leave to cool a little, then blend the mixture with a blender to a purée or mash with a potato masher until free of lumps.

Heat the oil in a saucepan and add the mustard seeds. When they crackle, add the curry leaves, coriander seeds, chillies, cumin seeds and peppercorns and sauté over a medium heat for 3–4 minutes. Add the garlic and sauté until pale.

Add the puréed lentils and the tamarind pulp and bring slowly to the boil. Simmer, uncovered, for 10–15 minutes. Lightly whisk the coconut milk and stir it into the lentils. Discard the chillies if you wish.

Serve straight away or set aside and reheat later.

SOPA DE GOA / CALDO DE VERDURAS

Vegetable soup

PORTUGUESE IN ORIGIN, THIS SOUP WAS ADOPTED IN GOA AND THEN ADDED TO OVER THE YEARS, SO THERE ARE MANY DIFFERENT VERSIONS. THAT'S THE GREAT THING ABOUT SOUPS – THEY'RE EASY TO MAKE AND YOU CAN IMPOSE YOUR OWN STYLE ON THEM.

SERVES 6

EXTRA VIRGIN RAPESEED OIL 2 tablespoons

CUMIN SEEDS 1 heaped teaspoon

FRESH GREEN CHILLIES 1–2, coarsely chopped

GARLIC 4–5 cloves, chopped

ONION 1, chopped

BUTTER 30–40g (1–1½oz)

BAY LEAVES 2–3

CELERY 1 stick, destringed and chopped

POTATOES 2–3 large, cut into chunks

LEEKS 2, slit in half lengthways, cleaned and thinly sliced

MILK 200–300ml (7–10fl oz)

CHICKEN STOCK 1–1.4 litres (1¾–2½ pints)

FRESH KALE OR OTHER GREENS 1 handful of leaves

FRESH SPINACH 12–15 leaves, finely shredded

SINGLE CREAM 200ml (7fl oz)

FRESH CORIANDER 1 small handful, chopped

SALT AND FRESHLY GROUND BLACK PEPPER

TO SERVE

CHOPPED FRESH CHIVES OR SPRING ONION GREENS 1 tablespoon

FRESH CORIANDER a few leaves

EXTRA VIRGIN OLIVE OIL for drizzling

CROUTONS (see opposite) OR TOAST

Heat the oil in a flameproof casserole dish or saucepan and add the cumin seeds. Once they sizzle and give off a lovely aroma, add the chillies, garlic and onion, cover and sweat until the onion is pale. Add the butter and bay leaves. When the butter has melted, add the celery, potatoes and leeks and sauté for 6–8 minutes.

Pour in the milk and stock and bring gently to the boil, then simmer for 15–20 minutes, or until the potatoes are soft. Add the kale or other greens and spinach and simmer for 1–2 minutes.

Discard the bay leaves and allow the soup to cool a little, before puréeing it with a blender or passing it through a sieve. Return it to the pan, season with salt and pepper and stir in the cream and coriander. Reheat very gently.

To serve, sprinkle each serving with the chopped chives or spring onion greens, some fresh coriander leaves and a drizzle of olive oil. Scatter a few Croutons on top, or serve with toast.

Note

If using spring onions for garnish, the white parts can be added to the soup instead of the leeks.

GYMKHANA SOUP

Giblet soup

WHEN THE BRITISH ARMY WAS IN INDIA, GIBLET SOUP WAS OFTEN SERVED IN THE MESS HALLS, AND ITS GREY APPEARANCE GAVE RISE TO ITS NICKNAME – 'THE COLONEL'S DIRTY SOCK WATER'. NONETHELESS, IT HAD THE VIRTUES OF BEING VERY TASTY AND REALLY CHEAP. THE VERSION BELOW DOES NOT USE ALL THE OFFAL THAT ORIGINALLY WENT INTO THE SOUP – JUST SOME KIDNEY AND LIVER, PLUS A LITTLE DICED BEEF. THE SOUP IS SUPPOSED TO BE SOMEWHERE BETWEEN A CLEAR CONSOMMÉ AND A FRENCH ONION SOUP, BUT WITH RED CHILLI AND FRESH CORIANDER GIVING IT A BIT MORE OOMPH.

SERVES 6–8

EXTRA VIRGIN RAPESEED OIL
2 tablespoons

CLOVES 3–4

CUMIN SEEDS 1 heaped teaspoon

DRIED RED CHILLIES 2 large, deseeded and cut into 4 pieces

ONIONS 2 small, finely chopped

GARLIC 3 cloves, crushed

FRESH GREEN CHILLI 1, deseeded and very finely chopped

LEAN STEWING BEEF 250g (9oz), chopped into 5mm (¼in) cubes

BEEF STOCK 3–4 litres (5¼–7 pints)

STALE BREAD 6–8 crustless slices

LAMBS' LIVER 150–200g (5½–7oz), chopped into 5mm (¼in) cubes

LAMBS' KIDNEYS 3–4, any outer membranes and white cores removed, then chopped into 5mm (¼in) cubes

BUTTER for spreading

CHEDDAR CHEESE 50g (1¾oz) grated, for sprinkling (optional)

CHOPPED FRESH CORIANDER 1 heaped tablespoon

FRESH MINT 8–10 leaves, finely shredded

SALT AND FRESHLY GROUND BLACK PEPPER

LIME OR LEMON WEDGES 6–8, to serve

Heat the oil in a flameproof casserole dish or saucepan and fry the cloves over a medium heat for 2 minutes. Add the cumin seeds and, as soon as they change colour, add the red chillies and sauté until they change colour too.

Add the onions and sauté until deep brown. Spoon off and reserve a tablespoon or so of the oil in the pan, then add the garlic, green chilli and beef. Cook until the meat has browned, then add the stock. Bring to the boil and season with salt and pepper. Cover and simmer for 20–25 minutes, until the beef is tender.

Meanwhile, preheat the oven to 140°C/275°F/Gas Mark 1 and prepare your croutons. Cut each slice of bread into 6–8 cubes and arrange in a single layer on a baking tray. Place on the top shelf of the oven for 3–4 minutes, until browned, then turn them over and brown the other side.

While the croutons are browning, heat the reserved onion oil in a heavy-based frying pan and sauté the liver and kidneys, stirring to prevent sticking. Once seared, let them brown well, turning from time to time. Drain well on kitchen paper, then add them to the soup. Taste and adjust the seasoning as necessary.

Remove the bread from the oven and lower the temperature to 120°C/250°F/Gas Mark ½. Butter the croutons generously, then return them to the oven, this time on the middle shelf so that the butter doesn't burn. After 6–8 minutes, switch off the oven, leaving the croutons inside. Sprinkle them with the grated cheese, if you wish, and let it soften a bit before serving.

Just before serving the soup, discard the red chilli pieces and cloves, then stir in the coriander and mint. Serve each bowlful with a wedge of lime or lemon and a few croutons, either sprinkled on top or offered separately.

SHAKARKAND, KADDU AUR DAAL KA SOUP

Roasted sweet potato, pumpkin & lentil soup

SIMPLE THOUGH IT IS, THIS SOUP IS REALLY TASTY AND LENDS ITSELF TO CREATIVITY WITH THE FLAVOURINGS.

SERVES 5–6

YELLOW OR PINK LENTILS (TOOR OR MASOOR DAAL) 100g (3½oz)

RED SQUASH OR ANY OTHER SQUASH 250–300g (9–10½oz), unpeeled, cut in half and seeds removed

SWEET POTATO 1 small, unpeeled

ONION 1

GARLIC 2–3 cloves, peeled

EXTRA VIRGIN RAPESEED OIL 2 tablespoons

RED CHILLI POWDER 1 teaspoon

CUMIN SEEDS 1 teaspoon

CORIANDER SEEDS 1 teaspoon

BUTTER 30g (1oz)

FRESH GREEN CHILLI 1, slit lengthways into 4 strips

WATER 500ml (18fl oz)

SEA SALT

FRESHLY GROUND BLACK PEPPER (optional)

TO SERVE

CHOPPED FRESH CORIANDER 1 tablespoon

SINGLE CREAM for swirling (optional)

PLAIN COOKED LONG-GRAIN RICE (optional)

Wash the lentils well until the liquid clears. Transfer to a bowl, add enough water to cover by 2.5cm (1in) and leave to soak for at least 1–2 hours, but longer if possible.

Preheat the oven to 150°C/300°F/Gas Mark 2.

Cut the squash, sweet potato, onion and garlic into small pieces and place in a roasting tray. Add the oil and toss to coat. Mix in some sea salt, the chilli powder and cumin and coriander seeds, and roast for 20–25 minutes, turning now and again, until the vegetable skins are soft and lightly coloured.

Meanwhile, melt the butter gently in a saucepan. When foaming, add the green chilli and sauté for 1 minute. Add the lentils and their soaking liquid plus the measured water and bring gently to the boil. (If done too briskly, foam will rise to the surface and need to be skimmed off, which will take some of the butter with it.) Cover and simmer for 20 minutes, or until the lentils are fully cooked.

Add the roasted vegetables, scraping everything off the tray, and bring to the boil again. Purée the mixture with a blender to a smooth soup – a few bits will remain, but these add a pleasant texture. If you prefer the soup to be completely smooth, pass it through a fine sieve.

Taste and adjust the seasoning as necessary. Serve sprinkled with the fresh coriander, plus a swirl of cream and/or some plain long-grain rice, if you wish.

KHAEKDA NAY BATATA NO PATTICE

Crab & potato cakes with mustard & cumin

CRAB IS POPULAR NOT ONLY IN COASTAL REGIONS OF INDIA, BUT ALSO INLAND, WHERE FRESHWATER CRABS THRIVE ALONG RIVERBEDS, YET THE LATTER LACK THE DEPTH OF FLAVOUR OF THEIR SEAFARING COUSINS. THE RECIPE BELOW WORKS BEST WITH A COMBINATION OF WHITE AND BROWN CRABMEAT IN A 70:30 OR 80:20 RATIO.

SERVES 3–4 AS A MAIN COURSE OR 6–8 AS A STARTER OR CANAPÉ

EXTRA VIRGIN RAPESEED OIL
4 tablespoons

BLACK MUSTARD SEEDS ½ teaspoon

WHITE LENTILS (URAD DAAL) OR
YELLOW SPLIT PEAS (CHANNA DAAL)
1 heaped teaspoon

CUMIN SEEDS ½ teaspoon

CHOPPED FRESH ROOT GINGER
1 tablespoon

CHOPPED FRESH GREEN CHILLI
1 tablespoon

RED SHALLOTS 6, or 2 small red onions,
finely chopped

FRESHLY GRATED COCONUT
2 tablespoons, or 1 heaped tablespoon
desiccated coconut soaked in enough
warm water to just cover for 30 minutes

DICED TOMATO 1 tablespoon

WHITE CRABMEAT 250–300g (9–10½oz)

BROWN CRABMEAT 1–2 tablespoons

CHOPPED FRESH CORIANDER
1 heaped tablespoon

FLOURY POTATOES 3 large, roughly cubed

CURRY LEAVES 12–14, preferably fresh,
shredded; if using dried, soak in water for
10–12 minutes, and dry thoroughly before
shredding (optional)

EGGS 3–4

PLAIN FLOUR for dusting

RICE FLOUR, MEDIUM SEMOLINA OR
WHITE BREADCRUMBS 200g (7oz)

SALT AND FRESHLY GROUND BLACK PEPPER

SPICED MAYONNAISE (see page 22),
garnished with red chilli powder, to serve

Prepare and set out all your ingredients in the order listed.

Heat half the oil in a wok until nearly at smoking point, then reduce the heat to medium. Add the mustard seeds and hold a lid loosely above them so that they don't go all over the place when they crackle and pop. The moment you get a nutty aroma and the popping reduces, add the lentils. Stir, watching until they change colour slightly, then immediately add the cumin seeds. Continue heating and stirring until the lentils turn a little brown, but do not let them burn.

Add the ginger, chilli and shallots, and sauté until the shallots become soft and pale. Mix in the coconut and sauté for 2–3 minutes, stirring with a wooden spatula to prevent sticking. The idea is to drive off some of the moisture and lightly toast the coconut.

Lightly stir in the tomato, then add the crabmeats, stirring until heated through. Add the coriander and salt to taste. Transfer to a dish and set aside to cool.

Meanwhile, bring a large pan of water to the boil. When boiling, add some salt and the potatoes, and cook for about 8–10 minutes, until tender. Drain well, then return the potatoes to the pan and place them over a low heat, stirring with a wooden spatula from the bottom up until they look dry, slightly crushed and fluffy. Pass through a ricer or mash with a potato masher until free of lumps. Season with salt, pepper and the curry leaves, if using. Set aside to cool.

There are 2 ways to make the crab cakes. The first is to mix the potato and crab mixture together, then form it into small patties of whatever size you like. The second is the Indian way, which is to roll the mashed potato into balls of the preferred size, flatten them in the palm of your hand, add a tablespoon of the crab mixture, then carefully envelop in the potato. Whichever method you use, make sure the cakes are smooth and free of cracks before the next step.

Beat the eggs in a shallow bowl until fully combined. Place the plain flour in a second bowl and the rice flour, semolina or breadcrumbs in a third. Taking one cake at a time, dip it first in the egg, then in the second bowl and finally in the third.

Heat the remaining 2 tablespoons oil in a frying pan. When hot, fry the cakes on each side until brown. Drain on kitchen paper and serve with Spiced Mayonnaise.

FRITADA DE OSTRAS

Goan-style fried oysters with a choice of dressings

FLASH-FRIED OYSTERS COATED IN SEMOLINA ARE FAMOUS IN GOA, BUT WHY ARE THEY USUALLY FRIED? BECAUSE MOST OF THEM ARE WILD AND LIVE IN CLUMPS ON ROCKS, WHICH MEANS THEY CANNOT BE INDIVIDUALLY HARVESTED AND MUST THEREFORE BE SHUCKED. NONETHELESS, THEY'RE STILL YUMMY, AND I LIKE TO EXPERIMENT WITH DIFFERENT FLAVOURS AND SEASONINGS TO MAKE THEM EVEN MORE TANTALIZING. SOME OF MY FAVOURITES APPEAR OPPOSITE AND ON PAGE 22, BUT FRIED OYSTERS MAY ALSO BE SERVED WITH FRESH GREEN CHUTNEY (SEE PAGE 176).

SERVES 4 AS A STARTER

FRESHLY SHUCKED OYSTERS
4–5 per person

GROUND TURMERIC ½ teaspoon

LIME JUICE 1 squeeze

PIRI-PIRI MASALA (see page 207)
1 tablespoon per 20 oysters, finely
puréed, or **RED CHILLI POWDER**
1 tablespoon

GROUND CUMIN 1 teaspoon

GROUND CORIANDER 2 teaspoons

CLOVES 2, toasted and ground
(see page 56)

FRESH ROOT GINGER 5cm (2in)
piece, peeled and chopped

GARLIC 3 cloves, crushed

CIDER OR PALM VINEGAR
2 tablespoons, plus extra if needed

PLAIN FLOUR 2–3 tablespoons

MEDIUM SEMOLINA 100–150g
(3½–5½oz)

EGGS 2, beaten

EXTRA VIRGIN RAPESEED OIL
for frying

YOUR CHOICE OF DRESSING
(see opposite, and on page 22)

SALT AND FRESHLY GROUND
BLACK PEPPER

SALAD to serve (optional)

Place the oysters in a bowl, add the turmeric and lime juice and set aside to marinate. After 30 minutes, add the Piri-Piri Masala or red chilli powder.

Put the cumin, coriander and cloves in a mortar, add the ginger, garlic and vinegar and pound until as smooth as possible. Add a little more vinegar if necessary to make it a thick paste.

Stir the mixture into the marinated oysters, then check and adjust the seasoning. Place in a lidded plastic container and refrigerate for at least 3 hours.

When you're ready to cook the oysters, place the flour, semolina and eggs in 3 separate shallow bowls. Line a tray with kitchen paper.

Shake any excess moisture off the oysters and gently turn them in the flour to coat well. Taking one at a time, dip them next into the egg and then in the semolina. Press the coating lightly on both sides, dusting off any excess semolina. (If you want them extra crispy, you can roll them twice in the semolina.) When you've prepared about half, place a 1cm (½in) depth of oil in a frying pan over a medium heat. While it's heating, finish coating the remaining oysters, then start gently reheating the Spicy Tomato Sauce, if using.

When the oil is hot, add a small batch of the oysters and cook for just 20 seconds on each side: they should be crisp outside and juicy in the middle. Transfer to the prepared tray to drain. Cook the remaining oysters in the same way.

To serve, pour a little of your chosen dressing on to each serving plate and sit a few fried oysters on top. (If you want to serve the dish with a little salad, put it on the plates before pouring the dressing and adding the oysters.)

FOR DRESSING 1

Spicy tomato sauce

EXTRA VIRGIN OLIVE OIL 3 tablespoons
DRIED RED CHILLIES 2–3, each cut into 2 or 3 pieces
CINNAMON STICK 2 × 5cm (2in) pieces
GARLIC 4 cloves, finely chopped
FRESH GREEN CHILLIES 2 finger-type, finely chopped
BAY LEAVES 2–3
ONION 1, finely chopped
RED CHILLI POWDER 1 teaspoon
CIDER OR PALM VINEGAR 2–3 teaspoons, or to taste
WATER 2 tablespoons
CHOPPED TOMATOES 1 × 400g (14oz) can
MUSCOVADO SUGAR 1 teaspoon, or JAGGERY a small piece
SALT AND FRESHLY GROUND BLACK PEPPER

Heat the olive oil in a frying pan until hot but not smoking. Add the red chillies and cinnamon stick and fry over a medium heat until the chillies darken. Add the garlic, green chillies and bay leaves, and sauté until the garlic becomes pale golden.

Add the onion and sauté until pale and soft. Stir in the red chilli powder, vinegar and measured water, and continue cooking until the vinegar evaporates.

Mix in the tomatoes and sugar, then cover and simmer until the sauce has thickened to your liking. You can now purée the sauce with a blender, if you like, discarding the red chilli pieces and cinnamon stick if you wish. If you do decide to purée, cook the sauce a bit longer before puréeing. Season and set aside until needed. If storing, pour the sauce into a clean sterilized container, allow to cool without a lid, then chill (still uncovered), until cold. After that, cover and keep refrigerated.

This dressing can be made well in advance, and also goes with other things, such as Crab and Potato Cakes with Mustard and Cumin (see page 18), so why not make a double quantity? In that case, add 1–2 tablespoons extra oil and vinegar and store it tightly covered in the refrigerator. It will keep for up to 10 days if a little oil is poured on top.

FOR DRESSING 2

Soya nahm pla & chilli

FRESH ROOT GINGER 2.5cm (1in) piece, peeled and very finely chopped
LIGHT SOY SAUCE 100ml (3½fl oz)
NAHM PLA (THAI FISH SAUCE) 2 teaspoons
FRESH GREEN CHILLI 1 finger-type, deseeded and very finely chopped
RED CHILLI POWDER ½ teaspoon
MUSCOVADO SUGAR 1 teaspoon, or to taste
FRESH CORIANDER 3–4 sprigs, very finely chopped

Crush the chopped ginger in a mortar. Transfer to a small piece of muslin, twist tightly and squeeze the juice into a small bowl. Discard the solids left in the cloth, or leave to dry and use for tea.

Add all the remaining ingredients to the bowl and mix until the sugar dissolves. Taste and add more sugar if you wish. Transfer to a dropper-type bottle (if you have one) and dot or spoon a little of the dressing over each oyster.

This dressing keeps well, so make as much as you like and store it in a small bottle or plastic container in the refrigerator.

FOR DRESSING 3

Lime, red chilli & sweet basil dressing

LIME JUICE from 1 lime

RICE VINEGAR OR WHITE WINE VINEGAR
3 tablespoons

FRESH RED CHILLIES 2, finely chopped,
seeds included

WHITE SUGAR 1 teaspoon

BOILING WATER 150ml (5fl oz)

SWEET THAI BASIL leaves from 4–5 sprigs

FRESH CORIANDER leaves from 2–3 sprigs

FRESH MINT 10–12 leaves

CUMIN SEEDS ½ teaspoon, toasted and
crushed (see page 56)

TABASCO SAUCE (optional)

SALT

Put the lime juice and vinegar in a bowl. Add the red chillies and sugar, then pour in the measured boiling water. Stir well.

Crush the basil, coriander and mint leaves in a mortar and stir them into the chilli mixture with the cumin. Add salt to taste, then set aside to infuse for a few hours. Taste to check the flavour, and if you'd like it spicier, add a few drops of Tabasco.

This dressing keeps well if stored in a sealed bottle or plastic container in the refrigerator. Apart from being a great accompaniment to fried seafood, it's good with many other dishes too.

FOR DRESSING 4

Spiced mayonnaise

ENGLISH MUSTARD PASTE 2 tablespoons

WORCESTERSHIRE SAUCE 2 tablespoons

TOMATO KETCHUP 2 tablespoons

FRESH GREEN CHILLIES 1–2 finger-type,
deseeded and finely chopped

RED CHILLI POWDER 1 teaspoon

GARLIC 2 cloves, finely chopped

FINELY CHOPPED FRESH CORIANDER
1 tablespoon, finely chopped

HOMEMADE OR SHOP-BOUGHT MAYONNAISE
200g (7oz)

LIME JUICE to taste (optional)

SALT AND FRESHLY GROUND BLACK PEPPER

Combine the mustard, Worcestershire sauce, ketchup, chillies, chilli powder, garlic and coriander in a bowl and mix well with a spoon, almost beating them together, until the flavours are amalgamated.

Put the mayonnaise into a separate bowl and fold in the mustard mixture. Taste and season if necessary. Most ready-made mayonnaise is quite sharp because it contains acidic stabilizing agents, so it does need good seasoning. A few drops of lime juice might actually help too.

Baked doughnuts with prawns, chorizo & cheese

THIS RECIPE MIGHT SOUND A BIT ODD, BUT THE UNSWEETENED DOUGHNUT MIXTURE COMBINED WITH SAVOURY INGREDIENTS WORKS REALLY WELL. THE AIM IS TO PRODUCE SOMETHING LIGHT AND FLUFFY, BUT AS FLOURS DIFFER AND THE FAT CONTENT OF CHORIZO IS VARIABLE, THE TEXTURE OF THE FINAL DOUGHNUTS MAY SOMETIMES BE DENSER. IN ORDER TO MINIMIZE THE RISK OF THIS, BUY THE LEAST FATTY CHORIZO YOU CAN FIND AND DO EXPERIMENT WITH DIFFERENT TYPES. ONCE YOU'VE MASTERED THIS RECIPE, PLAY AROUND WITH IT TO FIND A FORMULA THAT PLEASES YOU. NOTE THAT YOU DO NEED TO HAVE A RING DOUGHNUT BAKING TRAY.

MAKES 12

SELF-RAISING FLOUR 200g (7oz)

MILK 200ml (7fl oz)

BUTTER (PREFERABLY UNSALTED) 150g (5½oz), at room temperature

EGGS 3

CHORIZO 100g (3½oz), skinned and finely chopped

RAW PEELED PRAWNS 100g (3½oz), finely chopped

HARD CHEESE, SUCH AS CHEDDAR OR PARMESAN 50g (1¾oz), finely grated

FRESH GREEN CHILLIES 2, finely chopped

SNIPPED DRIED RED CHILLI ½ teaspoon

FRESHLY GROUND BLACK PEPPER ½ teaspoon

Preheat the oven to 160°C/325°F/Gas Mark 3. Set out your ring doughnut baking tray (depending on size, you might need to bake the doughnuts in 2 batches).

Put the flour, milk, butter and eggs into a bowl and beat until you have a smooth batter, then pass through a sieve to remove any lumps. Stir in the remaining ingredients, then pour the batter evenly into the tray. Bake for 12–15 minutes, until risen and brown.

Transfer to a wire rack as soon as possible to prevent the doughnuts sweating in their hot tray.

Enjoy as a starter with a creamy sauce or simple curry, or eat just as they are.

MACHLI AMRITSARI

Fillet of white fish in spiced chickpea batter

RECIPES FOR THIS MOST POPULAR OF INDIA'S BATTERED FISH ABOUND, AND THERE MUST BE AT LEAST A HUNDRED VARIATIONS. WE FEEL THAT THE FLAVOURS USED IN OUR VERSION BELOW WORK BEST. USE ANY FIRM WHITE-FLESHED FISH, SUCH AS HADDOCK, GREY MULLET, SEA BASS, HALIBUT OR COLEY.

SERVES 4–5 AS A STARTER

SKINLESS FILLETS OF WHITE FISH 700–800g (1lb 9oz–1lb 12oz), cut into 7.5 × 7.5cm (3 × 3in) pieces about 1cm (½in) thick (you might have to slice thick fillets horizontally too)

CHICKPEA (GRAM) FLOUR 6 tablespoons

EXTRA VIRGIN RAPESEED OIL for frying

SALT

FOR THE MARINADE

THICK GREEK YOGURT 3 tablespoons

GINGER AND GARLIC PASTE (see page 199) 1½ tablespoons

CORIANDER SEEDS 1 heaped teaspoon, toasted and crushed (see page 56)

CUMIN SEEDS 1 teaspoon, toasted and crushed (see page 56)

RED CHILLI POWDER 1 teaspoon, or to taste

GROUND TURMERIC ½ teaspoon

CHOPPED FRESH GREEN CHILLI 1 heaped teaspoon

CHOPPED FRESH CORIANDER 1 heaped tablespoon

LIME JUICE 1 teaspoon

SALT 1 teaspoon, or to taste

FRESHLY GROUND WHITE OR BLACK PEPPER ½ teaspoon

TO SERVE

LIME WEDGES (optional)

CRISP GREEN SALAD WITH SLICED RED ONION

Combine all the marinade ingredients in a bowl and mix thoroughly. Rub the mixture well into the fish, then place in a dish, cover and chill for up to 1 hour.

Sift the chickpea flour over the fish and work it into the marinade so that it forms a batter and completely covers each piece of fillet.

Heat about 1–2cm (½–¾in) of oil in a frying pan and fry a few pieces of fish at a time, until crisp and well coloured. Take care not to overdo it, as fish cooks very fast.

Sprinkle with salt and serve with a wedge of lime, if you wish, and a nice crisp salad containing sliced red onion.

SHINANIO ANI TISREO NAARL GHALUN

Shinanio mussels & clams with coconut

BEING PLENTIFUL AND RELATIVELY CHEAP, MUSSELS AND CLAMS ARE VERY POPULAR AROUND THE WORLD, NOT LEAST IN GOA. HERE WE HAVE COOKED THEM WHOLE, TO BE SCOOPED OUT AT THE TABLE, BUT YOU COULD HALF-SHELL THEM IF YOU WISH. IN GOA DURING THE MANGO SEASON, THE EMPTY HALF-SHELLS ARE DUMPED UNDER READY-TO-PICK MANGO TREES, WHERE THEY ATTRACT ALL THE LARGE RED BULLY ANTS, LEAVING THE PICKERS TO DO THEIR WORK UNHAMPERED.

THE MARINADE BELOW CONTAINS TURMERIC BECAUSE IT KILLS BACTERIA, AND IS AN EXCELLENT COAGULANT, PREVENTING THE SEAFOOD FROM RELEASING TOO MUCH LIQUID. IN FACT, TURMERIC IS MIRACULOUS STUFF – IT CAN STOP HEAVY BLEEDING (USEFUL IN CASE OF KITCHEN ACCIDENTS) AND EVEN BE USED AS AN EMERGENCY REPAIR ON A RUPTURED CAR RADIATIOR!

SERVE THIS DISH ON ITS OWN OR WITH SOME PLAIN RICE AND PLAIN CURRY (BY WHICH I MEAN A SIMPLE CURRY CONTAINING NO MEAT OR VEGETABLES).

SERVES 4 AS A STARTER

MUSSELS 16 large, whole or on the half-shell

LARGE CLAMS 32, whole or on the half-shell

LIME JUICE from ½ lime

GROUND TURMERIC ½ teaspoon

EXTRA VIRGIN RAPESEED OIL 2 tablespoons

CURRY LEAVES 12–15, preferably fresh, shredded; if using dried, soak in water for 10–12 minutes, and dry thoroughly before shredding

DRIED RED CHILLIES 2, broken into small pieces

CUMIN SEEDS ½ teaspoon

GARLIC 4 cloves, crushed

ONIONS 2, finely chopped

FRESHLY GRATED COCONUT from ½ coconut, or 250g (9oz) frozen, defrosted before use

CHOPPED FRESH CORIANDER 2 tablespoons

SALT

Wash and scrub the mussels and clams, pulling away any beards from the mussels. Drain. Tip into a bowl, add the lime juice, turmeric and some salt and toss well.

Pour 1 tablespoon of the oil into a frying pan and heat until hazy. Add the curry leaves, red chillies and cumin seeds and stir until their fragrance is released. Add the garlic and fry for 1 minute, then add the onions and cook until soft and pale.

Stir in the coconut and cook for about 5 minutes, scraping the pan often, as it sticks easily.

Heat the remaining oil in a separate large frying pan. When smoking hot, add the mussels and clams, reserving the juices. Fry briskly for 3–4 minutes, or until all the shells have opened if using whole shellfish (discard any that remain closed), stirring or tossing occasionally so that all the shellfish come into contact with the heat, but do not overcook. (For a lovely variation, fry some black mustard seeds in the oil before cooking the seafood.)

Stir the reserved juices into the coconut mixture, then add the cooked shellfish and coriander and stir again. Taste and adjust the salt if necessary.

Serve the dish straight away. It's easiest to eat the shellfish with your fingers, which is messy but quite an experience.

SARDINHAS MARINADAS

Marinated sardines

WE HAVE BEEN SERVING MARINATED, NEARLY PICKLED, SARDINES OR SARDINE FILLETS IN OUR RESTAURANTS FOR YEARS, AND VERY POPULAR THEY ARE TOO. THEY ARE DELICIOUS WITH TOAST AS A CANAPÉ, OR CAN BE CHOPPED AND MADE INTO A PASTE. IN FACT, THE POSSIBILITIES ARE ENDLESS, SO USE YOUR IMAGINATION. THEY WILL KEEP FOR WEEKS IN THE REFRIGERATOR AS LONG AS THE OIL LEVEL REMAINS ABOVE THE SARDINES.

SERVES 15 AS A SNACK

WHOLE SARDINES 1kg (2lb 4oz), cleaned, scaled and filleted by your fishmonger

FOR THE MARINADE
OLIVE OIL 300ml (10fl oz)
WHITE WINE VINEGAR 1–2 tablespoons
LIME JUICE from 2 limes
GARLIC 6 cloves, crushed
FRESH GREEN CHILLIES 2–3 finger-type, chopped
CORIANDER STEMS from 1 bunch, chopped
SALT ½ tablespoon, or to taste
RED CHILLI POWDER 2 teaspoons
CUMIN SEEDS 1½ teaspoons, crushed

Combine all the marinade ingredients in a blender and whiz to a purée. Taste and adjust the seasoning. A little extra salt will help to preserve the fish.

Wash the sardines, drain them well and pat them dry with kitchen paper.

Stir the marinade, then pour some into the bottom of a baking dish. Arrange a layer of sardines on top, skin-side down, and spoon a little more marinade over them. Continue making layers in the same way until all the fish have been used and they are submerged in the marinade. Cover and place in the refrigerator for at least 8–10 hours.

Preheat the oven to its lowest setting and place the baking dish on the middle shelf for 30–40 minutes.

Set the fish aside to cool, then layer them into a lidded plastic container. The sardines are very delicate at this stage, so careful handling is necessary. Chill thoroughly and leave to mature for 1–2 days before using.

CHETTINAD KOZHI VARUVAL TIKKA

Hot pepper-flavoured chicken tikka

KOZHI (SOMETIMES PRONOUNCED 'KOHDLI' WITH A VIRTUALLY SILENT 'D') IS A SOUTH INDIAN CLASSIC, AND IS NOT NORMALLY A TIKKA OR CHARGRILLED RECIPE. HOWEVER, I THINK GRILLING IT PRESERVES THE ZING AND WORKS RATHER WELL, THOUGH I'M AWARE IT MIGHT UPSET TRADITIONALISTS. AS WITH ALL MARINATED DISHES, LETTING THE MEAT SIT OVERNIGHT GIVES IT THE BEST FLAVOUR.

SERVES 6 AS A SNACK OR STARTER

BONELESS, SKINLESS CHICKEN 600g (1lb 5oz) leg and breast meat, cut into 3–4cm (1¼–1½in) cubes

GINGER AND GARLIC PASTE (see page 199) 1½ tablespoons

GROUND CORIANDER 1½ tablespoons

GROUND TURMERIC 1 teaspoon

RED CHILLI POWDER 1 tablespoon

THICK GREEK YOGURT 2 heaped tablespoons

CINNAMON STICK 5cm (2in) piece, broken into small bits

GREEN CARDAMOM PODS
3–4, lightly crushed

CLOVES 2–3

CUMIN SEEDS 1 teaspoon

DRIED BAY LEAVES 3–4

EXTRA VIRGIN RAPESEED OIL
2 tablespoons

RED OR PINK ONION 1, chopped

CURRY LEAVES 8–10, preferably fresh, finely chopped; if using dried, soak in water for 10–12 minutes, and dry thoroughly before chopping

TOMATO PURÉE 1 tablespoon

WATER 50–100ml (2–3½fl oz)

LIME JUICE 2 teaspoons

BLACK PEPPERCORNS 2–3 teaspoons, crushed

SALT

TO SERVE (optional)
MIXED RAITA (see page 194)
HOT BUTTERED BREAD such as sourdough, or NAAN (see page 173)

Put the chicken in a bowl and add half the Ginger and Garlic Paste, half the coriander, turmeric and chilli powder and all the yogurt. Mix well, scraping down the sides of the bowl. Cover and refrigerate for 2 hours.

Meanwhile, put the cinnamon stick, cardamom pods, cloves, cumin seeds and bay leaves in a heavy-based frying pan and heat gently until toasted and crisp. Transfer to a mortar or grinder and pound or whiz to a powder. Stir this mixture into the chicken when the 2 hours is up, then return the bowl to the refrigerator.

Heat the oil in a frying pan, add the onion and sauté until nicely browned. Add the curry leaves and sauté for a minute or so.

Put the remaining Ginger and Garlic Paste, coriander, turmeric and chilli powder into a heatproof jug. Add the tomato purée and the measured water and mix well. Add this to the onion mixture and continue cooking until virtually dried out.

Add the lime juice and crushed peppercorns and season with salt. Set aside to cool, then mix into the chicken. Cover and chill overnight if possible, but for at least a few hours.

Preheat the grill on a high heat or light a barbecue and cook the chicken, placing a drip tray below if necessary, for 6–8 minutes, turning often. Check to see if the chicken is cooked through by cutting a piece in half with a knife; if the meat is still pink, cook it for a few more minutes and then try again.

Serve with some thick Mixed Raita and hot buttered bread or Naan, if you wish.

MALAI MURG TIKKA

Creamy chicken tikka

HERE IS A DELICATE AND MILD CREAMY CHICKEN TIKKA THAT WILL PLEASE THE MOST
CHILLI-FEARING AND UNADVENTUROUS, WHILE STILL PACKING PLENTY OF FLAVOUR
FOR EVERYONE ELSE.

SERVES 4 AS A STARTER
OR 2 AS A MAIN COURSE

BONELESS, SKINLESS CHICKEN BREASTS
3, each cut into 4 equal pieces

LEMON JUICE 1 teaspoon

BUTTER 15–30g (½–1oz), melted, for
basting (optional)

SALT

FOR THE TIKKA PASTE

DOUBLE CREAM 1 tablespoon

THICK GREEK YOGURT 3 tablespoons

GRATED CHEDDAR CHEESE
1½ tablespoons

GINGER AND GARLIC PASTE (see page
199) 1 tablespoon

GROUND CARDAMOM ½ teaspoon

GROUND CUMIN ½ teaspoon

FRESH GREEN CHILLI 1 small, finely
chopped (optional)

MUSTARD OIL OR VEGETABLE OIL
1 tablespoon

SAFFRON THREADS a good pinch, gently
toasted, then cooled and crumbled

Put the chicken pieces in a bowl, sprinkle with the lemon
juice and some salt, then set aside.

Combine all the ingredients for the tikka paste in another
bowl and whisk until the cheese blends in. (If using ready-
grated cheese, which can be quite chunky, chop it finely
before adding so that it combines quickly, as the cream
can split with overbeating.) Once blended, taste for seasoning,
adding more salt if necessary.

Mix in the chicken, scraping down the sides of the bowl.
Cover and place in the refrigerator for at least 6–8 hours.

Like other tikkas, this is best chargrilled, in which case, light
the barbecue and thread the chicken on to metal skewers.
Place the skewers, supported just above the rack at either
end (use props for this; I use halved raw potatoes), and cook
for 4–5 minutes, turning often, until well coloured. Check to
see if the chicken is cooked through by cutting a piece in half
with a knife; if the meat is still pink, cook it for a few more
minutes and then try again.

If you are cooking the chicken under a grill, place the pieces
close together (sides touching) in a grill pan. Baste with the
melted butter and cook under a medium heat on one side for
3–4 minutes, until golden brown. Turn carefully so that the
pieces do not separate and cook on the other side for another
3–4 minutes. The coating will colour quickly because of the
cheese and cream, so do not have the heat too high – you
want to ensure that the chicken cooks gradually from within.
Check for doneness, as above. When ready, it will have both
a beautiful colour and texture. Serve immediately.

MASALA MA TATRAVELI KALEJI PURR BATAER NU EEDU

Chicken liver masala

A DELICIOUS ACCOMPANIMENT, STARTER OR SNACK, THIS SIMPLE RECIPE IS GREAT SERVED WITH TOASTED BREAD OR CHAPATTIS. IT IS VERY POPULAR IN MUMBAI, WHERE IT IS CHOPPED MORE COARSELY THAN WE HAVE IT HERE. WE OFTEN SERVE IT WITH CODDLED EGGS – IDEALLY CHICKEN OR DUCK EGGS – OR FRIED QUAIL EGGS, FOR A REALLY HEAVENLY TREAT.

SERVES 4 AS A STARTER

CLEANED CHICKEN LIVERS 500g
(1lb 2oz)

CRUSHED FRESH ROOT GINGER
1 heaped teaspoon

CRUSHED GARLIC 1 heaped
teaspoon

GROUND TURMERIC ¼ teaspoon

GROUND CUMIN 1 teaspoon

GROUND CORIANDER 1 teaspoon

RED CHILLI POWDER ½ teaspoon

LIME JUICE from ½ lime

EXTRA VIRGIN RAPESEED OIL
2 tablespoons

RED ONION 1, finely chopped

CHOPPED FRESH GREEN CHILLI
1 heaped teaspoon

TOMATOES 2, finely chopped

CHOPPED FRESH CORIANDER
1 tablespoon

SHREDDED FRESH MINT
1 tablespoon

SALT AND FRESHLY GROUND
BLACK PEPPER

Wash and drain the livers, then chop into tiny pieces, discarding any sinew. Place in a bowl and mix in the ginger, garlic, turmeric, cumin, ground coriander, chilli powder and lime juice.

Heat a heavy-based frying pan until really hot, then add the oil. When smoking, add the chicken livers and sauté them over a high heat for just 1 minute, stirring to keep the pieces separate. Remove the pan from the heat and, using a slotted spoon, transfer the livers to a plate.

Add the onion and green chilli to the hot oil left in the pan and stir well with a spatula for 2 minutes. Add a little water and scrape up any tasty bits stuck on the bottom. Mix in the tomato, then return the pan to the heat for a minute or so, without stirring, to let the pan reheat. Sprinkle in some salt plus the chopped coriander and mint, and mix again, ensuring that nothing sticks to the bottom. Cook until thick and no liquid is visible at the sides.

Finally, add the cooked livers and their juices. Taste for seasoning, adding more salt, if necessary, and pepper, and then sauté for a minute or so. Serve as you wish.

Notes

The livers are also good with coddled eggs. To do this, we Parsees commonly divide the liver mixture between 4–6 ramekins, filling them no more than three-quarters full. We then make a dent in the middle of each one and break in an egg so that the yolk sits in the centre. The dishes are then placed in a large frying pan or roasting tray with a little water around them, covered and placed on the hob until steam forms and cooks the eggs to your liking.

These also work with poached eggs. Simply put a shallow depth of water in a pan or tray and break the eggs into it, spacing them at intervals. Cover and cook over a low heat until the steam cooks the eggs to your liking. Season and serve.

BHEENDA BATATA PURR EEDU

Okra & eggs on potato

EGGS ARE THE BEDROCK OF PARSEE CUISINE, AND I BELIEVE THAT NO OTHER CULTURE IN THE WORLD REVERES THEM AS MUCH AS WE DO. EVEN CELEBRATORY MEALS TEND TO BEGIN WITH AN EGG-BASED DISH. IT WOULD THEREFORE BE IMPOSSIBLE FOR ME TO WRITE A BOOK THAT DOESN'T FEATURE THEM, SO HERE IS A RECIPE, ALBEIT ONE THAT MANY OF MY FELLOW PARSEES MIGHT DO SLIGHTLY DIFFERENTLY.

SERVE WITH CHUTNEY AND CRUSTY ROLLS, BAGUETTE OR CHAPATTIS. IN INDIA WE HAVE THE MOST GORGEOUS BREADS, AND I WOULD SERVE THIS DISH WITH LADI PAO, A TRAY BREAD THAT LOOKS LIKE SMALL BATCH LOAVES.

SERVES 2–4

EXTRA VIRGIN RAPESEED OIL or HALF OIL/HALF BUTTER 2–3 tablespoons (I like to add a good knob of butter once the cumin has coloured)

CUMIN SEEDS 1 teaspoon

FRESH GREEN CHILLI 1 finger-type, finely chopped

FRESH ROOT GINGER 5cm (2in) piece, peeled and finely chopped

GARLIC 2 cloves, finely chopped

ONION 1, thinly sliced

GROUND TURMERIC ½ teaspoon

POTATOES 2, cut into 3mm (⅛in) slices, preferably using a mandoline

OKRA 8–10 pods, washed, thoroughly dried and sliced 1cm (½in) thick

SPRING ONION 1, finely chopped, white and green parts alike

FINELY CHOPPED FRESH CORIANDER 1 heaped tablespoon, or to taste

EGGS 4

SALT

Heat the oil in a frying pan large enough to hold 4 eggs. When hot, add the cumin seeds and sizzle on a medium heat until they change colour – watch closely for this. Then add the butter, if using.

Add the green chilli, ginger and garlic and sauté for 1–2 minutes, until the garlic becomes pale but does not colour. Add the onion and sauté for 1–2 minutes more, until translucent, then add the turmeric, stirring over a low heat for another minute or so.

Now add the potato slices and sauté for at least 3–4 minutes. Add the okra and a sprinkling of salt and stir together. Pour in a dash of water, cover the pan and cook over a low heat until the potatoes are just tender, not falling apart (about 4 minutes).

Gently stir in the spring onion and coriander, then adjust the seasoning as necessary. Scrape down the sides of the pan.

Using the tapered end of an egg, make 4 four dents in the mixture, spacing them well apart and about 4cm (1½in) from the sides of the pan. Break an egg into each dent, taking care to get the yolk in the middle of it. Cover the pan and cook over a very low heat so that the potatoes don't burn but the eggs poach in the steam. When done to your liking, cut the potato base into 4 segments, each one including an egg, and serve straight away.

If you prefer, the eggs can be cooked for 12–15 minutes on the middle shelf of an oven preheated to 120°C/250°F/Gas Mark ½. Keep checking until the yolks are cooked just right.

OMELETE DE BATATA E ESPINAFRE

Potato & spinach omelette

ALTHOUGH THIS DISH RESEMBLES A SPANISH OMELETTE, I BELIEVE THAT THIS VERSION ORIGINATED IN PERSIA, AND WAS SUBSEQUENTLY SPREAD BY THE MOORS OF NORTH AFRICA, WHO TOOK A SHINE TO IT. IN FACT, IT IS STILL MADE IN IRAN IN VARYING FORMS, AND THAT PERHAPS EXPLAINS WHY PARSEES LOVE EGGS SO MUCH – IT'S SIMPLY GENETIC!

SERVES 8

WAXY POTATOES, SUCH AS CHARLOTTE 500–600g (1lb 2oz–1lb 5oz), unpeeled

FRESH SPINACH 115g (4oz)

BUTTER 20–35g (¾–1¼oz), as you wish

CUMIN SEEDS 1 heaped teaspoon

ONIONS 2–3 small, halved and thinly sliced

GARLIC 2 cloves, finely chopped

FRESH GREEN CHILLIES 2, finely chopped

RED PEPPER 1 small, cored, deseeded and finely diced

EGGS 4

CHOPPED FRESH CORIANDER 1–2 tablespoons

SALT AND FRESHLY GROUND BLACK PEPPER

Cook the potatoes in a saucepan of boiling water for 8–10 minutes, until just tender. Drain, retaining the cooking water. Allow the potatoes to cool, then refrigerate.

Return the potato water to the pan and bring back to the boil. Switch off the heat, add the spinach leaves and stir until wilted. Drain, again reserving the water to use in soup or another dish if you like. Cool the spinach quickly under running cold water to prevent colour loss, then squeeze out any remaining liquid. Transfer to a board and shred or chop the leaves.

Peel the cold potatoes and cut them into slices about 3mm (¹/₈in) thick. Set aside and keep cool.

Place the butter on another board and mix in the cumin seeds. Once combined, chop until the seeds are in tiny pieces.

Put the butter in a large frying pan over a medium heat. Once the butter foams and the cumin colours a bit, add the onions, garlic, green chillies and red pepper, and sauté until the garlic is light brown.

Add the sliced potatoes and sauté for a few minutes, turning regularly. Season well with pepper now, or wait and later season just the eggs with salt. Stir in the blanched spinach leaves.

Break all 4 eggs into a jug or bowl and beat gently until fully combined. Reduce the heat under your pan and pour the eggs evenly over the potato mixture, pressing down slightly so that the egg oozes through. Cover the pan and let the mixture gently steam in its own heat for 4–5 minutes. Check from time to time to see if it is setting well.

Preheat your grill. Meanwhile, lift the potatoes gently with a spatula to see if the bottom is well browned. When it is, place the pan under the hot grill with the door open and the handle jutting out. Keep moving the handle from side to side, until the top layer is well browned and firmly set.

Loosen the potato cake around the edges by running a spatula around it, then slide it on to a flat serving dish. Serve hot or cold.

KABOOTAR LAAL MASALA

Pigeon in red masala

IF YOU LIKE GAME, YOU'LL LOVE PIGEON. BUT EVEN IF YOU DON'T, A GREEN SALAD WILL OFFSET THE INTENSE FLAVOUR AND MAKE IT MORE THAN ACCEPTABLE. WE OFTEN INCLUDE PIGEON BREAST ON OUR MENU AND IT HAS ALWAYS BEEN POPULAR, SO HERE'S A SIMPLE RECIPE FOR YOU TO TRY. SERVE WITH ORIENTAL OR MUMBAI-STYLE COLESLAW (SEE PAGE 136) OR A YOGURT-BASED SALAD.

SERVES 4 AS A STARTER

BONELESS, SKINLESS PIGEON BREASTS 8
SALT 1 teaspoon
GROUND TURMERIC ¾ teaspoon
LIME JUICE from ½ lime

FOR THE MASALA
DRIED RED CHILLIES 5–6 large, deseeded and crumbled
BLACK PEPPERCORNS 6–8
CLOVES 2–3
CUMIN SEEDS ½ teaspoon
CORIANDER SEEDS 1 teaspoon
SEEDLESS TAMARIND 2.5cm (1in) ball, or 2 tablespoons light pulp (add carefully, as some tamarind preparations are extremely strong)
GARLIC 2 cloves, coarsely chopped
EXTRA VIRGIN RAPESEED OIL 2–3 tablespoons
SALT (optional)

Make light diagonal gashes on the top of each pigeon breast.

Combine the salt, turmeric and lime juice in a bowl, then rub this mixture into the pigeon breasts. Set aside in a cool place.

Put the chillies, peppercorns, cloves and cumin and coriander seeds in a dry, heavy-based frying pan over a low heat and toast until aromatic. Transfer the mixture to a grinder or mortar and whiz or pound to a powder. Add the tamarind, garlic and oil, then transfer the mixture to a hand-held blender and whiz to a paste. Pass the mixture through a fine sieve, discarding the tamarind fibres, and whiz again to a smooth purée. Taste and add salt if you wish.

Rub the masala into the pigeon breasts. Transfer to a covered container and refrigerate overnight, or for at least 8 hours.

Light a barbecue, or heat your grill to its highest setting. Cook the breasts for about 2–3 minutes on each side, until browned on all sides, but no more than medium–rare in the middle. Pigeon meat tends to dry out quickly, so watch carefully and test often. Serve immediately.

LIGHT DISHES
& STREET FOOD

TARKARI NA PUFF

Curried vegetable puffs

IN MUMBAI CURRIED LAMB PUFFS, INTRODUCED BY THE PARSEES AND THE GOAN COMMUNITIES, ARE PROBABLY THE MOST POPULAR OF SNACKS, THOUGH THE VEGETARIAN VARIETY IS A GREAT FAVOURITE TOO. IN FACT, THERE ARE MANY FILLING OPTIONS, ALL OF THEM ENCASED IN FLAKY OR PUFF PASTRY, AND SOLD IN DELIS RIGHT ACROSS THE CITY.

MAKES 24–30

VEGETABLES 500g (1lb 2oz) – a combination of carrots, peas, French beans, potato and spinach is ideal, finely diced

SUNFLOWER OIL 3 tablespoons, plus extra for greasing (optional)

FRESH ROOT GINGER 7.5cm (3in) piece, peeled and finely chopped

GARLIC 4–5 cloves, finely chopped

FRESH GREEN CHILLIES 2 large, finely chopped

ONIONS 2–3, finely chopped

GROUND TURMERIC 1 teaspoon

GROUND CORIANDER 1 tablespoon

GROUND CUMIN 2 tablespoons

RED CHILLI POWDER 1 heaped teaspoon

FRESH OR CANNED TOMATOES 200g (7oz), chopped

LIME JUICE 1 teaspoon

WHITE SUGAR 1 teaspoon

CHOPPED FRESH CORIANDER 2 heaped tablespoons

PLAIN FLOUR for dusting

READY-ROLLED PUFF PASTRY 2–3 sheets

EGG 1, beaten, for brushing

SALT

Blanch the vegetables (except the spinach) in boiling water for 1 minute, then drain and set aside. If using fresh spinach, blanch for just 5 seconds, then drain and cool quickly in cold water to preserve the colour. Drain well, then chop and set aside.

Heat the oil in a large frying pan or a flameproof casserole dish. When hot, sauté the ginger, garlic and green chillies. When the garlic begins to change colour, add the onions and sauté until pale brown.

Put the ground spices and chilli powder in a cup and mix with just enough water to make a paste of pouring consistency. Add to the pan and stir well. If you notice things beginning to stick to the bottom of the pan, rinse a little water around the emptied cup and add to the pan. This will prevent the spices from burning and turning the dish bitter. Once you see oil being released at the bottom of the pan, it indicates that the spices are cooked.

Add the tomatoes and cook until the liquid has almost evaporated. Stir in the lime juice and sugar, and then the vegetables, adding the chopped spinach once the others have been combined. Cook for a minute or so, then taste and adjust the salt content. Add the chopped coriander and set the pan aside to cool.

Lightly dust a work surface with flour and place a puff pastry sheet on it. Cut into 7.5cm (3in) squares – you want 24–30 in total.

Place a spoonful of the vegetable mixture in the centre of each square, brush around the edges with the beaten egg and fold over, either in the shape of a triangle or a rectangle.

Arrange the parcels on greased or nonstick baking trays and place in the refrigerator or freezer until the pastry becomes firm (30–40 minutes). Meanwhile, preheat the oven to 220°C/425°F/ Gas Mark 7.

Brush the chilled pastries with beaten egg and bake for 15–18 minutes, until golden. Turn off the oven, but leave the pastries inside with the door slightly ajar to dry a little. Serve hot or warm. These puffs need no accompaniment, but some people like tomato ketchup with them. They will keep for a couple of days as long as they are tightly covered and stored in the refrigerator.

VADA PAAV

Spiced potato patties with garlic chutney

SOMEBODY ONCE SAID THAT EATING THESE PATTIES IS A DIRECT BLOW TO THE HEART, WHICH, LIKE OTHER MUMBAIKARS, I TAKE TO MEAN THE SHEER LOVE THEY INSPIRE. THE FRITTERS OR BALLS OF CRUSHED SPICED POTATO ARE DIPPED IN CHICKPEA BATTER AND DEEP-FRIED, THEN SERVED IN SOFT BREAD ROLLS WITH HOT GARLIC CHUTNEY. HOWEVER, THE PATTIES CAN ALSO BE SERVED JUST AS THEY ARE, OR WITH HOT POORIES, OR EVEN IN A TOASTED SANDWICH. MUMBAIKARS LOVE THEM WITH CHEESE!

MAKES ABOUT 15

GROUND TURMERIC 1 teaspoon

FLOURY POTATOES 2–3 medium, roughly cubed

SUNFLOWER OR EXTRA VIRGIN RAPESEED OIL 2 tablespoons, plus extra for deep-frying

BLACK MUSTARD SEEDS 1 heaped tablespoon

CUMIN SEEDS 1 teaspoon

WHITE LENTILS (URAD DAAL) OR YELLOW SPLIT PEAS (CHANNA DAAL) 2 tablespoons

FRESH ROOT GINGER 7.5cm (3in) piece, peeled and chopped

FRESH GREEN CHILLIES 2 finger-type, chopped

CURRY LEAVES 10–15, preferably fresh, shredded; if using dried, soak in water for 10–12 minutes, and dry thoroughly before shredding

ONION 1 small, chopped

CHOPPED FRESH CORIANDER 1 tablespoon

CHICKPEA (GRAM) FLOUR 150–200g (5½–7oz)

SALT

FOR THE GARLIC CHUTNEY

GARLIC 10–12 cloves

DRIED RED CHILLIES 2–4, deseeded

CUMIN SEEDS 2 teaspoons

SKINNED AND ROASTED PEANUTS OR CANNED OR COOKED CHICKPEAS 2 tablespoons

LIME JUICE to taste

EXTRA VIRGIN RAPESEED OIL (optional)

TO SERVE

SOFT BREAD ROLLS

CHILLI KETCHUP

Bring a large pan of water to the boil. When boiling, add some salt, the turmeric and the potatoes, and cook for about 8–10 minutes, until tender. Drain well, then return the potatoes to the pan and place them over a low heat, stirring with a wooden spatula from the bottom up until they look dry, slightly crushed and fluffy. Spread them out on a tray and set aside to cool.

Heat the 2 tablespoons of oil in a small pan until you see a heat haze. Add the mustard seeds and cover with a lid until they crackle and release a nutty aroma (this takes just a few seconds). Quickly add the cumin seeds and lentils, lower the heat slightly and let them brown just a little. Immediately add the ginger, chillies and curry leaves and sauté for 30 seconds or so, then add the onion. Cook until translucent, then tip in the cooled potatoes, scraping the pan thoroughly. Sprinkle the coriander on top and mix well. Taste and adjust the salt if necessary. Once the mixture has cooled, shape it into balls about 4cm (1½in) in diameter and set aside on a plate.

Heat a 5–7.5cm (2–3in) depth of oil in a deep-fat fryer or deep frying pan.

Meanwhile, sift the chickpea flour into a bowl and mix in some chilled water, a spoonful at a time, until you have a batter with the consistency of double cream. Season with salt.

Test if the oil is now hot enough by adding a few drops of batter to it: they should bob up instantly. If not, continue heating and testing, but do not overheat. When ready, dip the potato balls in the batter with your fingers, let the excess drip off and gently lower them into the hot oil. Fry for about 2–3 minutes, taking care not to overcrowd the pan, which will lower the oil temperature too much. Drain on kitchen paper.

For the chutney, put all the ingredients (apart from the oil) into a blender and whiz to a smooth paste. Add oil only if the mixture does not purée without it.

To serve, cut open the bread rolls, spread some chutney on both halves and sandwich them together with a vada. Alternatively, serve as a snack without bread, offering the chutney and perhaps some chilli ketchup for dipping.

See image overleaf

MANKYO FRY

Deep-fried squid with coriander, mint & basil dip

WITH THIS DISH YOU NEED TO HAVE ALL THE INGREDIENTS READY BEFORE YOU START COOKING BECAUSE IT IS BEST SERVED REALLY HOT AND CRISP, WHILE THE CENTRE REMAINS SOFT TO THE BITE. OF COURSE, THIS MEANS THAT IT'S IMPORTANT TO HAVE THE OIL AT THE RIGHT TEMPERATURE, WHICH IS BEST ACHIEVED IN A WOK. IF YOU DON'T HAVE ONE, TEST THE OIL WITH A THERMOMETER AND MAKE SURE IT REGISTERS 180°C (350°F).

SERVES 4 AS STARTER OR SNACK

BABY SQUID TUBES 800g (1lb 12oz) cleaned
LIME JUICE from ½ lime
EXTRA VIRGIN RAPESEED OIL for frying
SELF-RAISING FLOUR 100g (3½oz), plus extra for dusting
CORNFLOUR 150g (5½oz)
CHILLED SPARKLING WATER 300–325ml (10–11fl oz)
SALT AND FRESHLY GROUND BLACK PEPPER

FOR THE DIP

FRESH CORIANDER 10–12 stems with leaves
FRESH MINT LEAVES 30–35
FRESH BASIL LEAVES 25–30
FRESH THAI BASIL LEAVES 25–30 (optional)
FRESH GREEN CHILLIES 1–2, deseeded
GARLIC 1 clove, finely chopped
GROUND CUMIN ½ teaspoon
WHITE SUGAR 1 heaped teaspoon
CIDER VINEGAR 1 teaspoon
NAHM PLA (THAI FISH SAUCE) 2–3 tablespoons

CHILLI SEASONING (OPTIONAL)
RED CHILLI POWDER 1 teaspoon
GROUND CUMIN 2 teaspoons, toasted (see page 56)
MANGO POWDER (AAMCHUR) 2 teaspoons
RED ROCK SALT 1 teaspoon
FRESHLY GROUND BLACK PEPPER 1 teaspoon

TO SERVE (optional)
SPRING ONION 1, chopped
FRESH GREEN CHILLI 1 finger-type, chopped

Slit the squid tubes lengthways and cut into small squares or cut widthways into strips about 5mm (¼in) wide. Rinse well, then drain and pat dry on kitchen paper. Place in a bowl, add the lime juice and seasoning and mix well. Cover and refrigerate for 2–3 hours.

Put all the dip ingredients into a blender and purée them to a fine paste. Pass through a sieve, if you wish, then season and place in a clean sterilized screwtop jar (see Note, page 189). (To preserve this for future use, pour some oil over the surface of the dip to prevent it drying out and oxidizing.)

If you are making the extra seasoning, combine all the ingredients for it in a bowl. It goes well with all sorts of fried seafood, so why not make some for future use and store it in a dark airtight container?

Heat a 7.5cm (3in) depth of oil in a deep-fat fryer or deep frying pan.

Meanwhile, dust a shallow baking tray with flour. Using a slotted spoon, lift the squid out of its bowl, draining off as much marinade as possible, then dust it thoroughly in the floured tray.

Sift the measured flours into a bowl and mix well. Whisk in the sparkling water until you have a smooth batter.

As soon as the oil is smoking hot or at least 180°C (350°F), dip the floured squid pieces in the batter, then carefully lower them into the oil. Fry for a minute or so, until nicely browned. Drain on kitchen paper.

Sprinkle with the chilli seasoning, if using, and serve the dip alongside. A little chopped spring onion and chilli sprinkled on top are good additions, if you happen to have them.

KERALA NYANND MASALA

Keralan-style crab with coconut

HERE IS A SIMPLE ADAPTATION OF A GREAT CRAB DISH FROM KERALA. IT TASTES FABULOUS, BUT YOU CAN ADD SOME CUMIN SEEDS, WHITE LENTILS AND ASAFOETIDA IF YOU WANT TO RING THE CHANGES. BROWN MUSTARD SEEDS CAN BE USED INSTEAD OF BLACK, BUT NOTE THAT THE FLAVOUR WILL BE DIFFERENT. SERVE WITH RICE AND/OR A PLAIN GOAN OR KERALAN-STYLE COCONUT CURRY, SOME STEAMED RICE DUMPLINGS OR THICK SAVOURY PANCAKES. ALTERNATIVELY, EAT WITH BREAD, TORTILLAS OR ROLLS WITH SOME SALAD.

SERVES 4 AS A STARTER

WHITE CRABMEAT 300–400g (10½–14oz)

EXTRA VIRGIN RAPESEED OIL 2 tablespoons

BLACK MUSTARD SEEDS 2 teaspoons

FRESH ROOT GINGER 2.5cm (1in) piece, peeled and chopped

GARLIC 2 cloves, finely chopped

CURRY LEAVES 6–8, preferably fresh, finely shredded; if using dried, soak in water for 10–12 minutes, and dry thoroughly before shredding

FRESH GREEN CHILLIES 2 finger-type, chopped

DRIED RED CHILLI 1, soaked in hot water for 8–10 minutes, then chopped

SHALLOTS 2–3 small, finely chopped

FRESHLY GRATED COCONUT 150–200g (5½–7oz), or 3 tablespoons desiccated coconut soaked in enough warm water to just cover for 30 minutes

RED CHILLI POWDER 1 heaped teaspoon

GROUND TURMERIC ½ teaspoon

TOMATOES 2 small plum-type, chopped and seeds/juice saved for another recipe

CHOPPED FRESH CORIANDER 2 tablespoons

SALT (optional)

Pick over the crabmeat to remove any hidden bits of shell or cartilage. Prepare and set out all the other ingredients.

In a wok or kadhai, heat the oil until it forms a haze. Test by adding a couple of mustard seeds: if they crackle immediately, the oil is hot enough. Lower the heat slightly, add the mustard seeds and cover with a lid while they crackle to prevent them flying off all over the place. As soon as the crackling stops and the seeds smell aromatic, add the ginger, garlic, curry leaves and the green and red chillies. Stir until the garlic turns pale, then add the shallots and continue to sauté until they soften.

Mix in the coconut and sauté for 3–4 minutes, then add the chilli powder and turmeric. Sauté for about 30 seconds, then add the crabmeat, tossing well for about 1 minute.

Add the tomatoes and fresh coriander. Taste and add salt if necessary, then serve immediately.

BOLINHOS DE MARISCO

Portuguese seafood cakes

HERE IS ANOTHER PORTUGUESE RECIPE THAT MADE ITS WAY TO GOA, WHERE THE LOCALS ADDED THEIR OWN TOUCHES. YOU TOO CAN PERSONALIZE IT, SWAPPING INGREDIENTS AND MAKING WHATEVER VARIATIONS YOU WISH. IT'S GREAT FOR USING WITH ANY TAIL PIECES YOU MIGHT HAVE SAVED IN THE FREEZER.

MAKES ABOUT 20 OR MORE IF SERVED AS SMALL CANAPÉS

FLOURY POTATOES 400–500g (14oz–1lb 2oz), coarsely chopped

SKINLESS FILLETS OF WHITE FISH 200–250g (7–9oz)

RAW PRAWNS 200–250g (7–9oz), peeled and deveined

LIME JUICE 1 teaspoon

CHOPPED FRESH CORIANDER 2 heaped tablespoons

FRESH GREEN CHILLIES 1–2, according to taste

CUMIN SEEDS 1 heaped teaspoon, toasted and crushed (see page 56)

GARLIC 3 cloves, crushed

WHITE BREAD 2–3 slices, crusts removed (optional)

SUNFLOWER OIL for frying

FRESH GREEN CHUTNEY (see page 176) to serve

SALT AND FRESHLY GROUND BLACK PEPPER

FOR THE COATING

PLAIN FLOUR 50–100g (1¾–3½oz)

EGGS 3–4, lightly beaten

MEDIUM SEMOLINA 200g (7oz)

Cook the potatoes in boiling water for about 8–10 minutes, until tender. Drain, return to the pan and shake over a low heat until dry and floury. Set aside to cool.

If you have a steamer, place the fish in it and steam until cooked (about 7–8 minutes). Otherwise, place in a pan of very shallow boiling water and poach until cooked (about 1–2 minutes). Drain and allow to cool, then cover and chill.

Steam or poach the prawns in the same liquid used for the fish – this should take no more than 2–3 minutes at a simmer because you want them tender, not rubbery. Set aside to cool.

Mince the fish and prawns together. Alternatively, mash the fish with a fork, and chop the prawns with a knife, then mix them together.

Mash the cooled potatoes until fine and smooth. Add the fish mixture, lime juice, coriander, chillies, cumin seeds and garlic and stir well. If the mixture is too sticky, soak the bread in a little water and squeeze dry, then work it into the potato. Taste and season with salt and pepper. Divide the seafood mixture into 20 equal pieces and roll them into balls.

Put the flour, egg and semolina into 3 separate shallow bowls. Taking 1 ball at a time, flatten to about 1cm (½in) thick and first dust in the flour, then dip in the egg and finally roll in the semolina, ensuring it is well coated. Transfer to a tray and repeat this process until you have 20 coated patties. Chill for 1 hour to firm up.

Heat a 5cm (2in) depth of oil in a deep pan. When hot, fry the patties a few at a time until crisp and golden. Drain on kitchen paper.

Serve hot or warm with Fresh Green Chutney.

KOLMI NAY KHAEKDA NO PORO

Prawn & crab masala omelette

OMELETTES ARE HUGELY POPULAR IN INDIA, THOUGH THE MASALA OMELETTE REIGNS SUPREME. PARSEES, OF COURSE, ALWAYS GO FURTHER WITH THEIR EGG RECIPES AND ADD MANY EXTRAS, AS BELOW. ENJOY THIS OMELETTE WITH WELL-BUTTERED TOAST AND PERHAPS SOME TOMATO KETCHUP ON THE SIDE.

SERVES 4

RAW PEELED PRAWNS 250–300g
(9–10½oz), fresh or defrosted

WHITE CRABMEAT 150–200g
(5½–7oz), fresh, defrosted or
canned

EXTRA VIRGIN RAPESEED OIL
3–4 tablespoons

CUMIN SEEDS ½ teaspoon

FRESH GREEN CHILLIES 1–2
finger-type, finely chopped

ONION 1, chopped

EGGS 8–12, depending on appetite

CHOPPED FRESH CORIANDER
1 tablespoon, plus extra sprigs
to garnish

TOMATO 1 plum-type, deseeded
and chopped

GRATED CHEDDAR CHEESE
3–4 tablespoons, for sprinkling
(optional)

SALT

TO SERVE

WELL-BUTTERED TOAST

TOMATO KETCHUP (optional)

Devein and chop the prawns. Squeeze any excess water out of the crabmeat, then break into flakes.

Heat a generous tablespoon of the oil in a frying pan. When hot, add the cumin seeds. As soon as they change colour, add the chilli(es) and sauté for a few seconds, then add the onion and cook until pale.

Add the prawns, increase the heat to high and sauté for 1 minute, until the liquid has evaporated.

Add the crabmeat and stir well, then turn off the heat. Transfer the mixture to a small tray and spread it out so that it cools fast.

Beat 2 or 3 of the eggs in a bowl, then mix in a quarter of the seafood mixture, a quarter of the coriander and a quarter of the tomato. Add salt to taste.

Put a little of the remaining oil in your omelette pan and place over a high heat until it comes almost to smoking point. Pour in the egg mixture and cook until the bottom is lightly browned and the centre is still slightly moist. Add some grated cheese now and fold the omelette in half, if you wish, then slide on to a plate. Cook the other omelettes in the same way.

Serve immediately, garnished with fresh coriander sprigs and accompanied by well-buttered toast, and tomato ketchup, if you wish.

PÃO COM CHOURIÇO, QUEIJO E FEIJÃO

Chorizo & spiced cheese rolls with spiced baked beans

SPICY CHEESE ROLLS ARE COMMONLY SERVED FOR BREAKFAST IN PORTUGAL AND BRAZIL, WHILE CHORIZO-FILLED ROLLS ARE VERY POPULAR AS A SNACK. HERE WE HAVE COMBINED THE TWO FILLINGS IN A HOMEMADE BREAD TO MAKE A TASTY TREAT FOR EATING AT ANY TIME.

SERVES 8

FAST-ACTION DRIED YEAST 1 tablespoon

FINE SEMOLINA 100g (3½oz)

PLAIN FLOUR 400g (14oz), plus extra for dusting

SALT 1 teaspoon

WARM WATER 250ml (9fl oz), at 40–45°C (104–113°F)

BUTTER 1 tablespoon, melted, for brushing, plus extra for greasing

FOR THE CHORIZO FILLING

CHORIZO 300g (10½oz), skinned and chopped

ONIONS 2 small, finely chopped

RED CHILLI POWDER 1–2 teaspoons

FRESH GREEN CHILLI 1, chopped

FOR THE CHILLI CHEESE FILLING

SÃO JORGE CHEESE 150g (5½oz)

NISA CHEESE 150g (5½oz)

FRESH GREEN CHILLIES 2, finely chopped

GARLIC 1 clove, chopped

FRESH CORIANDER 4 sprigs, chopped

FOR THE SPICED BAKED BEANS

BUTTER 30g (1oz)

CUMIN SEEDS 1 teaspoon

GARLIC 4–5 cloves, chopped

FRESH GREEN CHILLIES 3 finger-type, finely chopped

ONIONS 2, halved and chopped

BAKED BEANS 1 × 400g (14oz) can

CHOPPED FRESH CORIANDER 1 tablespoon

First make the chorizo filling. Place all the ingredients for it in a saucepan over a low heat until the fat begins to render out of the sausage. Gently build up the heat and cook for 10–15 minutes. Drain off the fat and set the mixture aside to cool.

Now make the chilli cheese filling. Grate both the cheeses into a bowl, add the other ingredients and mix well. Cover and chill until needed.

The dough for the rolls can be made in a food processor or by hand. If using a food processor, attach a metal chopping blade. Place the yeast, semolina, flour and salt in the bowl and pulse for about 4–5 seconds. Add the water and pulse for another 10–20 seconds. Scrape down the sides of the bowl with a plastic spatula, cover with a damp cloth and set aside in a warm place until doubled in size (about 1 hour). Pulse the risen dough 4 or 5 times to knock out the air, then churn it non-stop for 20 seconds. Cover the bowl tightly and leave to rest for 5 minutes, then process non-stop for another 20 seconds. The dough will roll into a ball and leave the sides of the bowl reasonably clean.

If making the dough by hand, put all the dry ingredients into a large bowl or in a heap on a clean work surface. Make a well in the middle, pour in the measured water and work with your hands to form the dough. Knead it for 5–6 minutes, then shape into a ball. Place in a bowl, cover with a damp cloth and set aside in a warm place until doubled in size (about 1 hour). Punch the risen dough firmly to knock out the air, then knead for about 5 minutes, until smooth and elastic. Shape into a ball. Turn the knocked-back dough on to a lightly floured surface, roll it in the flour, then return it to the bowl, cover tightly and leave until doubled in size again (about 1 hour). Knock the air out of the risen dough again.

Divide the dough into 8–10 equal pieces and roll them into balls. Lightly flour a work surface and flatten each ball of dough into a 15cm (6in) circle.

Spoon an equal amount of the chilli cheese filling into the centre of each circle. Top with the chorizo filling. Brush water around the edges with your fingers, then fold the dough over and roll into a ball between your palms. Place the rolls on a greased baking tray, spacing them 5–7.5cm (2–3in) apart. Cover and set aside in a warm place until nearly doubled in size (about 20 minutes).

Preheat the oven to 240°C/475°F/Gas Mark 9. Brush the rolls with the melted butter and bake for 20–25 minutes, until beautifully coloured.

Meanwhile, make the spiced baked beans. Melt the butter in a saucepan over a medium heat, add the cumin seeds and sauté for 1 minute, until browned and fragrant. Add the garlic, chillies and onions, and cook until soft.

Pour in the beans and mix well, then cover and simmer for 10–12 minutes, until the beans are hot. Stir in the coriander and serve alongside the rolls.

See images overleaf

Notes

Food processors can overheat the dough and kill the yeast, so it is best to pulse rather than mix non-stop.

Baking the bread in a very hot oven gives it elasticity and makes it nice and chewy. However, ovens vary in their ferocity, so if there is any sign of overbrowning, do lower the temperature. It is better for the rolls to be thoroughly baked than burnt.

RISSÓIS DE BACALHAU

Cod rissoles

A TRADITIONAL SNACK IN PORTUGAL AND, ONCE UPON A TIME, IN GOA, WHEN BACALHÃO (DRIED SALT COD) WAS READILY AVAILABLE. THIS RECIPE IS A SLIGHT VARIATION OF THE ORIGINAL, TAILORED TO SUIT A SPICIER PALATE. SALT COD VARIES GREATLY IN ITS DEGREE OF SALTINESS, SO THE SOAKING TIME IT REQUIRES TO LOWER THE SALT CONTENT VARIES TOO. IDEALLY, CHANGE ITS SOAKING WATER EVERY HOUR AND DO SO THREE OR FOUR TIMES.

MAKES 12–15

FLOURY POTATOES 3–4 largish ones, roughly cubed

DRIED SALT COD 250g (9oz), soaked in several changes of fresh water (see recipe introduction)

CUMIN SEEDS 1 heaped teaspoon, toasted and crushed (see Note below)

FRESH GREEN CHILLIES 2 finger-type, finely chopped

FRESH ROOT GINGER 7.5cm (3in) piece, peeled and finely chopped

ENGLISH MUSTARD PASTE 2 tablespoons

CHOPPED FRESH CORIANDER 1 heaped tablespoon

FRESHLY GROUND BLACK PEPPER ½ teaspoon

FRESH WHITE BREADCRUMBS (optional)

EXTRA VIRGIN RAPESEED OIL for frying

SALT (optional)

MAYONNAISE-BASED DRESSING to serve

FOR THE COATING

PLAIN FLOUR 3–4 tablespoons

EGGS 2–3, beaten

COARSE SEMOLINA 3–4 tablespoons

Bring a large pan of water to the boil. When boiling, add some salt and the potatoes, and cook for about 8–10 minutes, until tender. Drain well, then return the potatoes to the pan and place them over a low heat, stirring with a wooden spatula from the bottom up until they look dry, slightly crushed and fluffy. Pass them through a ricer or mash them with a masher or fork until as smooth as possible. Set aside to cool.

Drain and rinse the cod. Break it into pieces, then flake with a fork into fine fragments. Add to the potato along with the remaining ingredients (apart from the breadcrumbs and oil) and mix well. If the mixture seems too wet (you should be able to shape a handful into a ball without it sticking to your hands), add some fresh breadcrumbs until the consistency is correct. Taste and season with salt if necessary.

Heat a 7.5cm (3in) depth of oil in a deep pan. Place the coating ingredients in 3 separate shallow bowls. Divide the dough into equal pieces of the size you wish to make. Roll them first into balls and then in the flour. Now mould them into sausage-shaped rissoles and dip them in the egg. Let the excess drip off, then roll them in the semolina. (Take care not to apply the semolina too thickly or the rissole will crack as the heat builds up inside.)

When the oil is hot, fry the rissoles until crisp and golden all over (semolina does not brown in the same way as breadcrumbs, so don't expect a deep colour). Drain on kitchen paper and serve hot or warm with any mayonnaise-based dressing.

Note

To toast nuts, seeds or spices, use one of the following methods. For smaller quantities, put the nuts, seeds or spices in a heavy-based frying pan, place it over a low heat and toast, gently swirling the pan now and then in a circular motion, until the nuts, seeds or spices turn deep brown (not black) and give off a lovely aroma. For larger quantities, preheat the oven to 140°C/275°F/Gas Mark 1 and spread the nuts, seeds or spices on a baking tray. Toast in the oven for 4–5 minutes, and then turn off the oven, leaving the baking tray inside for a further 30 minutes.

Remove the nuts, seeds or spices from the frying pan or the baking tray and set aside to cool, then crush coarsely in a mortar or spice grinder, or use as required.

Crispy chicken strips

HERE IS A QUICK AND EASY RECIPE FOR FRYING CHICKEN WITHOUT IT BECOMING GREASY AND STICKY. THE MEAT CAN BE DICED IF YOU PREFER, IN WHICH CASE YOU CAN CALL IT POPCORN CHICKEN, WHICH WILL APPEAL TO CHILDREN. THE RECIPE CAN ALSO BE MADE WITH SQUID OR PRAWNS. AS WITH ALL STIR-FRIES, PREPARE ALL THE INGREDIENTS BEFORE YOU START COOKING AND HAVE THE OIL GOOD AND HOT.

SERVES 5–6 AS A SNACK

BONELESS, SKINLESS CHICKEN BREASTS 2

POTATO FLOUR 2–3 tablespoons

CORNFLOUR 2 tablespoons, plus extra if needed

FINELY CHOPPED FRESH ROOT GINGER 1 tablespoon

FINELY CHOPPED GARLIC ½ tablespoon

FRESH GREEN CHILLIES 2 finger-type, finely chopped

SPRING ONION 1, white part only, finely chopped

LIGHT SOY SAUCE 2 tablespoons

NAHM PLA (THAI FISH SAUCE) 1 tablespoon

EXTRA VIRGIN RAPESEED OIL for frying

EGGS 2

RED CHILLI POWDER ½ teaspoon

CRUSHED BLACK PEPPERCORNS ½ teaspoon

SALT

DIP OF YOUR CHOICE, such as Mustard, Garlic and Chilli Mayonnaise (see page 204), to serve

Chill the chicken breasts in the freezer for about 1½–2 hours, until almost frozen but still soft enough to be dented with a finger. Now slit each breast horizontally into 3 slices and shred into thin strips.

Put the 2 flours into a bowl, add the ginger, garlic, chillies and spring onion, then mix lightly to coat. Set aside to rest.

Put the shredded chicken into a bowl. Add the soy sauce and nahm pla and mix well, then cover and place in the refrigerator for about 30 minutes.

Heat a 7.5cm (3in) depth of oil in a deep pan. Place a slotted spoon and colander alongside.

Meanwhile, add the chicken mixture to the bowl of floured vegetables, break in the eggs, add the chilli powder, crushed peppercorns and some salt and mix well. The batter needs to be really firm and sticky; if not, add a bit more cornflour.

When the oil is smoking hot, add a few strips of chicken at a time until the surface area is covered. Stir a bit, then fry for a minute or so, until opaque. Drain in the colander. (There is no need to keep the meat warm.) Let the oil reheat, then add another batch of chicken and cook as before.

When all the chicken is done, let the oil reheat, then flash-fry the chicken in batches for just a few seconds. Drain on kitchen paper, then serve with a dip of your choice.

MURG KABAB PAAV

Mumbai-style chicken burger

AS FAR AS I AM CONCERNED, MUMBAI – A MELTING POT OF CULTURES, RELIGIONS AND COOKING – IS THE FOOD CAPITAL OF INDIA. ESPECIALLY STREET FOOD. OF COURSE, 'BURGER' IS NOT THE WORD LOCALS USE FOR THIS SNACK; KAVAAB, KEBAB, CUTLET OR PATTIE ARE ALL MORE LIKELY.

MAKES 4 MEDIUM-SIZED OR 8 SMALL BURGERS

CHICKEN LEG MEAT 500g (1lb 2oz)
GARLIC 4–5 cloves, coarsely chopped
FRESH CORIANDER 10–15 sprigs
FRESH MINT 30–40 leaves with stems
FRESH ROOT GINGER 5cm (2in) piece, peeled and coarsely chopped
FRESH GREEN CHILLIES 2 finger-type
GARAM MASALA (see below) 1 teaspoon
GROUND CUMIN 1 teaspoon
GROUND CORIANDER 1 teaspoon
GROUND TURMERIC ½ teaspoon
RED CHILLI POWDER ½ teaspoon
LIME JUICE 1 teaspoon
WHITE BREAD 3 slices, crusts removed
EXTRA VIRGIN RAPESEED OIL for griddling (optional)
SALT

FOR THE GARAM MASALA

GREEN CARDAMOM PODS 6–8, crushed and seeds extracted for use
CINNAMON STICK 2 × 7.5cm (3in) pieces
CLOVES 5–6
CUMIN SEEDS 1 tablespoon
CORIANDER SEEDS 2 tablespoons
BLACK PEPPERCORNS 1 teaspoon

TO SERVE

SPLIT, TOASTED BUNS 4 medium or 8 small
TOMATOES sliced
RED ONION sliced
FRESH GREEN CHUTNEY (see page 176)

First make the garam masala. Preheat the oven to 130°C/260°F/ Gas Mark ¾. Place all the spices on a baking tray and place on the middle shelf of the oven for 10–12 minutes. After this time, turn off the oven, leaving the tray inside for another 20 minutes. Remove the spices from the oven and allow to cool.

Transfer the spice mixture to a grinder or mortar and whiz or pound to a fine powder. If using a grinder and it gets too hot, the powder will stick to the edges of the bowl, so every now and again loosen the coarse pieces of spice from the sides, then grind some more. Transfer the powder to a sterilized small airtight jar (see page 189) and store in the refrigerator.

Remove all the sinew and gristle from the chicken, but keep the fat attached. Cut into small pieces. Fit a mincer with a medium cutting plate and push the chicken, garlic, fresh herbs and chillies through it and into a bowl.

Add all the ground spices and the lime juice and knead well.

Soak the bread in water, then squeeze into a ball as dry as you can make it. Knead it thoroughly into the mince. Fry a small amount of the mixture to check the seasoning, then season the raw mixture with salt as necessary. Cover and refrigerate for 1–2 hours, until nice and firm.

Light a barbecue or heat an oiled griddle pan until very hot.

Meanwhile, shape the chicken mixture into equal-sized patties of your chosen size. Cook them on one side for about 3–4 minutes, until well coloured, then turn and cook the other side for about 3–4 minutes. Take care not to overcook them – when done, they should feel spongy and be slightly juicy inside.

Serve in toasted buns with sliced tomatoes, sliced red onions and Fresh Green Chutney.

JUNGLI SOOVER NI SEEK BOTI

Game kebabs

A KEBAB, OR KAVAAB AS INDIANS CALL IT, MADE EXCLUSIVELY FROM GAME MEAT HAS A FANTASTIC FLAVOUR. ALTHOUGH THIS RECIPE IS LONG, IT IS EASY TO FOLLOW ONCE YOU HAVE READ IT THOROUGHLY (I SUGGEST YOU DO THIS AT LEAST TWICE) AND ALLOW IT TO SINK IN. IDEALLY, PREPARATION SHOULD START THE DAY BEFORE COOKING, AS GAME BENEFITS GREATLY IN TEXTURE AND FLAVOUR FROM LENGTHY MARINATION. THE KEBABS CAN BE COOKED ON A BARBECUE, IN A GRIDDLE PAN OR UNDER A GRILL, IF PREFERRED.

SERVES 4 AS A STARTER OR 10–12 AS CANAPÉS

WILD BOAR OR VENISON about 600g (1lb 5oz), cut into 1cm (½in) dice

BUTTER 30g (1oz)

FRESH GREEN CHILLIES 1 or 2 finger-type, very finely chopped

FRESH CORIANDER as much as you like, chopped

FRESH MINT a few leaves

FRESH ROOT GINGER 2.5cm (1in) piece, peeled and very finely chopped

EXTRA VIRGIN RAPESEED OIL for frying

SALT

SWEET CHUTNEY, CHILLI SAUCE OR SPICY KETCHUP to serve

FOR THE MARINADE

FRESH ROOT GINGER 5–7.5cm (2–3in) piece, peeled and finely chopped

GARLIC 4–5 cloves, chopped

GROUND TURMERIC 1 teaspoon

GROUND CORIANDER 2 teaspoons

GROUND CUMIN 1 teaspoon

RED CHILLI POWDER 1 teaspoon

GARAM MASALA (see page 58) ½ teaspoon

ONION 1 small

THICK GREEK YOGURT 3 tablespoons

ENGLISH MUSTARD PASTE 1 tablespoon

OIL (ANY EXCEPT OLIVE OIL) 3 tablespoons

SALT 1 teaspoon

LIME JUICE 1 tablespoon

FOR THE COATING

EGGS 2–3

PLAIN FLOUR 3–4 tablespoons

Place the meat in a large bowl. Put all the marinade ingredients into a blender and purée to a smooth paste. Add the mixture to the meat and stir well. Cover well and set aside at room temperature for 1–2 hours. After that, place in the refrigerator overnight, or for at least 8–10 hours.

Melt the butter in a flameproof casserole dish that has a tight-fitting lid (game needs a bit of added fat, as it is generally lean). Spread it over the bottom of the pan and add the meat and its marinade. Stir occasionally for 6–8 minutes, until the mixture is heated through. Cover tightly and simmer for 30–40 minutes, then taste to see if the meat is nearly cooked. If not, cover and cook for another 5–10 minutes. If ready, place the pan on the hob, take the lid off and heat briskly to drive off the liquid, stirring from the bottom upwards to prevent sticking. When the meat has a thick, nearly dry coating, switch off the heat and stir in the chopped chillies, fresh herbs and ginger. Set aside to cool.

When cool enough to handle, mix and taste for salt. When satisfied, set out 4 metal or presoaked bamboo skewers and make sure they will fit in your frying pan, or cut the latter to length. Thread 3–4 pieces of meat on to each skewer. (If making canapés, use presoaked wooden cocktail sticks rather than skewers.)

Beat the eggs and a pinch of salt in a shallow bowl wide enough to fit the kebabs. (My mother would always beat the whites first and then fold in the yolks to give a fluffier result, but that method allows more oil to be absorbed when the temperature drops, so you might prefer not to do this.) Place the flour in another shallow bowl.

Heat a 1cm (½in) depth of oil in a frying pan until smoking hot. Roll each kebab in the flour, then dip in the beaten egg. Fry for 3–4 minutes, just until the kebabs are heated through.

Note that if the oil becomes overheated, the coating around the kebabs will brown instantly and the meat will not heat right through. If this happens, place the kebabs on a roasting tray lined with kitchen paper and finish cooking in a moderate oven (180°C/350°F/Gas Mark 4) for a few minutes before serving.

Serve the kebabs with any sweet chutney, a chilli sauce or a spicy ketchup.

MEAT &
POULTRY

SEKELU MASALA GOSHT

Spiced shoulder of lamb

MOST PARSEE, GOAN, EAST INDIAN AND ANGLO-INDIAN HOMES EAT ROASTED LAMB OR MUTTON VERY OFTEN, AND EACH FAMILY USES ITS OWN SECRET COMBINATION OF SPICES. THEY ALSO TEND TO PART-STEAM THE MEAT AFTER ITS INITIAL ROASTING BECAUSE IT TENDERIZES IT MORE QUICKLY AND SAVES ENERGY.

LIKE THE BRITISH, WE EAT LAMB AS A ROAST WITH POTATOES AND WHATEVER ELSE TAKES OUR FANCY, BUT I THINK THE LEFTOVERS ARE BEST. THEY CAN BE MADE INTO LITTLE PUFF PASTRY PARCELS (SEE PAGE 40), AND I FONDLY REMEMBER THE ROAST MUTTON SANDWICHES MY MOTHER WOULD MAKE WHENEVER WE WENT ON A JOURNEY. WE ALL ADORED THE AMAZING FLAVOUR AND THE KICK OF THE HAND-GROUND MUSTARD SHE ADDED. MY SISTER CONTINUES THE TRADITION, AND MAKES THEM IN JUST THE SAME WAY.

SERVES 4–5

EXTRA VIRGIN RAPESEED OIL 1 tablespoon

SHOULDER OF LAMB about 1.5kg (3lb 5oz), boned, rolled and tied

CINNAMON STICK 7.5cm (3in) piece

DRIED RED CHILLIES (preferably Kashmiri) 2, broken into pieces

GINGER AND GARLIC PASTE (see page 199) 1 tablespoon

WATER 100ml (3½fl oz)

GROUND CUMIN 1 teaspoon

GROUND CORIANDER 2 teaspoons

SALT 1 teaspoon, or to taste

BLACK PEPPERCORNS 3, lightly crushed

ROAST POTATOES to serve (optional)

Preheat the oven to 180°C/350°F/Gas Mark 4.

Heat the oil in a pressure cooker or large flameproof casserole dish and brown the lamb well on all sides. Transfer to a roasting tray and place in the oven for 20 minutes.

Add the cinnamon stick and red chillies to the oil left in the pan and sauté until sizzling and aromatic. Stir in the Ginger and Garlic Paste and measured water. As soon as the water boils, add the cumin, coriander, salt and crushed peppercorns, and simmer for 5–10 minutes, until the masala starts to form and oil oozes out again.

If using a pressure cooker, transfer the lamb to it, adding a little more water if needed. Seal tightly and bring up to pressure. Alternatively, return the meat to the casserole and cover with a tight-fitting lid. In either case, cook over a low heat for 20 minutes.

Remove the lamb from the sauce (allowing the pressure cooker to cool first), cover it with foil and let it rest for at least 10 minutes.

Meanwhile, you can discard the cinnamon stick and purée the sauce if you wish. Taste and adjust the seasoning as necessary.

Carve the rested meat and serve with your chosen accompaniments, such as roast potatoes.

GOSHT PASANDA TAMATARWALA

Mini rolled escalopes of lamb in tomato sauce

AN ESCALOPE IS A FLATTENED PIECE OF MEAT GENERALLY FRIED OR SAUTÉED AND FINISHED WITH A SAUCE – IN THIS CASE, A SIMPLE TOMATO MIXTURE THAT IS ALSO GREAT WITH OTHER DISHES, SUCH AS CROQUETTES AND FRIED CHICKEN OR FISH. THE DIFFERENCE HERE IS THAT THE ESCALOPES ARE ROLLED AND SIMMERED IN THE SAUCE. IN INDIA THEY ARE CALLED PASANDA, A TERM THAT HAS BEEN GROSSLY MISUSED IN THE UK TO DESCRIBE A MILD, CREAMY CURRY. NO MATTER – BOTH FORMS OF PASANDA ARE DELICIOUS IN THEIR DIFFERENT WAYS. SERVE WITH VEGETABLES AND POTATOES, OR WITH BREAD OR RICE.

SERVES 4

BONELESS LEG OF LAMB 800g–1kg (1lb 12oz–2lb 4oz)
EXTRA VIRGIN RAPESEED OIL for frying
BUTTER 20g (¾oz)
CHOPPED FRESH CORIANDER 1–2 tablespoons, for sprinkling (optional)
SALT AND FRESHLY GROUND BLACK PEPPER

FOR THE MARINADE

FRESH ROOT GINGER 7.5cm (3in) piece, peeled and finely chopped, then crushed in a mortar
GARLIC 4–5 cloves, crushed
GROUND CUMIN 1 tablespoon
GROUND CORIANDER 2 tablespoons
GROUND TURMERIC 1 teaspoon
WORCESTERSHIRE SAUCE to taste

FOR THE TOMATO SAUCE

EXTRA VIRGIN RAPESEED OIL 1 tablespoon
CINNAMON STICK 2 × 10cm (4in) pieces
DRIED RED CHILLIES 4, each broken into 3 pieces and deseeded
FRESH GREEN CHILLIES 3–4, slit lengthways into 4 pieces
ONIONS 2, finely chopped
MALT VINEGAR 1 tablespoon
RAW CANE OR MUSCOVADO SUGAR 2 teaspoons
FRESH OR CANNED TOMATOES 400g (14oz), chopped

Remove all the gristle, sinews and fat from the lamb. Cut the meat into equal pieces weighing roughly 100g (3½oz) each. Place a piece at a time inside a strong plastic bag or between 2 sheets of clingfilm and flatten it with a meat mallet or heavy-based saucepan, turning it after every hit to make it as round as possible.

Mix all the marinade ingredients in a bowl, seasoning to taste with salt and pepper. Spread the paste over all the escalopes in a dish, then cover and refrigerate for 3–4 hours.

Meanwhile, prepare the sauce. Heat the oil in saucepan or flameproof casserole dish. When hot, add the cinnamon stick and sauté for a few seconds, before adding the dried red chillies. As soon as the chillies darken, add the fresh green chillies and onions. Sauté until the onions are soft.

Add the vinegar and sugar and simmer for a few minutes, then add the tomatoes. Cook gently until the mixture thickens slightly. Season with salt and pepper and set aside.

Scrape the excess marinade off the escalopes, reserving it for later. Tightly roll up each piece of meat and fasten with a wooden cocktail stick.

Heat a little oil in a frying pan. When hot, brown the escalopes on all sides. Transfer to a plate.

Pour a little water into the pan and scrape up the tasty bits stuck to the bottom. Stir in the reserved marinade, then add the butter and heat for just a few minutes. Pour in the tomato sauce and bring to a simmer. Add the browned escalopes and cook for 3–4 minutes. They should be well cooked by now, but do check by tasting a bit.

Taste and adjust the seasoning, adding a sprinkling of chopped coriander if you wish.

Lamb piccata stuffed with mushrooms & feta

PICCATA IS BASICALLY ANOTHER NAME FOR AN ESCALOPE. IN THIS CASE, THE FILLING IS SPREAD OVER EACH PIECE OF MEAT, WHICH IS THEN ROLLED UP AND SIMMERED IN THE SAUCE SO THAT FLAVOUR AND SUCCULENCE ARE ADDED FROM THE INSIDE AS WELL AS THE OUTSIDE. SERVE WITH VEGETABLES AND POTATOES, OR WITH BREAD OR RICE.

SERVES 8 AS A STARTER OR 4 AS A MAIN COURSE

BONELESS LEG OF LAMB 800g–1kg (1lb 12oz–2lb 4oz)

MARINADE (see page 67) 1 quantity

EXTRA VIRGIN RAPESEED OIL for frying

BUTTER 20g (¾oz)

TOMATO SAUCE (see page 67) 1 quantity

CHOPPED FRESH CORIANDER 1–2 tablespoons, for sprinkling (optional)

SALT AND FRESHLY GROUND BLACK PEPPER

FOR THE STUFFING

EXTRA VIRGIN RAPESEED OIL 2 tablespoons

MUSHROOMS 250g (9oz), chopped

ONION 1 small, chopped

CUMIN SEEDS 1 teaspoon, crushed

CELERY 1 stick, destringed and finely chopped

FETA CHEESE 150g (5½oz)

Remove all the gristle, sinews and fat from the lamb. Cut the meat into equal pieces weighing roughly 100g (3½oz) each. Place a piece at a time inside a strong plastic bag or between 2 sheets of clingfilm and flatten it with a meat mallet or heavy-based saucepan, turning it after every hit to make it as round as possible.

Spread the marinade paste over all the piccatas in a dish, then cover and refrigerate for 3–4 hours.

To make the stuffing, heat the oil in a frying pan until it just starts smoking, then add the mushrooms. (If the oil is not very hot, they will release too much moisture.) Stir occasionally until they sizzle and start to dry out. Lower the heat to medium, add the onion, cumin seeds and celery and sauté until the onions soften. Strain the mixture if it seems watery, then set aside to cool.

Crumble the feta into the cooled mushrooms and stir to combine. Taste and adjust the seasoning with salt and pepper as necessary.

Scrape the excess marinade off the meat, reserving it for later. Place the piccatas in a row on a work surface and spoon the filling equally on top of them. Roll up as tightly as possible and fasten each one with a wooden cocktail stick.

Heat a little oil in a frying pan. When hot, brown the piccatas on all sides. Transfer to a plate.

Pour a little water into the pan and scrape up the tasty bits stuck to the bottom. Stir in the reserved marinade, then add the butter and heat for just a few minutes. Pour in the Tomato Sauce and bring to a simmer. Add the browned escalopes and cook for 3–4 minutes. They should be well cooked by now, but do check by tasting a bit.

Taste and adjust the seasoning, adding a sprinkling of chopped coriander if you wish. Serve immediately.

CHANFANA DE CABRITO

Portuguese goat stew

THE TRADITIONAL FLAVOURINGS USED IN THIS DISH ARE PAPRIKA, PEPPER, PARSLEY AND BAY LEAVES. AS WE INDIANS LIKE A BIT MORE SPICE, WE'VE CREATED OUR OWN VERSION OF CHANFANA, AND WE SERVE IT A BIT DIFFERENTLY: WE PURÉE THE STEWING LIQUID AND SERVE IT ALONGSIDE THE MEAT WITH SOME RICE. GOAT MEAT IS READILY AVAILABLE IN THE UK THESE DAYS, BUT LAMB OR MUTTON CAN BE USED INSTEAD.

SERVES 4–5 AS A MAIN COURSE

SHOULDER OF GOAT 1–1.25kg (2lb 4oz–2lb 12oz), on the bone, but shoulder blade removed

ONIONS 2, chopped

GARLIC 5–6 cloves, crushed

FRESH ROOT GINGER 7.5cm (3in) piece, peeled and coarsely chopped

BAY LEAVES 4–5, broken into small pieces

CLOVES 4, crushed

GREEN CARDAMOM PODS 3, lightly crushed

CUMIN SEEDS 1 teaspoon, crushed

FRESH GREEN CHILLIES 3–4, coarsely chopped

CORIANDER SPRIGS 8–10, coarsely chopped

RED CHILLI POWDER 3 teaspoons

GROUND WHITE PEPPER 2–3 teaspoons

SALT 3–4 teaspoons

DRY RED WINE (PREFERABLY PORTUGUESE) about 1 × 75cl bottle

OLIVE OIL 4–5 tablespoons

STEAMED SHORT-GRAIN RICE to serve

Open out the meat and remove the gristle, sinews and fat. Chop into 7.5cm (3in) chunks on the bone.

Put all the remaining ingredients (apart from the wine and olive oil) in a bowl and mix well. Sprinkle one-third of the mixture in the bottom of a flameproof casserole dish. Arrange a single layer of meat over it. Sprinkle another third of the spice mixture on top and cover with the remaining meat. Pour in enough wine almost to submerge the meat. Pour the olive oil on top, then press the meat down so that it is completely immersed. Cover tightly with a lid and place in the refrigerator for at least 3–4 hours.

Preheat the oven to 200°C/400°F/Gas Mark 6.

Place the casserole dish on the middle shelf of the oven for 30–40 minutes. Stir well, reduce the temperature to 150°C/300°F/Gas Mark 2 and cook, still covered, for a further hour. Stir again, then reduce the temperature to 140°C/275°F/Gas Mark 1 and cook, covered, for another 1–1½ hours.

Using just a spoon or a fork, test to see if the meat is tender; it should cut easily with no need for a knife. If not, re-cover and return to the oven for another 10–15 minutes, or until the meat passes the spoon test. (The cooking time will vary, depending on the type of meat used and the age of the animal it comes from.) When ready, taste and adjust the seasoning.

If you wish, purée the gravy and serve alongside the stew with steamed short-grain rice.

ADRAK KAY PUNJEY

Rack of lamb with mango & chilli salad

THE INDIAN NAME OF THIS DISH TRANSLATES LITERALLY AS 'FIVE FINGERS OF GINGER', BUT 'FINGERS' ALLUDES TO THE BONES IN A SMALL RACK OF LAMB. USE GOOD-QUALITY MEAT, AS THE COOKING PROCESS IS SHORT AND DOES NOT ALLOW FOR TENDERIZING. ALSO, THE BETTER THE MEAT, THE BETTER THE SPICES WILL PENETRATE.

SERVES 4–5

RACKS OF LAMB 4 × 4-bone racks, about 800g (1lb 12oz) total weight

SALT 2 teaspoons, or to taste

LEMON JUICE 1 tablespoon

GROUND TURMERIC ½ teaspoon

CUMIN SEEDS 1 teaspoon

GREEN CARDAMOM PODS 4, lightly crushed

CINNAMON STICK 2.5cm (1in) piece

CLOVES 3–4

FRESH ROOT GINGER 7.5cm (3in) piece, peeled

GARLIC 4–5 cloves, peeled

FRESH GREEN CHILLIES 2 large finger-type

BLACK PEPPERCORNS 4–5

THICK GREEK YOGURT 200ml (7fl oz)

CHOPPED CORIANDER STEMS 1 tablespoon

SUNFLOWER OIL 2 tablespoons, plus extra for greasing (optional)

BOILED POTATOES to serve (optional)

FOR THE GRAVY

ONIONS 2, sliced

SUNFLOWER OIL 1 tablespoon

TOMATOES, 2 chopped

CHOPPED FRESH CORIANDER OR MINT 1–2 tablespoons, for sprinkling (optional)

SALT AND FRESHLY GROUND BLACK PEPPER

FOR THE SALAD

RED ONION 1, thinly sliced

MANGO 1 small and ripe, stoned, peeled and cut into chunks

FRESH GREEN CHILLI 1, sliced

BABY PLUM TOMATOES 6, halved

FRESH MINT 1 handful

CUCUMBER ½, sliced

LIME JUICE from 1 lime

SUNFLOWER OIL 1 tablespoon

Score the fat part of the racks in a regular criss-cross pattern with a sharp knife. Rub in some of the salt, lemon juice and turmeric, then set aside in a lidded container or dish just large enough to hold them. If you wish, you may cut the racks into portions of 3 or 4 bones each, depending on how many people you are serving.

Put the cumin, cardamom, cinnamon and cloves in a small frying pan and toast them gently over a low heat until aromatic and lightly coloured. They must not burn, so keep shaking the pan.

Transfer the contents of the pan to a blender and add all the remaining ingredients. Whiz to a fine paste. Taste and add more salt if necessary.

Coat the racks thoroughly with the paste, then cover tightly and leave at cool room temperature for 2–3 hours. Transfer to the refrigerator and marinate for 1–4 days.

Preheat the oven to 200°C/400°F/Gas Mark 6.

Transfer the racks to a lightly greased or nonstick roasting tray, fat-side up. Place in the oven and immediately lower the temperature to 180°C/350°F/Gas Mark 4. Roast for about 20 minutes, turning once or twice, then lower the temperature to 150°C/300°F/Gas Mark 2 and roast for about another 8 minutes – the time depends on how long the racks have marinated. Remember that the meat should remain slightly pink inside, otherwise it is overcooked. Set the racks aside and keep warm.

To make the gravy, take a clean pan and fry the onions in the oil. When the onions are soft and translucent, add the tomatoes and fry for 1–2 minutes. Tip in the juices from the roasting tray and mix well. Taste and adjust the seasoning if necessary, then add the chopped coriander or mint, if using.

Combine all the salad ingredients in a large bowl and toss well.

Serve the meat with the salad and some boiled potatoes, if you wish, offering the gravy separately.

Note

The racks can be grilled or barbecued if you wish, but in that case, scrape off most of the marinade so that they will cook thoroughly. The excess marinade can be used to make a gravy, or kept for use in another dish.

KHEEMA PURR BATATA

Spiced shepherd's pie

KHEEMA (SPICED MINCEMEAT) IS A MUCH-LOVED STAPLE FOOD THROUGHOUT THE SUBCONTINENT, EVEN AT BREAKFAST, WHEN IT IS COMBINED WITH EGGS AND TOMATOES. OF COURSE, IT IS ALSO MIXED INTO COOKED RICE, BAKED (AS IN THIS PIE) OR ENJOYED WITH SOFT ROLLS, BREAD OR CHAPATTIS. IT CAN EVEN BE USED AS A VOL-AU-VENT FILLING. SERVE THIS PIE WITH THE VEGETABLES OF YOUR CHOICE.

SERVES 4–6

RED CHILLI POWDER 1 teaspoon

GARAM MASALA (see page 58) ½ teaspoon

GROUND TURMERIC ½ teaspoon

GROUND CORIANDER 2 teaspoons

GROUND CUMIN 1 teaspoon

WATER 200ml (7fl oz)

SUNFLOWER OIL 3 tablespoons

GINGER AND GARLIC PASTE (see page 199) 2 tablespoons

FRESH GREEN CHILLIES 4–5, chopped

ONIONS 2, chopped

LEAN MINCED LAMB, MUTTON OR GOAT 500g (1lb 2oz)

LIME JUICE from ½ lime

CHOPPED FRESH CORIANDER 1 heaped tablespoon

SALT

FOR THE TOPPING

FLOURY POTATOES 400g (14oz), roughly cubed

BUTTER 15–30g (½–1oz)

CUMIN SEEDS ½ teaspoon

FRESH GREEN CHILLI 1 finger-type, finely chopped

FRESHLY GROUND BLACK PEPPER ½ teaspoon

2–3 egg yolks (optional)

Combine the dried spices in a small bowl and mix with the measured water. Cover and set aside.

Heat a flameproof casserole dish and add the oil. When a haze forms, add the Ginger and Garlic Paste and green chillies. Sauté, stirring well to prevent sticking. Once the paste becomes pale and aromatic, add the onions and continue to sauté over a low heat until they are reduced almost to a pulp. You might need to add a little water now and then to deglaze the bottom of the pan.

Stir the soaked spices, adding a little more water to the bowl if they are stuck to the sides, then add to the onions. Sauté until the oil emerges, adding a little water again if the mixture shows signs of sticking.

Turn off the heat and add the minced meat, breaking it up with a spatula and combining it thoroughly. I sometimes add a little water to help this process along. Return the pan to the heat and cook gently, stirring regularly, for 20–25 minutes, until the minced meat is cooked. Add salt to taste, then stir in the lime juice and fresh coriander.

While the meat is simmering, preheat the oven to 160°C/325°F/Gas Mark 3. Bring a large pan of water to the boil. When boiling, add some salt and the potatoes, and cook for about 8–10 minutes, until tender. Drain well, then return the potatoes to the pan and place them over a low heat, stirring with a wooden spatula from the bottom up until they look dry, slightly crushed and fluffy. Mash well. Put the butter and cumin seeds on a board and chop them together. Add to the potato along with the green chilli and black pepper, and beat again until creamy. (For extra richness, you can add more butter or the egg yolks, if you wish.)

Tip the meat mixture into a deep pie dish and spoon the mashed potato on top. Spread it out using the back of a fork to give the topping character. Place in the oven for 12–15 minutes, turning the dish from time to time so that the top browns evenly. Serve immediately.

Notes

Chopped tomatoes can be added to the minced meat if you wish (3–4 should be enough).

To give the meat a lovely sheen, add 3 tablespoons tomato ketchup and cook until it is absorbed.

Harissa-marinated shoulder of lamb

LAMB HAS A GREAT WAY OF ABSORBING FLAVOURS, BUT ITS FAT DOES NOT BLEND WELL WITH SPICES, SO IN THIS RECIPE, AS ELSEWHERE, IT IS REMOVED. FORTUNATELY, THE MEAT IS VERY RECEPTIVE TO MARINADES, AND I CREATED THE ONE BELOW WHILE STAYING WITH SOME FRIENDS IN GERMANY. THE SHOULDER JOINT WAS PRETTY BIG, WHICH TOLD ME IT WAS A WELL-AGED ANIMAL, IDEAL FOR SLOW ROASTING. IT CERTAINLY WENT DOWN WELL.

SERVES 6

BONELESS SHOULDER OF LAMB 2kg (4lb 8oz) or more

ONIONS 3, thinly sliced

NEW POTATOES 20 small, peeled and peelings reserved (keep the potatoes and peelings in water to prevent discoloration)

BUTTER 30g (1oz)

CUMIN SEEDS 1 teaspoon

EXTRA VIRGIN RAPESEED OIL 1 tablespoon

GROUND CUMIN 1 teaspoon, for sprinkling

CHOPPED FRESH CORIANDER 1 tablespoon

SALT AND FRESHLY GROUND BLACK PEPPER

FOR THE MARINADE

HARISSA PASTE 3–4 heaped tablespoons

GARLIC 6 cloves, finely chopped

FRESH ROOT GINGER 7.5cm (3in) piece, peeled and finely chopped

FRESH ROSEMARY LEAVES from 3–4 sprigs, chopped

FRESH THYME LEAVES from 3 sprigs

DRIED RED CHILLIES 2 large finger-type, chopped

CUMIN SEEDS 1 teaspoon

BAY LEAVES 2, finely crushed

EXTRA VIRGIN RAPESEED OIL 4 tablespoons

Open out the meat and remove the gristle, sinews and fat. Place the joint in a tray or dish and make some small incisions all over it.

Mix the marinade ingredients in a bowl, seasoning to taste with salt and pepper. Rub the mixture over the meat and into the incisions. Cover and set aside at cool room temperature for 1 hour. Transfer to the refrigerator and leave for at least 3–4 hours (we went gallivanting and left it all day).

When you're ready to cook the lamb, preheat the oven to 180°C/350°F/Gas Mark 4. Scrape the marinade off the lamb and place it in a large flameproof casserole dish. Roll the meat up as best you can and secure it with thin metal skewers or presoaked bamboo skewers or wooden cocktail sticks.

Put the casserole dish over a medium heat and warm the marinade until the oil separates. Push the solids to one side, then add the lamb and brown well on all sides. Set the meat aside on a plate, then add the onions and cook until soft and pale.

Meanwhile, drain the potato peelings and cut into 2.5cm (1in) pieces. Add them to the pan and sauté for a few minutes, until softened. Place the lamb on top of the onion mixture and cover the dish. Transfer to the bottom shelf of the oven and immediately reduce the temperature to 160°C/325°F/Gas Mark 3. Cook for 20 minutes, then lower the heat to 140°C/275°F/Gas Mark 1 and cook for another hour. Turn the lamb, then cover and return to the oven for another 30–40 minutes. The joint is cooked if the juices run clear when it is pierced with a thin skewer, or when a meat thermometer registers the core temperature at 70°C (160°F). If not, cook for a liitle longer, then test again.

While the meat is cooking, drain the potatoes and cook them in boiling salted water for about 10–15 minutes, until tender. Drain again.

Put the butter and cumin seeds on a board and chop them together. Transfer to a roasting tray or frying pan with the oil and heat until melted. Add the boiled potatoes and roast or sauté for about 20 minutes, until brown and crisp. Sprinkle with the ground cumin.

Transfer the cooked joint to a meat plate. Cover with foil and leave to rest in a warm place for 15–20 minutes. Meanwhile, purée the mixture left in the dish, adding a little water if it seems too thick for a sauce. Taste and adjust the seasoning to taste, stirring in the coriander at the last moment.

Carve the meat and serve with the roast potatoes and sauce.

FEIJOADA À GOESA

Goan pork & bean stew

ORIGINALLY FROM PORTUGAL, THIS RECIPE HAS TRAVELLED AROUND THE WORLD, AND VARIATIONS OF IT CAN BE FOUND IN FORMER PORTUGUESE COLONIES. IN BRAZIL, FOR INSTANCE, IT IS MADE WITH ALMOST ANY PART OF THE PIG AND COMBINED WITH BLACK KIDNEY BEANS. IN GOA, ON THE OTHER HAND, YOU WILL OFTEN FIND IT MADE WITH SPICY SAUSAGE AND RED KIDNEY BEANS. MY OWN RECIPE BELOW, WHICH I HOPE WILL APPEAL TO AN EVEN WIDER AUDIENCE, COMBINES SLOW-ROASTED PORK LOIN MEAT WITH SPICY SAUSAGE AND HARICOT BEANS.

SERVES 4–5

LOIN OF PORK 500g (1lb 2oz)

LARGE ONION 1, finely diced

TOMATOES 2, finely diced

CHORIZO OR OTHER SPICY SAUSAGE 200g (7oz), skinned and thickly sliced

HARICOT BEANS 1 × 400g (14oz) can, drained

SALT (optional)

FOR THE MARINADE

CIDER VINEGAR 150ml (5fl oz)

RED CHILLI POWDER 1 teaspoon

GROUND CORIANDER 1 teaspoon

GROUND CUMIN ½ teaspoon

GROUND TURMERIC ½ teaspoon

SALT 1 teaspoon

CRUSHED BLACK PEPPER ¼ teaspoon

FRESH ROOT GINGER 2.5cm (1in) piece, peeled and chopped, then crushed in a mortar

GARLIC 2 cloves, crushed

Combine all the marinade ingredients in a bowl. Add the pork, turning it to coat in the mixture. Cover and set aside to marinate at cool room temperature for 2–3 hours.

Preheat the oven to 150°C/300°F/Gas Mark 2. Transfer the meat to a roasting tray, cover loosely with foil and roast for 40–45 minutes. Pour the roasting fat into a frying pan, then set the meat aside to cool.

Add the onion to the frying pan and fry until brown. Stir in the tomatoes and cook until pulpy. Add the chorizo or spicy sausage and fry until its fat is released.

Cut the cooled pork into thick slices, then add to the tomato mixture along with the beans and a cupful of water. Stir well, then cover and simmer for 4–5 minutes, until the liquid has thickened and everything is heated through. Taste and add more salt only if necessary.

Notes

The pork may be diced rather than sliced if you wish, and you can use different types of bean, such as butter beans.

For a different flavour, add some diced green and red peppers towards the end of the cooking time.

PHILIPPINE DUKERACHE POT SUNGTA LEPA ANI NAARL CHE ROSU GHALUN

Philippine belly of pork with shrimp paste & coconut cream

THIS IS AN ADAPTATION OF A CLASSIC PHILIPPINE RECIPE SENT TO ME BY A FABULOUS COOK CALLED DES RODRIGUEZ TORRES (NOW DECEASED), WHO DID MUCH TO INCREASE AWARENESS OF HER NATION'S CUISINE. WE DEDICATED THIS VERSION TO HER WHEN WE USED IT TO RAISE FUNDS FOR THE PHILIPPINE HURRICANE DISASTER OF 2013. IT IS REALLY QUITE SIMPLE, AND YOU CAN ADJUST THE BAGOONG (SHRIMP PASTE) TO SUIT YOUR TASTE. THE PASTE IS WIDELY AVAILABLE IN THE UK, AND THERE IS NO NEED TO SEEK OUT A SPECIFICALLY FILIPINO PRODUCT.

SERVE WITH STEAMED RICE OR NOODLES AND OTHER VEGETABLES.

SERVES 4–6

BELLY OF PORK 1kg (2lb 4oz), cut into 2.5cm (1in) squares

GARLIC 8–10 cloves, peeled

CRUSHED BLACK PEPPERCORNS 1 tablespoon

CINNAMON STICK 3 × 7.5cm (3in) pieces

SEA SALT 1 teaspoon

CIDER OR WHITE WINE VINEGAR 150ml (5fl oz)

GROUND CUMIN 1 tablespoon

GROUND CORIANDER 1½ tablespoons

RED CHILLI POWDER 2 teaspoons

WATER 150ml (5fl oz)

COCONUT MILK 2 × 400ml (14fl oz) cans, well shaken, or 400g (14oz) powdered coconut mixed with 800ml (1⅓ pints) water

FRESH GREEN CHILLIES 4–5 small, slit lengthways into 4 strips

SHRIMP PASTE 1 tablespoon, or to taste

CHOPPED FRESH CORIANDER 1–2 tablespoons, chopped

SALT AND FRESHLY GROUND BLACK PEPPER (optional)

Place the pork in a bowl. Put the garlic and peppercorns into a mortar and crush to a paste. Add the paste to the pork and rub it in well. Cover and set aside at cool room temperature for 30–40 minutes.

Place the pork in a deep pan, add the cinnamon stick, salt and vinegar and bring to boil, uncovered. Lower the heat and simmer for about 30 minutes, until the liquid has reduced slightly.

Meanwhile, put the cumin, coriander, chilli powder and measured water in a bowl and mix to a paste. Add to the reduced pork liquid and heat until it has almost evaporated – the fat released by the meat will help with this process.

Stir in half the coconut milk, then add the green chillies and cook, covered, over a medium heat for about 20–25 minutes, until the pork is tender.

Add the remaining coconut milk and the shrimp paste and simmer for 5–6 minutes. Check the seasoning, adding salt and pepper if you wish, then stir in the fresh coriander. Serve immediately.

Any pork leftovers can be covered and chilled, and will have a fabulous flavour the following day.

Brined belly of pork with cashew nuts & spinach

AT ONE TIME BELLY OF PORK WAS CONSIDERED CHEAP AND CHEERFUL. BUT OF LATE IT HAS BECOME RATHER FASHIONABLE AND MORE EXPENSIVE. I PARTICULARLY LIKE IT WHEN IT COMES FROM FREE-RANGE AND RARE BREEDS OF PORK – SO MUCH MORE FLAVOURSOME THAN INTENSIVELY FARMED MEAT. WITH THIS RECIPE, YOU NEED TO START THE BRINING PROCESS A DAY BEFORE YOU WANT TO COOK THE MEAT. PATIENT PREPARATION AND SLOW COOKING ARE KEY FACTORS.

SERVES 4–5

UNSCORED PORK BELLY 1kg (2lb 4oz), cut into 7.5cm (3in) squares

BUTTER AND EXTRA VIRGIN RAPESEED OIL 1 tablespoon of each (optional)

CUMIN SEEDS 1 heaped teaspoon

RAW CASHEW NUTS OR 50:50 ALMONDS AND PINE NUTS 150g (5½oz)

GARLIC 3 cloves, finely chopped

FRESH SPINACH 450g (1lb)

SALT AND FRESHLY GROUND BLACK PEPPER

FOR THE BRINE

CIDER VINEGAR 1 litre (1¾ pints)

MUSCOVADO SUGAR OR JAGGERY 300g (10½oz)

COARSE SEA SALT 150–200g (5½–7oz)

CINNAMON STICK 2 × 7.5cm (3in) pieces

DRIED RED CHILLIES 5–6 large, broken in half

LIME JUICE from 1 lime

FOR THE HERBED JUS

GOOD CHICKEN STOCK 500–600ml (18–20fl oz)

CHOPPED CORIANDER STEMS 2 tablespoons

CHOPPED CURRY LEAVES 1 tablespoon, preferably fresh; if using dried, soak in water for 10–12 minutes, and dry thoroughly before chopping

GARLIC 2 cloves, finely chopped

FINELY CHOPPED FRESH ROOT GINGER 1 tablespoon

FRESH GREEN CHILLI 1, finely chopped

CLOVES 3–4, lightly crushed

Place all the brine ingredients in a stainless steel saucepan and bring to the boil over the heat and simmer for 3–4 minutes, then switch off the heat and set aside to cool.

Place the pork pieces in a large plastic container and add the brining liquid. Seal tightly and refrigerate for at least 12–15 hours, turning now and then.

Combine all the jus ingredients in a pan and bring to the boil. Then simmer for about 4–5 minutes, wiping down the sides of the pan with a wet brush from time to time, until the liquid has reduced by two-thirds. Strain and check the seasoning, adding salt if needed. (If you wish, pepper can be added just before serving.) The jus can be used straight away, or covered and refrigerated for up to 3 days.

Preheat the oven to 200°C/400°F/Gas Mark 6.

Drain the pork well. Place a deep flameproof casserole dish over a low heat. Add the pork pieces in a single layer skin-side down (you might need to work in batches), and gradually increase the heat until the skin side only is well browned. Set the meat aside on a plate, draining the fat into a frying pan.

Return all the meat to the casserole dish and pour in the chilled jus. Bring to the boil, then place on the middle shelf of the oven, uncovered, for 15 minutes. Lower the temperature to 120°C/250°F/Gas Mark ½, cover with a lid and cook for 3–4 hours, until done to your liking. It should be virtually falling apart to the touch.

Heat the pork fat reserved in the frying pan. (If you didn't get much, heat the optional butter and oil.) Add the cumin seeds, nuts and garlic, and stir over a gentle heat until all change colour. As soon as that happens, add the spinach, tossing until it has wilted.

Serve the pork with the reheated jus and vegetables, and whatever else you fancy eating it with.

See image overleaf

CACHAÇO DE PORCO MARINADO

Marinated pork collar slices

HERE IS A FINE EXAMPLE OF THE MARRIAGE BETWEEN PORTUGUESE AND GOAN CUISINE. PORK IS A VERY POPULAR MEAT IN BOTH CULTURES, BUT IN GOA IT IS OFTEN COMBINED WITH A SPICY MARINADE – GREAT FOR CHARGRILLING KEBABS OR CHOPS, BUT ALSO EXCELLENT FOR ROASTING LARGE JOINTS. I LIKE TO USE A RATHER OVERLOOKED CUT, PORK COLLAR, AND PREPARE IT IN A PRESSURE COOKER – THOUGH IT CAN BE ROASTED OR, IF YOU CUT THE MEAT INTO SMALL PIECES, BARBECUED OR GRIDDLED.

NOTE THAT THE MARINADE IS ALSO SUITABLE FOR CHICKEN, BUT NOT FOR LAMB OR BEEF.

SERVES 4–6

COLLAR OF PORK 1.5kg (3lb 5oz), cut into 4–6 slices (ask your butcher to do this)
EXTRA VIRGIN RAPESEED OIL 2–3 tablespoons
ONIONS 2, sliced
STOCK OR WATER 250–300ml (9–10fl oz)
FRIED POTATO SLICES to serve

FOR THE MARINADE

DRIED RED CHILLIES 20g (¾oz), preferably large
BLACK PEPPERCORNS 4–6
CINNAMON STICK 7.5–10cm (3–4in) piece, broken into smaller bits
CLOVES 3–4
CUMIN SEEDS 1 heaped teaspoon
GARLIC 8–10 cloves, peeled
FRESH ROOT GINGER 7.5cm (3in) piece, peeled and coarsely chopped
FRESH GREEN CHILLIES, 2–3 finger-type, coarsely chopped
LEMON JUICE 2 tablespoons
PALM OR CIDER VINEGAR about 100ml (3½fl oz)
SALT

Place all the marinade ingredients in a blender and whiz to a paste, adding more vinegar if needed to make it smooth and fine.

Spread the marinade all over the pork in a dish, then cover and refrigerate overnight, or for at least 8 hours.

Heat the oil in a large frying pan. Scrape the excess marinade off the pork, reserving it for later, and brown the meat, skin-side down at first, then all over. Set aside on a plate.

Add the onions and a little of the stock or water to the frying pan and cook over a high heat until the liquid has evaporated. Lower the heat and continue to cook the onions until they are soft. Add the reserved marinade and cook for 8–10 minutes, until the chillies are thoroughly cooked.

Place the onions in a pressure cooker (if you have one), pour in the remaining stock or water and sit the pork on top. Seal the cooker tightly and bring up to pressure, placing over a high heat for 5 minutes, then a medium heat for 5 minutes and finally a very low heat for 30 minutes. Allow the cooker to cool, then open and check that the meat is cooked through and the sauce sufficiently reduced. If not, return to the heat without the lid and cook until the sauce has reduced to the desired consistency.

Alternatively, preheat the oven to 140°C/275°F/Gas Mark 1. Place the onions in a flameproof casserole dish, cover tightly and cook in the oven for 40–45 minutes. Gently turn the meat over and test to see if it is cooked through and the sauce sufficiently reduced. If not, return to the heat without the lid and cook for another 5–10 minutes, until the sauce has reduced to the desired consistency.

Serve the pork with the sauce poured over, with fried potato slices.

CARIL DE FRANGO COM MARINADA DE RUM

Chicken curry with butternut squash, potato & rum

IT IS A COMMON HABIT IN GOA TO ADD EITHER PALM OR CASHEW FENI LIQUEUR TO MEAT DISHES. AS FENI IS NOT AVAILABLE IN THE UK, I HAVE USED DARK RUM INSTEAD. THIS IS STILL QUITE AUTHENTIC, AS INDIA IS ONE OF THE WORLD'S LARGEST PRODUCERS OF RUM.

SERVES 6–8

CHICKEN LEGS 6–8, with skin, chopped in half through the bone

SALT 1 teaspoon, plus extra to taste (optional)

FRESHLY GROUND BLACK PEPPER ½ teaspoon, plus extra to taste (optional)

SUNFLOWER, GROUNDNUT OR EXTRA VIRGIN RAPESEED OIL 4 tablespoons

RED ONIONS 2, chopped

BUTTERNUT SQUASH 500g (1lb 2oz), deseeded and cut into 5cm (2in) cubes

WAXY POTATOES, 2–3 large, cut into 4cm (1½in) pieces

COCONUT MILK 1 × 400ml (14fl oz) can, well shaken

CHICKEN STOCK 500ml (18fl oz)

TAMARIND PASTE OR PULP 1 tablespoon, or to taste, as some tamarind preparations are very strong

BAY LEAVES 3

DARK RUM 1½–2 tablespoons

LIME JUICE from ½ lime

CHOPPED FRESH CORIANDER 1–2 tablespoons (optional)

STEAMED OR BOILED RICE to serve (optional)

FOR THE MARINADE

GROUND TURMERIC ¼ teaspoon

GROUND CORIANDER 2 teaspoons

BLACK MUSTARD SEEDS 1 teaspoon

GARLIC 4 cloves, roughly chopped

FRESH GREEN CHILLIES 2–3 finger-type, coarsely chopped

SEA SALT 1 teaspoon

Combine all the marinade ingredients in a blender with a little water and whiz to a smooth paste.

Put the chicken in a bowl, rub in the salt and pepper, then stir in the marinade. Cover and refrigerate for at least 2–3 hours.

When you're ready to start cooking, heat half the oil in a large, heavy-based saucepan or flameproof casserole dish over a medium heat. Scrape the excess marinade off the chicken pieces, reserving it for later. Sauté the meat for 3–4 minutes on each side, turning regularly until browned all over. Transfer to a plate and keep warm.

Heat the remaining oil in the empty pan, then add the onions and sauté for about 6–8 minutes, until soft.

Add the squash and potatoes and sauté for 5–7 minutes, stirring regularly, until just soft and pale golden brown.

Add the reserved marinade to the pan and stir well to coat the vegetables. Cook for another 3–4 minutes, stirring often, until the spices are fragrant.

Return the browned chicken to the pan and add the coconut milk, chicken stock, tamarind paste or pulp (a bit at a time, tasting as you go) and the bay leaves. Stir well and bring the mixture to the boil. Lower the heat and simmer until reasonably thick, then pour in the rum. Cover the pan and simmer for 20–30 minutes, or until the chicken is tender and the sauce has thickened. At that point, gently stir in the lime juice. Taste and adjust the seasoning as necessary. Sprinkle with the chopped coriander if you like.

Serve with steamed or boiled rice, if liked.

RESHMI KATHI KAAB IMLI KHAJOOR NI CHUTNEY

Chicken kebab rolls with date & tamarind chutney

IN INDIA THE WORD 'KAVAAB' IS USED NOT JUST FOR SKEWERED MEAT BUT ALSO FOR MEATBALLS, BURGERS AND SMALL CUTLETS. IN THIS RECIPE THE MEAT IS COMBINED WITH SPICES AND DRIED FRUITS AND ROLLED INTO SHEEK (SKEWER) KEBABS. THEY'RE GREAT WITH SALAD, TUCKED INSIDE A WRAP, ADDED TO A CROQUETTE MIXTURE OR EVEN CHOPPED AFTER BEING HALF-COOKED, THEN SIMMERED IN THE SAUCE.

MAKES 8–10 KEBABS AND ABOUT 1 LITRE (1¾ PINTS) CHUTNEY

MINCED CHICKEN LEG AND BREAST 500g (1lb 2oz)
WHITE BREAD 3–4 slices, crusts removed, cubed
FRESH CORIANDER STEMS 1 tablespoon, chopped
FRESH MINT 10–12 leaves, torn
FRESH ROOT GINGER 7.5cm (3in) piece, peeled and chopped
GARLIC 3–4 cloves, chopped
GROUND CARDAMOM ¼ teaspoon
GROUND CINNAMON ½ teaspoon
GROUND MACE ¼ teaspoon
FRESH GREEN CHILLIES 2
STONED DATES 10–12, coarsely chopped
SULTANAS 2 tablespoons
CASHEW NUTS 12–15
FRESHLY GROUND BLACK PEPPER ¼ teaspoon
SUNFLOWER OIL OR BUTTER for griddling
SALT

FOR THE CHUTNEY

TAMARIND PULP 150–200g (5½–7oz)
STONED DATES 250g (9oz)
JAGGERY OR MUSCOVADO SUGAR 250g (9oz)
RED CHILLI POWDER 1 teaspoon
CUMIN SEEDS 1 heaped teaspoon
BOILING WATER 1.7 litres (3 pints)

TO SERVE

FLOUR TORTILLAS 10–12 wraps, warmed until soft
FRESH SPINACH LEAVES shredded
EGG 1, beaten

First make the chutney. Place the tamarind in a deep saucepan with the dates, jaggery or sugar, chilli powder and cumin seeds. Pour the measured boiling water over and soak for 1 hour, stirring occasionally. Put the pan over a medium heat and bring to the boil, then part-cover and simmer for 40–50 minutes. Strain into a bowl. Remove any tamarind seeds or strands, then purée in a blender. Press through a sieve and blend with the liquid. Season with salt. Taste the chutney and add a bit more sugar if you wish. It will keep well for several months in the refrigerator if stored in a sterilized screwtop jar (see Note, page 189). Use as required, always with a dry spoon and wiping the rim and lid with kitchen paper before resealing.

For the kebabs, put all the ingredients (except the oil or butter) into a food processor and pulse until a soft dough forms. (If you don't have a processor, chop everything finely by hand and mix together in a bowl.) Take a small flat piece of the chicken mixture and pan-fry it. When you're ready to make the kebabs, cut along the sides of a plastic bag and open it out. Divide the mince into 6–8 equal pieces and roll each into a ball. Place a ball just below the fold in the bag. Flap the far side of the bag over it towards you. Take firm hold of the bottom sheet of the bag, place a ruler against the mince and push it away from you. A perfect sausage-shaped kebab forms right in front of your eyes! Stop pushing when it reaches about 1.5cm (⅝ in) thick. Open out the bag and trim the ends off the kebab, then place it on a tray lined with greaseproof paper. Scrape any remaining mixture off the bag and return it to the bowl. Repeat the rolling process until all the mixture has been used up. Refrigerate for 1–2 hours to firm up. Light a barbecue or preheat the grill. When very hot, put the kebabs on the rack, brush with oil or butter and cook for 6–8 minutes, turning often. Use a thermometer to make sure they are done right through (the core temperature should be 65–70°C /150–160°F).

To serve, spread chutney on each tortilla, leaving a thumb-width border around the edge. Top with spinach, then brush the border with beaten egg. Place a kebab about 7.5–10cm (3–4in) from one end, fold in both sides of the tortilla, then roll up and press to seal. Press down on the barbecue rack or a hot griddle pan, turning regularly, until hot right through and brown on all sides. Eat straight away with more chutney.

JUNGLI LAAL MAAS

Game in yogurt with spices & chilli

FOR CENTURIES, HUNTING WAS A FAVOURITE ACTIVITY IN RAJASTHAN, PARTICULARLY AMONG THE RULING MAHARANAS. INEVITABLY, MANY RECIPES WERE DEVISED TO USE WHAT WAS 'BAGGED', AND THIS STEW IS ONE OF THEM. IT GENERALLY FEATURES WILD BOAR, BUT ALSO GOES WELL WITH VENISON, BUFFALO, HARE AND GAME BIRDS. THIS SAUCE IS PUNGENT, BUT I BELIEVE YOU WILL RELISH EVERY MORSEL OF THE FINISHED DISH.

THE BLOOD, OFFAL AND MUSK GLAND OF THE DEER ALSO FOUND AN INTERESTING USE – IN A SAFFRON-SPICED LIQUEUR CALLED KESAR KASTOORI. IT MIGHT NOT SOUND APPETIZING, BUT IT TASTES GOOD AND IS WONDERFULLY WARMING ON A WINTER'S DAY.

SERVES 4

GAME MEAT 500g (1lb 2oz), cut into cubes
GROUND TURMERIC ½ teaspoon
FRESH ROOT GINGER 5cm (2in) piece, peeled and chopped
GARLIC 10–12 cloves, peeled
DARK RED CHILLIES 6–8 finger-type, coarsely chopped
CUMIN SEEDS 1 heaped teaspoon
CORIANDER SEEDS 1 tablespoon
GHEE 3–4 tablespoons
ONIONS 3–4, finely sliced
EXTRA VIRGIN RAPESEED OIL 2 tablespoons
CINNAMON STICK 5cm (2in) piece
GREEN CARDAMOM PODS 3–4, lightly crushed
CLOVES 3–4
MACE 2 blades
FRESH RED CHILLI 1 large, broken into 1cm (½in) pieces
THICK GREEK YOGURT 300ml (10fl oz)
TOMATOES 2, chopped
CHOPPED FRESH CORIANDER 1–2 tablespoons
SALT
HOT CHAPPATIS OR FLOUR TORTILLAS to serve

Put the meat into a shallow dish and mix in the turmeric and some salt. Cover and set aside.

Place the ginger, garlic, red chillies and cumin and coriander seeds in a blender with a little water and whiz to a paste.

Melt the ghee in a frying pan, add the onions and fry until golden brown and crisp. Drain the ghee into a flameproof casserole dish, then set the onions aside.

Add the oil to the ghee and place over a medium heat. When hot, add the cinnamon stick, cardamoms, cloves, mace blades and red chilli and sauté for 2 minutes, until the spices change colour and swell. The chilli should darken but not burn.

Add the meat and sauté for about 6–8 minutes, until evenly brown. Do not overstir or the fat will cool and the meat will release its juices.

Stir in the ginger paste and sauté for a further 4–5 minutes, until the fat is released. Add enough water to cover the meat by 1cm (½in), then put the lid on the casserole dish and simmer for 25–30 minutes, until the meat is three-quarters done.

Purée the fried onions with the yogurt in the blender, then stir the mixture into the meat. Add the tomatoes and scrape the sides of the pan clean, then cover again and cook until the meat is tender.

Check the seasoning, adding more salt if needed, then stir in the fresh coriander. The finished dish may look a bit oily, which is traditional in India because in the days before refrigeration a layer of fat on top of food helped to preserve it. However, you can spoon that off if you wish and save it for frying sliced potatoes.

Serve with hot chappatis or flour tortillas.

GALINHA CAFREAL COM RUM

Chicken cafreal with rum

INTRODUCED TO GOA BY THE PORTUGUESE, WHO BROUGHT IT FROM MOZAMBIQUE AND ANGOLA, CHICKEN CAFREAL IS A SPICY DISH THAT IS SOMEWHAT SIMILAR TO PERI-PERI CHICKEN. THE TRADITIONAL RECIPE CONTAINS NO ALCOHOL, BUT THE GOANS DECIDED TO ADD CASHEW FENI, A POWERFUL BREW THAT IS NOT WIDELY AVAILABLE OUTSIDE GOA. HERE I'VE USED RUM AS AN ALTERNATIVE.

SERVE WITH A SALAD OF YOUR CHOICE.

SERVES 4

BONELESS CHICKEN THIGHS 4, with skin, cubed or cut into strips

OLIVE OR EXTRA VIRGIN RAPESEED OIL 2–3 tablespoons

ONIONS 2, sliced

POTATOES 2 large, halved and cut into slices 5mm (¼in) thick

TOMATOES 3–4, thickly sliced

CHICKEN STOCK OR WATER 150–200ml (¼–⅓ pint)

CHOPPED FRESH CORIANDER 1 tablespoon, to garnish

SALT AND FRESHLY GROUND BLACK PEPPER

FOR THE MARINADE

GARLIC 6–8 cloves, roughly chopped

FRESH ROOT GINGER 7.5cm (3in) piece, peeled and roughly chopped

FRESH GREEN CHILLIES 2–3 finger-type

CORIANDER SEEDS 1 heaped teaspoon

FRESH CORIANDER 6–8 sprigs

GARAM MASALA (see page 58) ½ teaspoon

LIME JUICE 1 tablespoon

DARK RUM 2 tablespoons

Put all the marinade ingredients into a blender with some salt and pepper and whiz them to a smooth paste. Taste and adjust the seasoning.

Place the chicken in a bowl, add the marinade and mix thoroughly. Cover and refrigerate overnight, or for a least 2 hours.

When you're ready to start cooking, preheat the oven to 150°C/300°F/Gas Mark 2. Heat 1–2 tablespoons of the oil in a large frying pan and gently sauté the onions for 8–10 minutes, until soft and pale. Transfer to a flameproof casserole dish, spreading them out in the bottom.

Scrape the excess marinade off the chicken pieces, reserving it for later. Add the chicken to the empty pan and sauté over a medium heat until golden brown. Stir the reserved marinade into the cooked chicken, then arrange the chicken pieces on top of the onions.

Add a bit more oil to the pan if needed and fry the tomatoes for 1 minute on each side. Dot them among the chicken pieces.

Add a bit more oil to the pan if needed and fry the potatoes for about 10 minutes, until slightly crisp. Arrange them on top of the chicken and add the stock or water. Cover with a lid and cook in the oven for about 10 minutes, until the potatoes are tender and the chicken is cooked through.

Season to taste and garnish with the fresh coriander.

See image overleaf

BATTAKH MASALA

Duck masala

GUNTUR IN THE STATE OF ANDHRA PRADESH IS ONE OF THE BIGGEST PRODUCERS OF CHILLIES IN INDIA, SO THE REGION BOASTS SOME OF THE SPICIEST DISHES IN THE COUNTRY. THIS RECIPE IS A GOOD EXAMPLE. USUALLY MADE WITH LAMB OR MUTTON, IT'S ALSO FABULOUS WITH DUCK. SERVE WITH RAITA, OR BREAD AND YOGURT.

SERVES 4

SMALL OVEN-READY DUCK about 1.5kg (3lb 5oz), on the bone, chopped into small pieces

GROUND TURMERIC 1 teaspoon

RED CHILLI POWDER 1 tablespoon

EXTRA VIRGIN RAPESEED OIL 3 tablespoons (optional)

CURRY LEAVES 20–30, preferably fresh, chopped; if using dried, soak in water for 10–12 minutes, and dry thoroughly before chopping

ONIONS 3–4, chopped

GINGER AND GARLIC PASTE (see page 199) 1 heaped tablespoon

TOMATOES 3–4, chopped

CHOPPED FRESH CORIANDER 1½ tablespoons

GROUND WHITE PEPPER 1 tablespoon, or to taste

SALT

RAITA to serve

FOR THE SPICE MIXTURE

WHITE POPPY SEEDS 1 tablespoon

BLACK PEPPERCORNS 8–10

CORIANDER SEEDS 1 tablespoon

CUMIN SEEDS 2 teaspoons

CINNAMON STICK 2 × 5cm (2in) pieces

CLOVES 4–5

GREEN CARDAMOM PODS 4–5, lightly crushed

First make the spice mixture. Soak the poppy seeds in warm water for 2 hours. Skim the scum off them, drain well and spread out in a small roasting tray.

Preheat the oven to 120°C/250°F/Gas Mark ½.

Put the other spices in a separate roasting tray. Place both trays in the oven for 20–30 minutes. Remove the larger tray, then turn off the oven and leave the poppy seeds inside with the door closed until dried and toasted, stirring from time to time to prevent sticking.

When all the spices are toasted, grind them together in a mortar or grinder to a fine powder.

Put the duck in a bowl, add the turmeric, red chilli powder and some salt, and mix well. Transfer to a pressure cooker, seal tightly, bring up to pressure and cook over a medium–low heat for 15–20 minutes, then set aside to cool down. Alternatively, place the meat in a flameproof casserole dish, add a cupful of water and cook, covered, over a medium–low heat for 30–40 minutes, until the duck is cooked through.

Drain well, reserving the liquid. If set aside to cool, the fat will rise and solidify, which makes it easy to lift off. If you wish, you can use this fat instead of the oil when cooking the rest of the dish.

Heat the oil or a similar amount of reserved duck fat in a frying pan. When hot, add the curry leaves, which will splutter, and stir briefly. Add the chopped onions and sauté until well browned. Stir in the Ginger and Garlic Paste, heating it until its oil is released.

Add the tomatoes and cooked meat and cook over a high heat until the tomatoes are soft.

Sprinkle the spice mixture into the pan and sauté for 5 minutes. Pour in the reserved duck liquid and bring to the boil over a medium heat. Continue cooking until most of the liquid evaporates, leaving a nice thick sauce on which the fat or oil is clearly visible.

Stir in the coriander, then add the white pepper, or to taste. Serve immediately with raita.

Note

If you would like to try making this dish with lamb, use 800g (1lb 12oz) shoulder meat, trimmed and cut into 1cm (½in) pieces. There is no need to remove the fat from the stock, as lamb is much less fatty than duck.

Beef curry Marie Kiteria

AUNTY MARIE WAS A PART-TIME COOK EMPLOYED AT THE HOTEL WHERE I WORKED IN GOA. SHE CAME IN THE MORNING, PREPARED A FEW OF THE SPECIALS (WITH WHICH WE WERE NOT THEN FAMILIAR) AND THEN LEFT. SOME OF THE DISHES SHE CREATED, SUCH AS THIS ONE AND HER RAZOR CLAMS IN COCONUT (SEE PAGE 111), WERE SIMPLY FABULOUS. I BELIEVE SHE WAS BETTER THAN ALL OF US IN THE KITCHEN PUT TOGETHER. THIS IS GREAT SERVED WITH RICE OR POTATOES, OR JUST SOME WARM CRUSTY BREAD.

SERVES 4–6 DEPENDING ON ACCOMPANIMENTS

ONIONS 750g (1lb 10oz), roughly chopped

EXTRA VIRGIN RAPESEED OIL 2 tablespoons

THICK GREEK YOGURT 200ml (7fl oz)

GARLIC 4–6 cloves, finely chopped

TOMATO PURÉE 3 tablespoons

FRESH ROOT GINGER 2 × 5cm (2in) pieces, peeled and finely chopped

CURRY LEAVES 12–15, preferably fresh; if using dried, soak in water for 10–12 minutes before adding

GROUND CUMIN 1 heaped teaspoon

GROUND CORIANDER 2 heaped teaspoons

RED CHILLI POWDER 3 heaped teaspoons

GROUND TURMERIC 1 teaspoon

BEEF RUMP 500g (1lb 2oz), cubed

GARAM MASALA (see page 58) 1 teaspoon (optional)

COCONUT MILK 1 × 400ml (14fl oz) can, well shaken

FRESH GREEN CHILLIES 2–3 finger-type, slit lengthways into 4 strips

SALT

Put the onions and oil in a blender and whiz to a smooth paste.

Pour the yogurt into a flameproof casserole dish, add the garlic, tomato purée, ginger, curry leaves and spices and mix well. Stir in the beef. Cover tightly and place over a medium heat for about 4–5 minutes, stirring regularly as it sticks easily. It is ready when the oil separates and the beef is tender. Taste and add some salt.

To finish the dish, beat the garam masala with the coconut milk until smooth. Pour into the casserole, add the green chillies and simmer for 6–8 minutes. Check the salt content and serve immediately.

CROQUETES DE CARNE DE VACA

Goan beef croquettes

WHEN LIVING IN GOA, MY WIFE PERVIN AND I OFTEN VISITED A LITTLE BAR AND RESTAURANT CALLED COPACABANA, WHICH WAS RUN BY A MAN CALLED UNCLE PAULI AND HIS DAUGHTER MARIA. HE SERVED THE MOST AMAZING CROQUETTES MADE BY HIS WIFE, AND THEY WERE AN IDEAL ACCOMPANIMENT TO SOME GOOD GROG! I HOPE YOU'LL TRY THIS RECIPE, INSPIRED BY THOSE SNACKS WE SO MUCH ENJOYED. IT CERTAINLY SHOWS THAT SIMPLE FOOD CAN BE GREAT.

MAKES 20

MINCED BEEF 750g (1lb 10oz)

ONION 3 small, finely chopped

GARLIC 5 cloves, chopped

FRESH GREEN CHILLIES 2 finger-type, chopped

CHOPPED FRESH ROOT GINGER 1 tablespoon

GROUND TURMERIC 1 teaspoon

GROUND CORIANDER 1 heaped tablespoon

GROUND CUMIN ½ tablespoon

RED CHILLI POWDER 2 teaspoons

EXTRA VIRGIN RAPESEED OIL 1 tablespoon, plus extra for deep-frying

WATER 250ml (9fl oz)

WHITE BREAD 4–6 slices, crusts removed

CHOPPED FRESH CORIANDER 1 heaped tablespoon

SALT

FOR THE COATING

PLAIN FLOUR about 100g (3½oz)

EGGS 2–3, lightly beaten

MEDIUM SEMOLINA about 150g (5½oz)

TO SERVE

MAYONNAISE-BASED SAUCE

TOMATO KETCHUP

Put the meat, onion, garlic, spices, oil and measured water into a flameproof casserole dish over a medium heat and mix well to break down all the lumps. Cook, stirring regularly, for about 20–25 minutes, until the meat is fully cooked and dry. Spread out on a tray to cool.

Transfer the cooled meat mixture to a food processor, if you have one. Break up the bread, add it to the meat mixture with the fresh coriander and process to a smooth, thick paste. Taste and adjust the salt content.

If you don't have a food processor (no one did when this recipe was created, so the meat mixture was ground using a pestle and mortar), put the meat mixture in a large bowl, removing as much fat as possible. Soak the bread in water for 1 minute, then squeeze dry. Work the bread and fresh coriander into the meat mixture by hand. Taste and adjust the salt content.

Divide the meat mixture into 20 equal pieces and form into sausage shapes.

Put the flour, beaten egg and semolina into 3 separate shallow dishes. Roll each croquette first in the flour, then the egg and finally the semolina, ensuring they are well covered. Transfer to a plate and chill for 30–40 minutes.

When you're ready to cook, heat a 7.5cm (3in) depth of oil in a deep pan until nearly smoking. Deep-fry the croquettes, straight from the refrigerator, for about 3–4 minutes, until crisp and golden outside and heated right to the middle.

Serve with a mayonnaise-based sauce and some tomato ketchup.

Massaman beef curry

PEOPLE SAY THAT THIS CURRY ORIGINATED IN 17TH-CENTURY THAILAND, ALTHOUGH THERE IS DISAGREEMENT ABOUT WHETHER IT IS FROM THE CENTRE OR THE SOUTH. THE ARGUMENT IN FAVOUR OF THE SOUTH IS THAT IT IS OBVIOUSLY INFLUENCED BY THE NEARBY MALAY CUISINES, AND THAT MASSAMAN COULD DERIVE FROM THE MALAY WORD MASAM (SOUR). HOWEVER, THE DISH WAS ALSO KNOWN AS MUSSULMAN CURRY, 'MUSSULMAN' BEING AN ARCHAIC INDIAN FORM OF THE WORD 'MUSLIM', PERHAPS PICKED UP FROM SOUTH INDIAN MUSLIM TRADERS. THE DISH MAY BE AN EARLY EXAMPLE OF 'FUSION FOOD', AS IT COMBINES TRADITIONAL INDIAN SPICES, SUCH AS CLOVES, STAR ANISE AND MACE, WITH TYPICALLY THAI INGREDIENTS, SUCH AS LEMON GRASS AND GALANGAL.

THIS CURRY IS MOST COMMONLY MADE WITH BEEF, PARTICULARLY AMONG STRICT MUSLIMS, BUT THERE ARE ALSO VARIATIONS THAT USE DUCK, CHICKEN, MUTTON, GOAT AND EVEN PORK. SERVE WITH JASMINE RICE.

SERVES 4

RAW SKINNED PEANUTS 3 tablespoons

COCONUT CREAM 1 × 400ml (14fl oz) can, well shaken

STEWING BEEF 600–700g (1lb 5oz–1lb 9oz), cut into 2.5cm (1in) pieces and slightly flattened

WATER 250ml (9fl oz)

RED ONION 1, sliced

KAFFIR LIME LEAVES 4, finely shredded

CINNAMON STICK 7.5cm (3in) piece

TAMARIND PASTE 1 tablespoon, or to taste

SOFT BROWN SUGAR OR PALM SUGAR 1 tablespoon

NAHM PLA (THAI FISH SAUCE) 1 tablespoon

WAXY POTATOES 500g (1lb 2oz) small

FRESH RED CHILLIES 1 or 2, finely sliced for sprinkling

FRESH CORIANDER 3–4 sprigs

SALT

FOR THE MASSAMAN PASTE

DRIED RED CHILLIES 15 large

CORIANDER SEEDS 2 tablespoons

CUMIN SEEDS 1 tablespoon

CINNAMON STICK 7.5cm (3in) piece

CLOVES 3–4

BLACK PEPPERCORNS 5

CHOPPED GARLIC 4 tablespoons

CHOPPED PINK SHALLOTS 6 heaped tablespoons

SHRIMP PASTE 1 heaped teaspoon, or to taste

LEMON GRASS 1–2 stems, very finely chopped

COARSELY CHOPPED FRESH GALANGAL ROOT 1 tablespoon

NAHM PLA (THAI FISH SAUCE) 1–2 teaspoons

Start by making the massaman paste. Soak the chillies in warm water for 15–20 minutes, until soft. Meanwhile, toast the coriander, cumin, cinnamon, cloves and peppercorns in a wok or dry frying pan to release the flavours. Transfer to a mortar or blender and grind finely.

Drain the chillies and add to the mortar or blender with the remaining paste ingredients. Pound or process until smooth. (The paste can be made in advance and stored in a sterilized screwtop jar – see Note, page 189 – covered with a layer of oil. It will keep in the refrigerator for up to 3 months.)

To make the curry, preheat the oven to 120°C/250°F/Gas Mark ½. Put the peanuts on a baking tray on the middle shelf of the oven for 15–20 minutes, then switch off the heat, leaving the peanuts inside. By the time you need them, they should be nice and crisp.

Heat the oven again, this time to 150°C/300°F/Gas Mark 2.

Place 2–3 tablespoons of the coconut cream in a flameproof casserole dish and bring it to the boil. Once it has reduced a little, add the massaman paste and stir well to prevent it from sticking to the bottom. Cook for 2 minutes, until aromatic.

Add the beef and cook over a medium-high heat for 10–12 minutes, until the meat is well browned. Stir in the remaining coconut cream and the measured water, then add the onion, lime leaves, cinnamon stick, tamarind, sugar and nahm pla. Coarsely chop about two-thirds of the peanuts and add those too. Bring to a simmer, then cover tightly and place on the middle shelf of the oven for 1 hour. Add the potatoes, stir briefly and return to the oven for 30 minutes. When done, stir well, then taste and adjust the salt content.

Allow the curry to sit for a few minutes, then sprinkle with the red chillies, the remaining peanuts and fresh coriander.

See image overleaf

FISH & SHELLFISH

PURÉ DE BATATA COM PEIXE, BACON, COUVE FLOR E PIMENTA

Baked mashed potato with fish, bacon, cauliflower & chilli

IT MIGHT COME AS A SURPRISE TO SOME PEOPLE THAT MANY INDIAN HOMES REGULARLY MAKE BAKED CAULIFLOWER. MOST ADD CHILLI AND SPICES, AND SOME WILL MIX FISH, POTATO OR PEAS IN IT. MY RECIPE GIVES IT AN INDIAN TWIST TOO.

SERVES 4–6

FLOURY POTATOES 4, roughly cubed

ENGLISH MUSTARD PASTE 1 tablespoon

GRATED HARD CHEESE 2–3 tablespoons (pecorino or São Jorge are particularly good for this)

CAULIFLOWER 1 small, cut into small pieces

WHITE FISH FILLETS 500g (1lb 2oz), skinned and diced

BUTTER 40g (1½oz), at room temperature, plus extra for greasing

FRESH GREEN CHILLIES 2, chopped

CUMIN SEEDS ½ teaspoon

SMOKED STREAKY BACON 6–8 rashers, derinded and chopped

EGGS 3, separated

SALT AND FRESHLY GROUND BLACK PEPPER

TO SERVE (optional)
YOUR CHOICE OF VEGETABLES
HOT CRUSTY BREAD

Bring a large pan of water to the boil. When boiling, add some salt and the potatoes, and cook for about 8–10 minutes, until tender. Drain well, reserving the water, then return the potatoes to the pan and place them over a low heat, stirring with a wooden spatula from the bottom up until they look dry, slightly crushed and fluffy. Mash well or pass through a ricer or mouli. Season generously with black pepper, then stir in the mustard and cheese. Transfer to a bowl, cover with kitchen paper and refrigerate.

Return the potato water to the boil and cook the cauliflower in it for 3–4 minutes, until still slightly firm. Drain, again reserving the water, and set the cauli aside in a colander to cool.

Return the water to the pan and blanch the fish in it for 1–2 minutes, until just cooked. Drain, again reserving the water (you should have just a few tablespoons left – if not, heat to reduce it to that amount). Allow the fish to cool.

Place the butter on a chopping board, mix in the chillies and cumin seeds, then chop together. Place the mixture in a frying pan and warm gently until the butter has melted. Add the bacon and cook until crisp. Set aside to cool.

Add the egg yolks to the mashed potato and mix well. Add the cauliflower, fish and bacon and mix again. Taste and adjust the seasoning.

Preheat the oven to 180°C/350°F/Gas Mark 4. Butter a large baking dish.

Add a pinch of salt to the egg whites, then whisk into soft peaks. Add half to the potato mixture, folding it in with a spatula. Fold in the remainder, then add a little of the reserved fish water to get the desired consistency.

Tip into the prepared dish and place on the middle shelf of the oven for 15–20 minutes, moving it to the top shelf for the last 4–5 minutes so that it browns well. Test if it is cooked right through by inserting a knife or thermometer into the centre – the blade should feel hot, or the temperature should be 70–75°C (160–170°F).

Serve with other vegetables, if you wish, and some hot crusty bread.

SUNGTA CHE BARBEQUE JIRAY ANI MIRAY GHALUN

Barbecued king prawns with cumin & crushed pepper

TRADITIONALLY GOAN AND FIERY HOT. THIS RECIPE NEEDS TO BE PREPARED AT LEAST FOUR HOURS BEFORE YOU WANT TO START COOKING, AS THE PRAWNS MUST BE MARINATED. IT'S BEST TO USE WHOLE UNPEELED PRAWNS BECAUSE THE SHELL PROTECTS THEM FROM TURNING RUBBERY WHEN COOKED.

SERVE WITH SALAD AND BUTTERED RICE.

SERVES 4

RAW TIGER OR KING PRAWNS
12 large, in shells, defrosted slowly overnight in the refrigerator if frozen

FOR THE MARINADE

CUMIN SEEDS 1 teaspoon

BLACK PEPPERCORNS 10–12, or to taste

FRESH ROOT GINGER 5cm (2in) piece, peeled and coarsely chopped

RED CHILLI POWDER 1 teaspoon

LIME JUICE from 1 lime

SALT

EXTRA VIRGIN RAPESEED OIL
1–2 tablespoons

Using kitchen scissors, trim the prawns, cutting out the part just above the eyes to remove the antennae, and the sharp pointed spear on the head. Now cut along the top of the shell from head to tail. Slit the flesh to about halfway down and carefully lift out and discard the black vein. Rinse under the tap and see that it is all clean. After the third prawn you will become quite an expert. Drain well, then set aside in a bowl.

Put the cumin and peppercorns in a dry frying pan over a medium heat and toast until aromatic. Allow to cool slightly, then transfer to a blender and whiz until finely ground.

Crush the ginger in a mortar, then place in a small piece of muslin and squeeze the juice (1 tablespoon) into the blender. (Save the crushed ginger for making tea.)

Add the remaining marinade ingredients to the blender and whiz together. Taste and adjust the seasoning: you might like to make it hotter by adding more crushed peppercorns.

Pour the marinade over the prawns and mix well, getting as much as possible under the shells without breaking them. Cover and refrigerate for at least 4–6 hours. If leaving for longer (no more than 10–12 hours in total), make sure they are in a tightly sealed container.

When you're ready to cook, light a barbecue or heat a grill to its highest temperature. Thread the prawns on to metal or presoaked bamboo skewers, then place on a rack and cook for about 2 minutes on each side. Break open and taste a prawn to see if the flesh is cooked. Do not overcook!

Eat with your fingers.

MACHLI TIKKA DHUWARA

Hot smoked salmon tikka

WHILE SALMON IS NOT AN INDIAN FISH, THE REGIONS AROUND MUMBAI AND THE WEST COAST ON THE ARABIAN SEA BOAST A FABULOUS FISH CALLED 'RAWAS', NICKNAMED 'THE BOMBAY SALMON'. THIS MUCH-PRIZED AND EXPENSIVE FISH RESEMBLES SALMON IN SHAPE BUT IS WHITE FLESHED, VERY FLAKY AND DELICATE.

IN INDIAN COOKING, SMOKING OVER SPICES GOES BACK CENTURIES. HOWEVER, THE STYLE APPLIED IS DIFFERENT TO ELSEWHERE, WITH THE MEAT BEING SMOKED FOR JUST A FEW MINUTES TO PREVENT IT FROM BECOMING TOO FLAVOURED. THIS SALMON TIKKA IS EASY TO MAKE AND EASY TO SMOKE. TRY IT AND FIND OUT FOR YOURSELF!

SERVES 6

1.5–1.8 kg (3lb 5oz–4lb) salmon fillet, scaled, pin-boned and cut into 24 equal chunks

FOR THE MARINADE
CORIANDER SEEDS 1 tablespoon
CUMIN SEEDS 1 teaspoon
BLACK PEPPERCORNS 1 teaspoon
GROUND TURMERIC 2 tablespoons
RED CHILLI POWDER 1 tablespoon
GINGER AND GARLIC PASTE (see page 199) 3 tablespoons
HOT ENGLISH MUSTARD PASTE 4 tablespoons
HONEY 4 tablespoons
LEMON JUICE from 2 lemons
DILL 1 small bunch, chopped
SEA SALT 1 teaspoon
SCOTTISH MUSTARD OIL OR EXTRA VIRGIN RAPESEED OIL 2 tablespoons

FOR THE SMOKING
CLOVES 3–4, coarsely crushed
GREEN CARDAMOM PODS 5–6, lightly crushed
GHEE OR OIL 1–2 tablespoons

First make the marinade. Put the coriander, cumin and peppercorns into a frying pan and heat gently until aromatic and lightly toasted. Allow to cool slightly, then crush in a mortar.

Put all the remaining marinade ingredients into a bowl, add the toasted spices and mix well. Add the salmon chunks, tossing well to coat thoroughly, then cover and leave to marinate for 4–6 hours, or in the refrigerator overnight.

Remove all but the middle shelf from your oven and preheat it to 180°C/350°F/Gas Mark 4.

Meanwhile, put 4–5 chunks of charcoal into a metal or heatproof bowl. Light them and heat on the hob until glowing.

Sit a wire rack over a roasting tray and arrange the salmon pieces on it, leaving a gap between them. Place on the middle shelf of the oven. Put the bowl of glowing charcoal underneath and sprinkle with the cloves, cardamom and ghee or oil. It will immediately start smoking, so quickly shut the oven door. Leave for 2 minutes, then switch off the heat and leave for a further 10–12 minutes, until the salmon is cooked to your liking. Serve immediately.

See image overleaf

Note

The oven will need to air after the smoking is done so that all the smells disperse.

VAGHEO AURELIANO

Tiger prawns Aureliano

AN EXTREMELY POPULAR DISH IN MY RESTAURANT CAFÉ SPICE NAMASTE, THIS RECIPE WAS CREATED WHEN I WAS STILL LIVING IN GOA. IT IS NAMED AFTER ONE OF OUR CHEFS, AURELIO, WHO ALWAYS ENDED UP MAKING IT.

SERVE WITH FINELY SHREDDED SALAD AND/OR GARLIC BREAD, PREFERABLY CIABATTA. IF YOU ARE SERVING THESE AS A MAIN COURSE, OFFER THEM WITH CRUSHED SPICED POTATOES, VEGETABLES AND A LITTLE SALAD.

SERVES 4 AS A STARTER OR 2 AS A MAIN COURSE

RAW TIGER PRAWNS 4 large Madagascan-type (you get 4–5 per kg/2lb 4oz)

LIME JUICE ½ teaspoon, or to taste

EXTRA VIRGIN RAPESEED OIL 50ml (2fl oz)

FRESH GREEN CHILLIES 2 finger-type

GARLIC 3–4 cloves, finely chopped

GREEN PEPPER ½, cored, deseeded and diced

ONION 1, finely chopped

CUMIN SEEDS ½ teaspoon, crushed

GROUND CORIANDER ½ teaspoon

TOMATO 1, deseeded and chopped

PEELED PRAWNS 10–12 small, raw or cooked, chopped

SAFFRON THREADS a pinch, gently toasted, then soaked in a little water

EGG 1, hard boiled, shelled and white part chopped

CHOPPED FRESH CORIANDER 1 tablespoon

FRESH WHITE BREADCRUMBS from 2–3 crustless slices

GRATED PARMESAN CHEESE 1–2 tablespoons (optional)

BUTTER for dotting (optional)

SALT AND FRESHLY GROUND BLACK PEPPER

Using a small sharp knife, slit the prawns from head to tail, going almost to the bottom of the flesh but without cutting them in half. Carefully lift out and discard any black veins.

Thread the tiger prawns all the way through on presoaked bamboo skewers, then open them out like butterflies. Place the skewers in a baking dish, pour the lime juice over them and season with salt and pepper. Set aside.

Preheat the oven to 190°C/375°F/Gas Mark 5.

Heat the oil in a frying pan and sauté the green chillies and garlic until the garlic turns pale. Add the green pepper and onion and continue cooking gently until the onion becomes soft. Add the cumin seeds and ground coriander and stir for 1 minute, then add the tomato.

If your small prawns are raw, put them in now and sauté until they are just cooked. If they are already cooked, simply mix them in. Add the saffron and its soaking water.

Take the pan off the heat and mix in the chopped egg white and fresh coriander. Check for seasoning. Stuff the mixture into the slit tiger prawns. Combine the breadcrumbs with the Parmesan, if using, and spread over the prawns. Alternatively, dot with butter if you wish.

Bake on the top shelf of the oven for 10–12 minutes, checking often to ensure the prawns don't overcook. If the crumbs haven't browned, place the dish under a hot grill for just a minute. Serve immediately.

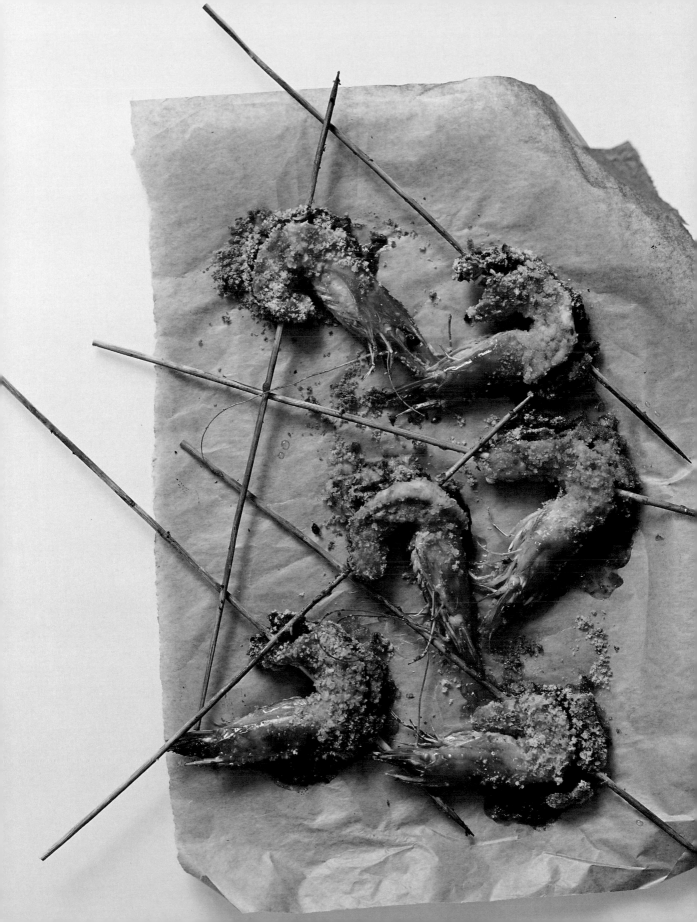

NAARLANTUL TISREO

Razor clams in coconut

I HAVE NEVER COME ACROSS RAZOR CLAMS IN INDIA, SO THIS RECIPE IS USUALLY MADE WITH ORDINARY CLAMS OR OTHER BIVALVES. HOWEVER, RAZOR CLAMS ARE FABULOUS MEATY BEASTS WITH GREAT FLAVOUR, AND WORK BRILLIANTLY HERE. THEY NEED CAREFUL CLEANING, SO BUILD IN TIME FOR THAT WHEN MAKING THIS DISH.

SERVES 3–4 AS A STARTER

CORIANDER SEEDS 1 heaped teaspoon

CUMIN SEEDS ½ teaspoon

FRESH ROOT GINGER 7.5cm (3in) piece, peeled and finely chopped

GARLIC 3–4 cloves, finely chopped

COCONUT OR OTHER OIL 2 tablespoons

BLACK MUSTARD SEEDS 1 heaped teaspoon

FRESH GREEN CHILLIES 1–2 finger-type, chopped

DRIED RED CHILLI 1, deseeded and sliced

CURRY LEAVES 15–20, preferably fresh, finely shredded; if using dried, soak in water for 10–12 minutes, and dry thoroughly before shredding

ONION 1, chopped

KOKUM (BUTTERNUT) BERRY 1, shredded, or ½ dried sour plum or raw mango (optional)

GROUND TURMERIC ½ teaspoon

RED CHILLI POWDER ½ teaspoon

FRESHLY GRATED COCONUT from ½ a large coconut, or 200g (7oz) frozen coconut, defrosted, or 100g (3½oz) desiccated coconut, soaked in enough warm water to just cover for 30 minutes

LIME JUICE from ½ lime

TOMATO 1 plum-type, diced

RAZOR CLAMS 500g (1lb 2oz), preferably fresh, cleaned and opened (see Note below)

FRESH CORIANDER a few leaves, torn or coarsely chopped

SALT

Set out all the ingredients, along with the sterilized half-shells (see Note below).

Place a frying pan over a medium heat, add the coriander and cumin seeds and toast until aromatic. Allow to cool slightly, then crush well in a mortar. Add the ginger and garlic and crush together.

Heat the oil in a wok, kadhai or large saucepan until a couple of mustard seeds sizzle straight away when dropped in the pan. Add the remaining mustard seeds and cover loosely with a lid while they pop and splutter.

Stir in the toasted seed mixture, adding a little water if it sticks to the pan. Add the green and red chillies and the curry leaves, and sauté for 30–60 seconds, then add the onion and kokum or sour plum or raw mango, if using. When the onion turns pale, add the turmeric and red chilli powder plus a little water and cook for 1–2 minutes. Drain the coconut, if necessary, and add it to the pan, heating and stirring to prevent burning, until it releases its aroma. Taste, then add the lime juice a bit at a time until you are happy with the flavour.

Stir in the tomato, add the clams and increase the heat to maximum. Toss briefly, then cook without stirring or shaking for 30 seconds. Repeat this step 3 more times so that the clams cook for just 2 minutes in total. Season to taste with salt.

Sprinkle in the fresh coriander and serve the clams straight away on the half-shells.

Note

Razor clams are straightforward to prepare, but allow at least 30 minutes for this if you've never done it before.

1. Rinse your clams under cold running water to remove all the sand. Transfer them to the freezer for 30–40 minutes so that they are unconscious for the next step.

2. Place the clams in a colander in the sink and pour boiling water over them (don't let them soak or the meat will become rubbery and cook). The shells will pop open in about 5 seconds, at which point immerse them in cold water.

3. Using a small sharp knife, prise the shells fully open and remove the meat by running the tip of the knife along the inside and cutting through the muscle. Set the meat aside.

4. Retain one half of each shell, rinse well, then pour boiling water over them to sterilize.

5. Using kitchen scissors and squeezing the clam, cut open the body from top to tail and snip out all the dark parts.

6. Rinse the meat gently in cold water and it's ready to cook.

BHARELU SHAYVUT

Stuffed lobster

ARE YOU FRIGHTENED OF PREPARING LOBSTER AT HOME? WELL, DON'T BE! THIS RECIPE IS VERY EASY AND WILL MAKE YOU FEEL VERY ACCOMPLISHED. ALTHOUGH LOBSTER CAN BE A BIT PRICEY, IT'S A GREAT TREAT FOR A SPECIAL OCCASION. TRY TO USE FRESH LOBSTERS IF POSSIBLE. FROZEN RAW LOBSTERS (GENTLY DEFROSTED IN THE REFRIGERATOR OVERNIGHT) CAN BE USED INSTEAD, BUT THE FLAVOUR WILL NOT BE THE SAME.

SERVES 4

LOBSTERS 4, about 300–400g (10½–14oz) each

LEMON JUICE 1 teaspoon

GROUND TURMERIC ½ teaspoon

BUTTER 30g (1oz)

GARLIC 8–10 cloves, finely chopped

FRESH GREEN CHILLIES 2, deseeded if you wish and finely chopped

ONIONS 2, finely chopped

GROUND CUMIN 1 heaped teaspoon

GROUND CORIANDER 2 heaped teaspoons

SPRING ONIONS 4, chopped

CHOPPED FRESH CORIANDER 2 heaped tablespoons, or to taste

EGGS 2, hard boiled, shelled and chopped (optional)

TOMATO 1, deseeded and diced (optional)

PULAO OR PLAIN STEAMED RICE to serve

If using live lobsters, place them in the freezer for about 30 minutes to render them comatose. Break off the claws and crack their shells lightly with a hammer (to help them cook). Using a pointed knife, pierce the lobster just below the base of the head and use a firm sawing motion to slit the lobster open without cutting right through it. Turn the lobster around and slit the head in the same way.

Remove the meat and coral from the shells, discarding the pasty part in the centre. Wash the shells well.

Put the cracked claws and empty shells in a pan of boiling water over a high heat for 2 minutes. Remove the claws, but let the shells remain in the water until they are bright red. Drain and rinse under cold running water, then flip them over, place your thumbs inside the cavity and carefully pull the shell open while still flexible. Bend the tail and tuck it just behind the head to hold its position. Place a chopping board over them so that they do not curl. (This process is called butterflying.)

Using a large, heavy knife, hit the narrow edge of each claw, slightly twisting the blade as you do so, and it should crack across the middle. Gently pull to remove the meat from the claws (in one piece if you can) and set it aside.

Dice the rest of the lobster meat into 1cm (½in) pieces. Place in a bowl and toss with the lemon juice and turmeric. Now add the claw meat, keeping it whole if possible.

Put the butter in a flameproof casserole dish over a medium heat. When hot and frothing, add the garlic and chillies and sauté for 2 minutes. Mix in the onions and continue sautéeing until they are soft.

Add the cumin and ground coriander and sauté for 1–2 minutes. Increase the heat to high and mix in the lobster meat (reserving the claw meat) and spring onions. Allow to cook without stirring for 1 minute, then stir once and leave for another minute. Repeat this once or twice more, until the meat is cooked but not rubbery. Season and set aside, but keep warm.

Stuff the lobster mixture into the shells on individual plates, placing the claw meat alongside as a garnish.

There will be juice left in the pan, so put it back on the heat and reduce slightly. Stir in the fresh coriander, plus the chopped eggs and diced tomato, if using. Spoon this mixture over each lobster and serve immediately with pulao or plain steamed rice.

BHARELU KOOLYO

Goan-style stuffed crab

CRABS ARE FOUND ABUNDANTLY IN ALL COASTAL REGIONS OF INDIA, AND FRESHWATER CRABS ARE ALSO CAUGHT IN SOME PARTS OF CENTRAL INDIA. IT HAS TO BE SAID THAT STUFFING CRABS IS NOT PARTICULARLY INDIAN, BUT THE PORTUGUESE HABIT INFILTRATED GOA, WHERE IT WAS GIVEN AN INDIAN TWIST.

SERVES 4–5 AS A STARTER

DRESSED CRABS 6, or 500g (1lb 2oz) white and brown crabmeat (a 70:30 split is fine)

OLIVE OIL 2 tablespoons

FRESH ROOT GINGER 5–7.5cm (2–3in) piece, peeled and finely chopped

GARLIC 4–5 cloves, finely chopped

FRESH GREEN CHILLIES 2 finger-type, finely chopped with seeds

RED ONIONS 2 small, finely chopped

PIRI-PIRI MASALA (see page 207)
2–3 teaspoons

PLUM TOMATOES 2, pulp reserved and flesh diced

CHOPPED FRESH CORIANDER 1 heaped tablespoon

FRESH OR FROZEN PEAS 4 tablespoons, cooked and cooled

LEMON OR LIME JUICE to taste (optional)

EGGS 2–3, hard boiled, shelled and chopped

GRATED MATURE CHEDDAR CHEESE 2–3 tablespoons, for sprinkling

SALT

SALAD to serve

If using dressed crab, remove the meat, then wash and dry the shells. Otherwise, use washed scallop shells or shallow dishes.

Place the oil in a large, heavy-based frying pan over a medium heat. When hot but not smoking, add the ginger, garlic and chillies and sauté for a minute or so, then add the onions. When they become pale, stir in the Piri-Piri Masala and cook until its oil is released.

Add the tomato pulp to the mixture and cook until slightly reduced, then add the tomato flesh and warm through.

Take the pan off the heat and mix in the crab meat, coriander and peas. Stir well and check for seasoning: you might like to add a little lemon or lime juice, as well as salt.

Preheat the grill. Meanwhile, set out the prepared shells or 4 shallow dishes and divide the mixture equally between them. Sprinkle with the chopped egg, followed by the grated cheese. Place under the hot grill until the cheese has melted and is lightly browned.

Serve hot with a salad.

Notes

For a change, top the crab with just the chopped egg and roll up in warmed or griddled chappatis.

Alternatively, toss the filling with some freshly diced cooked peeled prawns and serve over a salad.

Oriental fish parcels

FOR THIS RECIPE IT'S BEST TO USE WHOLE WHITE FISH, SUCH AS SMALL SEA BASS,
BREAM OR MACKEREL, WHICH ARE EASY TO BONE THROUGH THE MIDDLE.
FAILING THAT, USE GURNARD FILLETS OR SOMETHING SIMILAR.

SERVES 2 AS A MAIN COURSE
4 AS A STARTER

WHOLE FISH 2, about 400–450g (14oz–1lb) each, cleaned and scaled, heads left on if you like

LIME JUICE 1–2 teaspoons

EXTRA VIRGIN RAPESEED OIL 1–2 tablespoons

SEA SALT AND FRESHLY GROUND BLACK PEPPER

FOR THE FILLING

CELERY 1 stick, cut into thin strips

CARROT 1, cut into thin strips

SPRING ONIONS 2, cut into thin strips

KAFFIR LIME LEAVES 2–3, finely chopped

FRESH ROOT GINGER 5cm (2in) piece, peeled and finely sliced

GARLIC 2 cloves, finely sliced

FRESH GREEN CHILLI 1, slit lengthways, deseeded if required, then shredded

FRESH CORIANDER a few sprigs

LIME JUICE 1–2 teaspoons

RAW PRAWNS 250–300g (9–10½oz), peeled, deveined and finely chopped

LIGHT SOY SAUCE 2–3 teaspoons, plus extra to serve

NAHM PLA (FISH SAUCE) 1–2 teaspoons

CINNAMON STICK 5cm (2in) piece

MUSHROOM AND EGG FRIED RICE (see page 170), to serve

Slit the fish right along both sides of the backbone. Snip off the bone at either end and pull it out. Save for making stock or soup.

Wash the fish and pat dry with kitchen paper. Rub some salt, pepper and lime juice into both the inside and outside of the fish. Place on a plate, cover and refrigerate.

Preheat the oven to 200°C/400°F/Gas Mark 6. Line a baking dish with foil, leaving a short overhang on 3 sides, and a long overhang at one end that will flap right over the fish. Spread a fine layer of oil on the foil in the bottom of the dish.

Place the vegetables in a bowl and add the lime leaves, ginger, garlic, chilli and coriander. Mix well, then spoon roughly one-third of this mixture along the centre of the lined dish, spreading it wide enough to fit the fish. Sprinkle with a little salt and lime juice, then place the fish on top.

Combine the prawns with one-third of the remaining vegetable mixture and add the soy sauce and nahm pla to your taste. Spoon this mixture into the cavity of the fish, but do not overfill.

Sprinkle any remaining vegetables around the fish, place the cinnamon stick on top, then flap the foil over and crimp the edges tightly to keep in the steam. If possible, place the dish on a baking sheet and heat for 1–2 minutes on the hob. Transfer to the middle of the oven and cook for 15–20 minutes. The foil should puff up with steam.

Serve the fish at the table so that your family or guests can enjoy the aromas that are released when the parcel is opened. Offer the fish with Mushroom and Egg Fried Rice and a light soy sauce for drizzling if needed.

Note

If **serving this recipe as a starter,** it is best to remove the fish heads before cooking and cut each fish into 2 neat portions. These can then be stuffed to make 4 small parcels.

PATRA MA KOLMI NI BHARELI MACHCHI NAY PATIA

Prawn-stuffed fish in banana leaf & patia

PATIA IS A PARSEE CLASSIC, A DARK VINEGAR-BASED SAUCE IN WHICH FISH OR MEAT MAY BE
COOKED. I STRONGLY RECOMMEND USING IT WITH GREY MULLET, A FISH OFTEN OVERLOOKED
BUT WORTH GETTING TO KNOW. THE STUFFED FISH CAN ALSO BE SERVED WITHOUT THE PATIA
IF YOU WISH, AND BAKING PARCHMENT OR FOIL CAN BE USED INSTEAD OF BANANA LEAF.

THE FISH GOES WELL WITH STEAMED RICE AND PURÉED LENTILS, OR SALAD AND WARM BREAD.

SERVES 4

WHOLE SMALL WHITE FISH such as red or grey mullet 4, about 300–350g
(10½–12oz) each, cleaned, scaled and backbone removed
GROUND TURMERIC ¾ teaspoon
LIME JUICE from ½ lime
RAW PRAWNS 400–500g (14oz–1lb 2oz) small, peeled and deveined
FRESH GREEN CHILLIES 2–3 finger-type, peeled and finely chopped
FRESH ROOT GINGER 5cm (2in) piece, finely chopped
FRESH MINT 15–20 leaves, finely chopped
FRESH CORIANDER 6–8 sprigs, finely chopped
SALT ½ teaspoon
BANANA LEAF 1, if available
EXTRA VIRGIN RAPESEED OIL for brushing

FOR THE PATIA
EXTRA VIRGIN RAPESEED OIL 2–3 tablespoons
CINNAMON STICK 7.5cm (3in) piece
ONIONS 2, finely chopped
RED CHILLI POWDER 1 heaped teaspoon
GROUND CUMIN 2 teaspoons
GROUND CORIANDER 1 tablespoon
CANE OR CIDER VINEGAR 2 tablespoons
WATER 2–3 tablespoons
GARLIC 3 cloves, finely chopped
FRESH ROOT GINGER 5–7.5cm (2–3in) piece, peeled and chopped
FRESH GREEN CHILLIES 3, slit lengthways into 4 strips
TOMATOES 3–4, chopped
TAMARIND PULP 2–3 tablespoons, or to taste
RAW CANE SUGAR 1 tablespoon OR JAGGERY 5cm (2in) piece, or to taste
CHOPPED FRESH CORIANDER 2–3 tablespoons
SALT

Open out the fish and place them on a board with the inside uppermost. Mix the turmeric and half the lime juice in a small bowl and spread the paste inside the fish.

Chop the prawns and put them in a bowl. Mix in the chillies, ginger and herbs, then add the salt and stir in the remaining lime juice. Spoon this mixture equally into each fish, then press together with your hands to get them back into shape. Cover and refrigerate while you prepare the banana leaf, if using, or baking parchment.

Preheat the oven to 160°C/325°F/Gas Mark 3.

If using a banana leaf, wipe it clean with a warm, damp cloth, then trim off the thick membrane on one side and snip off any broken or brown edges. Spread the leaf out and divide it into 4 pieces large enough to wrap around each fish. Light a gas hob and, holding a piece of leaf at one end, drag it gently over the flame; this will soften the leaf and make it glossy, as well as killing any surface bacteria. Brush the brighter side of each piece with oil.

Alternatively, set out 4 separate pieces of baking parchment or foil and brush with oil.

Place the fish on the leaves, parchment or foil and wrap them up, tying with string at either end if necessary. (You might not need string if the overlap is big and the parcels are kept close together to stop them flapping open.)

Place in a baking dish or roasting tray and cook in the oven for 20–25 minutes. (The fish cooks more quickly in parchment or foil than banana leaf, in which case start checking if the fish is ready after about 15 minutes.) Set aside to rest while you make the patia.

Heat the oil in a deep saucepan, then add the cinnamon stick and stir-fry for 30 seconds. Add the onions and sauté over a medium heat, stirring regularly, until soft and browned.

Meanwhile, put the ground spices into a small bowl, add the vinegar and the measured water and mix to a smooth paste. Cover and set aside.

When the onions are well browned, add the garlic, ginger and fresh chillies, and sauté for 1–2 minutes, adding a little water if the mixture starts sticking to the pan.

Stir in the vinegar mixture and continue sautéeing until nearly dry. Add the tomatoes, tamarind and sugar or jaggery, and cook gently for a further 4–5 minutes. Taste and adjust the seasoning as you wish to make it sweeter or more sour. Stir in the fresh coriander and set aside.

Serve the fish parcels on individual plates, allowing people to open them at the table, and offer the patia on the side. It is traditional to eat off the banana leaf, but parchment or foil will need to be set aside. Put a platter on the table for these bundles and any bones.

See image overleaf

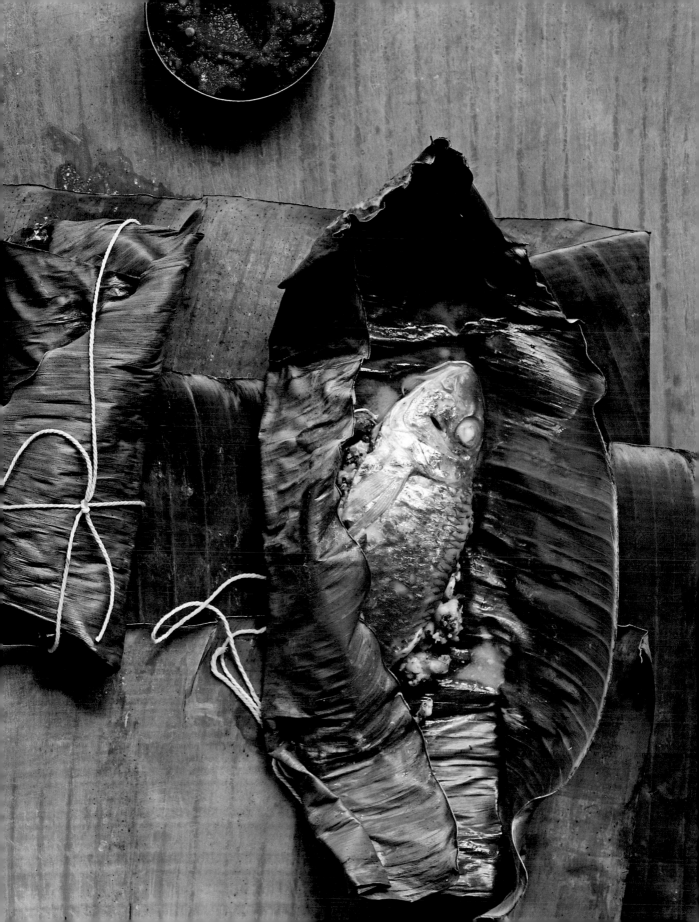

Haddock with mussels & clams

WHILE WORKING AT THE TAJ HOTEL IN GOA MANY MOONS AGO, I REGULARLY HAD TO CREATE SEVERAL OPTIONS OUTSIDE THE MAIN MENUS FOR LONG-TERM GUESTS, WHO QUICKLY EXHAUSTED ALL THE USUAL CHOICES ON OFFER. THE FISH MARKET WAS ONLY A FEW MILES AWAY, SO I WOULD HOP ON A BIKE AND GO TO SEE WHAT I COULD BUY TO TEMPT JADED PALATES. THE SELECTION WAS ENORMOUS – EVERYTHING FROM PRIME LOCAL FISH TO KING PRAWNS AND ROCK LOBSTERS – SO I OFTEN FOUND MYSELF MAKING SEAFOOD SOUPS AND STEWS, SUCH AS BOUILLABAISSE OR BOURRIDE. THIS RECIPE HAS FEWER INGREDIENTS THAN THOSE CREATIONS, BUT IS STILL SOMEWHAT STEW-LIKE.

SERVES 4–6

HADDOCK FILLET 500g (1lb 2oz), or fillets of sea bass, pollock, coley, tilapia or snapper (a combination of them can be used too)

MUSSELS about 50, washed, scrubbed and debearded

CLAMS about 50, washed and scrubbed

BUTTER 35g (1¼oz), at room temperature

CUMIN SEEDS 1 heaped teaspoon

FRESH GREEN CHILLI 1, roughly chopped

GARLIC 2–3 cloves, crushed

WHITE OR ROSÉ WINE 150–200ml (5–7fl oz) – Sauvignon, Pinot Gris or Riesling would be good

RED CHILLI POWDER 1 teaspoon

SHALLOTS 2–3 small, chopped

LEEK 1, thinly sliced, then cleaned and drained

BAY LEAVES 2

FRESH FENNEL 1 baby bulb, or ¼ standard bulb, cut into thin strips

PASSATA 200g (7oz)

CHOPPED FRESH CORIANDER 1 heaped tablespoon

FRESH DILL a few sprigs, chopped

SALT AND FRESHLY GROUND BLACK PEPPER

CRUSTY BREAD to serve (optional)

Cut the fish into bite-sized pieces and place in a bowl. Place the mussels and clams in a separate bowl. Cover both and refrigerate until needed.

Place the butter on a chopping board and mix in the cumin seeds, then chop until they are very tiny. Mix in the green chilli and garlic, then chop again until finely chopped.

Place a flameproof casserole dish over a high heat and add the wine. Bring to the boil and bubble until reduced by half. Add the mussels and clams, cover with a lid and shake the pan for about 1 minute, until the shells open (discard any that remain closed). Drain, reserving the juices. Set the shellfish aside.

Return the juices to the casserole, place over a medium heat and poach the fish for 1 minute, or just until the meat becomes opaque. Using a slotted spatula, transfer the fish to a plate. Pour the juices into a jug.

Put the flavoured butter into the empty casserole dish and melt over a medium heat. Sauté for 1–2 minutes, until the garlic in it just about changes colour, then add the red chilli powder, shallots, leek, bay leaves and fennel.

Sauté for a few minutes until aromatic, then pour in the reserved juices and passata. Simmer for 3–4 minutes.

Meanwhile, scoop most of the mussels and clams out of their shells, keeping just a few with the shells on for garnish. Add the shellfish meat and fish to the tomato mixture and check the seasoning. Gently stir in the coriander and dill, taking care not to break up the fish.

To serve, spoon equal amounts of the seafood into soup plates or bowls, then pour the liquid over them. Serve with crusty bread, if you wish.

BATATA PURR BHUJAELI MACHCHI

Masala grilled fish on a bed of potatoes

AS YOU KNOW BY NOW, PARSEES LOVE EGGS, BUT POTATOES RUN THEM A CLOSE SECOND. THEY ARE USED HERE AS A BASE FOR ANY WHITE-FLESHED FISH, BUT FILLET OF SEA BREAM WORKS PARTICULARLY WELL. WHOLE FISH CAN BE USED IF YOU PREFER, BUT I RECOMMEND YOU BONE THEM FIRST.

SERVES 4

SEA BREAM FILLETS 4, with skin, about 200g (7oz) each

GROUND CUMIN 1 heaped teaspoon

CORIANDER SEEDS 1 tablespoon, toasted and coarsely crushed (see page 56)

LIME JUICE from 1 lime

GINGER AND GARLIC PASTE (see page 199) 1 tablespoon

DRIED RED CHILLI FLAKES 2 teaspoons

SALT 1½ teaspoons

EXTRA VIRGIN RAPESEED OIL 2 tablespoons

SALT AND FRESHLY GROUND BLACK PEPPER

GREEN SALAD to serve (optional)

FOR THE POTATOES

BUTTER 30g (1oz), plus extra for brushing (optional)

CUMIN SEEDS 1 teaspoon

GARLIC 4–5 cloves, thinly sliced

RED ONIONS 2 small, sliced 3mm (⅛ in) thick

POTATOES 4, sliced 3mm (⅛ in) thick

Cut the fillets in half or leave them whole – whatever you wish. Place the remaining ingredients in a bowl, mix well, then taste and adjust the seasoning if necessary. Add the fillets, turning them in the masala to coat well. Cover and refrigerate until needed.

For the potatoes, put the butter in a large frying pan and melt over a medium heat. When foaming, add the cumin seeds and garlic, and sauté until the garlic turns pale brown.

Add the onions and sauté for 2 minutes, or until soft. Add the potatoes, sprinkle with a little salt and pepper and mix gently. Cover the pan with a lid and cook for about 10 minutes, turning the potatoes at least once until half done.

Preheat the oven to 200°C/400°F/Gas Mark 6.

Transfer the potato mixture to a baking dish and arrange the fillets on top, exposing as much of their skin as possible. Season again if you wish. Cook on the middle shelf of the oven for 12–15 minutes, then place on the top shelf or under a hot grill for another 3–4 minutes to crisp the skin on both sides. If you wish, brush the skin with a little softened butter before its final browning.

Serve straight from the dish, with a green salad, if you wish.

Grilled fish steak with quinoa & Indian chimichurri salad

HERE IS A WONDERFUL EXAMPLE OF FUSION FOOD: FISH STEAKS, FOUND GLOBALLY; QUINOA, AN INCREASINGLY POPULAR SOUTH AMERICAN GRAIN; AND CHIMICHURRI, A SALSA OR DRESSING, PERHAPS OF BASQUE ORIGIN, THAT INDIANS WOULD DESCRIBE AS A FRESH CHUTNEY. CHIMICHURRI IS BEST MADE A COUPLE OF DAYS IN ADVANCE SO THAT THE INGREDIENTS MELD TOGETHER AND ADD VIBRANT FLAVOUR TO THE FISH. ANY LEFTOVERS CAN BE PURÉED AND ADDED TO MAYONNAISE AS A CREAMY DRESSING.

THE TASTY AND SUBSTANTIAL SALAD CONTAINS QUINOA AND CHICKPEAS, BOTH OF WHICH NEED TO BE SOAKED BEFORE USE (UNLESS YOU BUY CANNED), SO BUILD THAT INTO YOUR PREPARATION TIME.

SERVES 4–6

EXTRA VIRGIN RAPESEED OIL 2 tablespoons
FISH STEAKS 4–6, thickly cut from a large salmon, trout or whatever you fancy, with skin
CUMIN SEEDS 1½ teaspoons, toasted and crushed (see page 56)
LIME JUICE from ½ lime
SALT AND FRESHLY GROUND BLACK PEPPER
CRUSTY BUTTERED BREAD to serve

FOR THE CHIMICHURRI
GARLIC 3 cloves, peeled
CHOPPED FLAT LEAF PARSLEY 1 tablespoon
CHOPPED FRESH CORIANDER 4 tablespoons
CHOPPED FRESH MINT 2 tablespoons
CHOPPED FRESH OR DRIED OREGANO ½ tablespoon
DRIED RED CHILLI FLAKES ½ teaspoon
CANE, MALTED, RED WINE OR CIDER VINEGAR 2 tablespoons
FRESH LIME JUICE 2 tablespoons
BLACK PEPPERCORNS ½ teaspoon, crushed
SALT ½ teaspoon, or to taste
OLIVE OIL OR EXTRA VIRGIN RAPESEED OIL about 75ml (2½fl oz)

FOR THE SALAD

CHICKPEAS 1 × 400g (14oz) can, or 200g (7oz) dried chickpeas,
soaked in water for at least 6–8 hours

BICARBONATE OF SODA ½ teaspoon (optional)

QUINOA 150–200g (5½–7oz), soaked in water for at least 1–2 hours,
or 300–400g (10½–14oz) ready-cooked quinoa

BUTTER 15g (½oz), for frying (optional)

FRESH MIXED GREENS 200g (7oz), such as baby kale, spinach leaves,
red amaranth, cress, mizuna leaves

First make the chimichurri, either by combining everything in a food
processor and pulsing to a coarse paste, or by finely chopping and combining
the ingredients by hand. Transfer the mixture to a sterilized screwtop jar
(see Note, page 189) and store in the refrigerator for 1–2 days before using.

To make the salad, drain the chickpeas. If cooking your own, place them
in a pan of water with the bicarbonate of soda and bring to the boil, then
cover and simmer for about 30–35 minutes, until soft. Drain and set aside
until cool.

Drain the quinoa, add it to a pan of boiling salted water and cook it for
15–20 minutes, until soft. Drain well.

If you wish, melt the butter in a large frying pan and gently sauté the
quinoa for 4–5 minutes, until lightly browned. Allow to cool.

When everything else is ready, it's time to cook the fish. Preheat the oven
to 180°C/350°F/Gas Mark 4.

Heat the oil in a large frying pan and cook the fish steaks on one side for
3–4 minutes, until the skin is brown and crisp. Turn and brown the skin on
the other side. Now put the fish on its flesh side and brown just a little (about
15 seconds). Repeat on the other flesh side. Season with the cumin. Transfer
to a baking dish and place in the oven for up to 10 minutes, depending on
what type of fish you're using and how cooked it already is – some fish cook
much quicker than others. You want it to be flaky and succulent.

When the fish is almost done, put the salad together. Combine the cooled
chickpeas and quinoa in a bowl and mix well. Add the salad greens, drizzle
some chimichurri over the top and toss well. Taste and season, adding more
dressing if necessary.

Serve the fish with some of the salad underneath it or alongside, and
sprinkled with the lime juice. Enjoy with some crusty bread and butter.

See image overleaf

EMPADINHAS DE CAMARÃO À GOA PORTUGUESA

Pasties stuffed with prawns & peas

EMPADINHAS (PRONOUNCED EM-PAH-DIN-YASH) ARE SMALL PIES THAT THE PORTUGUESE INTRODUCED TO THEIR VARIOUS COLONIES, SUCH AS BRAZIL AND GOA. THEY ARE VERY VERSATILE, CAN BE MADE WITH POULTRY, BEEF, LAMB, SEAFOOD OR VEGETABLES AND ARE GREAT FOR USING UP LEFTOVERS.

SERVES 6 AS A MAIN COURSE

EXTRA VIRGIN RAPESEED OIL 2 tablespoons
CUMIN SEEDS 1 teaspoon
GARLIC 4 cloves, crushed
FRESH GREEN CHILLI 1, chopped
ONIONS 2, finely chopped
BAY LEAVES 2
RED CHILLI POWDER 1 heaped teaspoon
PASSATA 100g (3½oz)
RAW PRAWNS 500g (1lb 2oz), peeled, deveined and chopped
PLAIN FLOUR 1 tablespoon
PEAS 200g fresh or frozen, cooked and drained
EGG 1, beaten, for glazing
CHOPPED FRESH CORIANDER 1–2 tablespoons
SALT AND FRESHLY GROUND BLACK PEPPER

FOR THE PASTRY

PLAIN FLOUR 600g (1lb 5oz), plus extra for dusting
SALT ½ teaspoon
EGGS 2, plus 1 extra yolk
BUTTER 1 × 250g (9oz) pack, slightly softened
WATER 375ml (13fl oz)

FOR THE SAUCE

COCONUT MILK 1 × 400ml (14fl oz) can, well shaken
RED CHILLI POWDER 1 teaspoon
FRESH ROOT GINGER 5cm (2in) piece, peeled and chopped
GROUND CORIANDER 1 teaspoon
GROUND CUMIN ½ teaspoon
GARLIC 3 cloves, peeled
ONION 1 small, coarsely chopped
TOMATO PURÉE 1 tablespoon
GROUND TURMERIC ½ teaspoon
FRESH CURRY LEAVES 1–2, shredded

First make the pastry. Sift the flour and salt on to a work surface and form a well in the centre. Break the eggs into the middle, add the butter and beat together with a fork or hand-held mixer. Stir in the measured water a bit at a time until a dough forms, then bring it together with your hands and work lightly until smooth. Place in a bowl, cover with a cloth and place in the refrigerator to chill for 30–40 minutes.

Meanwhile, heat the oil in a pan and add the cumin seeds. As soon as they change colour, add the garlic and green chilli, and sauté until the garlic turns golden brown.

Add the onions and bay leaves and stir well, then add a few tablespoons of water and continue to cook slowly until the onions soften. Stir in the red chili powder and sauté until you see oil being released in the pan. Now add the passata and cook for about 10–12 minutes, until the sauce thickens.

Stir in the prawns and sauté over a high heat for 1 minute. Lower the heat and sprinkle in the flour. Mix well, then cook for 1 minute before adding the peas. The mixture should be soft but feel dry to the touch. Season to taste and add some fresh coriander. Cool quickly by spreading the filling out on a tray or plate and ruffling it occasionally with a fork.

Meanwhile, roll the chilled pastry into a sausage shape and divide into 6 equal pieces. Form each into a ball, then use a rolling pin to roll out on a work surface lightly dusted with flour into a rough circle about the size of a saucer.

Divide the filling equally between the circles, placing it slightly off-centre. Flap the pastry over the filling and crimp the edges with a fork. Brush with beaten egg and place on a baking sheet. Chill for at least 30 minutes.

To make the sauce, pour the coconut milk into a blender and add all the remaining ingredients. Purée to a thin liquid, then strain into a saucepan and bring slowly to the boil. Simmer for 10–15 minutes. Taste and season with salt and pepper.

Preheat the oven to 190°C/375°F/Gas Mark 5. When ready, bake the pastries on the middle shelf for about 20 minutes, until golden brown.

Serve the empadinhas with the sauce offered alongside.

PHRIED PFISH YAND PICY CHIPSY

Mumbai-style fillet of gurnard & spiced chips

INDIANS LOVE FRIED FISH, AND IN THE REGIONS OF BOMBAY, GOA AND THE SOUTH THEY ALSO HAVE SOME STRANGE PRONUNCIATIONS. *YEVVERYTHING PHRIED* IS LOVED BY *YEVVERYBODY*, ESPECIALLY IF IT IS COATED IN KIRRIM (CRUMBS), AS IN THIS RECIPE.

GURNARD, LIKE MONKFISH, IS VERY UGLY BUT GOOD TO EAT, THOUGH IT IS NOT NEARLY SO WELL KNOWN. ASK YOUR FISHMONGER TO FILLET THE GURNARD FOR YOU, AND GIVE YOU THE BONES TOO, AS THEY MAKE EXCELLENT SOUP OR STOCK. THOUGH NOT AN INDIAN FISH, GURNARD COMBINES VERY WELL WITH SPICES.

SERVES 4

SKINLESS GURNARD FILLETS 8, about 200–250g (7–9oz) each

LIME JUICE from ½ lime

FRESH GREEN CHILLIES 2, very finely chopped

GARLIC 2 cloves, very finely chopped

WORCESTERSHIRE SAUCE 1 tablespoon

ENGLISH MUSTARD PASTE 1 tablespoon

SALT 1 teaspoon

EGGS 2

PLAIN FLOUR 150g (5½oz)

FRESH OR DRIED WHITE BREADCRUMBS 150–200g (5½–7oz)

KETCHUP, TARTARE OR A MAYONNAISE-BASED SAUCE to serve

FOR THE CHIPS

POTATOES 4–5 large, cut in half widthways, then into thick wedges

SALT ½–1 teaspoon, plus extra for cooking the potatoes

RED CHILLI POWDER 1 teaspoon

GROUND CUMIN ½ teaspoon

MANGO POWDER (AAMCHUR) ½ teaspoon

EXTRA VIRGIN RAPESEED OIL for deep-frying

Wash the fish and pat dry with kitchen paper. Place in a shallow dish and sprinkle with the lime juice.

Combine the chillies, garlic, Worcestershire sauce, mustard paste and salt in a bowl and mix well. Smear this paste over the fish, then cover and refrigerate until needed.

For the chips, cook the potatoes in boiling salted water for about 6–8 minutes, until just tender. Drain and set aside to cool a little.

Put the chilli powder in a bowl with the ½–1 teaspoon salt, the cumin and mango powder, if using, and mix well. Transfer to a shaker, if you have one.

Heat a 7.5cm (3in) depth of oil in a deep pan until it registers 180°C (350°F) on a thermometer, or a mustard seed sizzles straight away. Fry one-third of the potatoes for 4–5 minutes, until very pale brown. (It's important not to cook many at a time, as this may cause the oil to foam and drop too low in temperature.) Lift out with a slotted spoon and transfer to a sieve. Cook another 2 batches in the same way.

Allow the oil to reheat, then cook each batch of chips again for 2–3 minutes, until a little more brown. Set aside to cool well, keeping the pan of oil on a very low heat.

Whisk the eggs in a bowl and gradually beat in the flour until it forms a thick batter (you might not need all the flour). Place the breadcrumbs in a separate shallow dish.

Dip the marinated fish into the batter, coating each fillet thoroughly. Let the excess batter drip off, then press the fish into the breadcrumbs, coating every side.

Preheat the oven to 150°C/300°F/Gas Mark 2. Reheat the oil until hot (see above).

Fry the potatoes again, one-third at a time, until beautifully golden. Drain well, place in a tray lined with kitchen paper and put in the oven to keep warm.

Bring the oil back up to temperature, then fry the crumbed fish until beautifully crisp and brown. Drain on kitchen paper.

Sprinkle the chips with the spice mixture and serve with the fish, offering ketchup, tartare or a mayonnaise-based sauce separately.

VEGETABLES & VEGETARIAN DISHES

Mixed vegetable salad in yogurt

HERE IS A QUICK AND SIMPLE MAHARASHTRIAN-STYLE SALAD, SIMILAR TO COLESLAW. IT GOES WELL WITH MANY DISHES, INCLUDING CURRY, DAAL AND RICE, AND ALSO MAKES A GREAT SANDWICH FILLING. IT LENDS ITSELF TO VARIATION, SO YOU CAN EXPERIMENT WITH IT TO YOUR HEART'S CONTENT.

SERVES 6–8 AS A SIDE DISH

CARROTS 2, shredded

CUCUMBER 1, deseeded and finely grated (the seeds can be sprinkled with salt and red chilli powder and enjoyed separately)

CABBAGE LEAVES 3–4, shredded

RED ONIONS 2 small, finely sliced

CAULIFLOWER OR BROCCOLI 5–6 florets, finely sliced, chopped or grated

MANGETOUT 8–10 pods, finely sliced

EXTRA VIRGIN RAPESEED OIL 1 tablespoon

BLACK MUSTARD SEEDS 1 teaspoon (optional)

FOR THE DRESSING

THICK GREEK YOGURT 4–5 heaped tablespoons

ENGLISH MUSTARD PASTE 1 heaped tablespoon, or to taste

FRESH GREEN CHILLIES 2 finger-type, finely chopped

CHOPPED FRESH CORIANDER 1 heaped tablespoon, stems and leaves

FRESH MINT LEAVES 10–15, finely shredded

HIMALAYAN BLACK SALT OR SEA SALT ½ teaspoon, or to taste

First make the dressing. Put the yogurt in a bowl and add the mustard, chillies herbs and salt. Mix well and adjust the seasoning if necessary, then cover and refrigerate for 2 hours.

Combine all the vegetables in a bowl, then cover and chill for 1 hour.

Heat the oil in a wok, kadhai or large saucepan until a couple of mustard seeds sizzle straight away when dropped in the pan. Add the remaining mustard seeds and cover loosely with a lid while they pop and splutter.

Pour the dressing over the vegetables and toss well, then sprinkle with the fried mustard seeds, if using, and serve.

Note

Himalayan salt, commonly referred to as 'black salt', tastes strongly of sulphur, so add carefully, according to taste. Indians regard it as a cooling ingredient and good for the digestion, so tend to use it on most salads.

SHATAVARI CHILLI FRY

Asparagus chilli fry

NOWADAYS, VEGETABLES ARE IMPORTED FROM ALL AROUND THE WORLD, BUT
TO MY MIND, NOTHING BEATS GOOD ENGLISH ASPARAGUS. MY PARTICULAR
FAVOURITE COMES FROM THE ISLE OF WIGHT AND HAS PURPLE TIPS, THANKS
TO THE SEAWEED USED AS A FERTILIZER, WHICH RELEASES IODINE INTO THE
SOIL. MUCH PRIZED IN AYURVEDIC MEDICINE, ASPARAGUS HAS A WONDERFUL
FLAVOUR, SO IS BEST COOKED AND SERVED SIMPLY, AS HERE. THE CHILLI GIVES
IT A LIFT WITHOUT OVERPOWERING ITS UNIQUE TASTE.

SERVES 4 AS A STARTER

FRESH ASPARAGUS 1–2
bunches, about 20–24 spears
in total

EXTRA VIRGIN RAPESEED OIL
2 tablespoons

CUMIN SEEDS 1 teaspoon

RED ONION 1, finely sliced

GARLIC 2 cloves, finely
chopped

FRESH GREEN CHILLI
1 finger-type, cut lengthways
into thin strips

GREEN PEPPER ½, cored,
deseeded and thinly sliced

PLUM TOMATO 1, deseeded
and cut into thin strips

WORCESTERSHIRE SAUCE
a few dashes

FRESH CORIANDER 3–4 sprigs,
chopped

SALT AND FRESHLY GROUND
BLACK PEPPER

Cut each asparagus spear about 7.5cm (3in) from the
pointed end and set the tender spears aside. String
or thinly peel the separated stalks and cut into 2.5cm
(1in) lengths. Those bits nearest the base might be
fibrous and woody, in which case chop them finely
and save for making soup.

Heat a wok or frying pan and add half the oil. When
near smoking point, add all the asparagus and shake
the pan to even out the pieces. Allow to rest for about
20 seconds, then toss again. Repeat this process once
more, then eat a piece to see if it is ready. When done
to your liking, use a slotted spoon to transfer the
asparagus to a bowl and set aside.

Add the remaining oil to the pan and increase the
heat, but do not let it smoke. Add the cumin seeds and
let them sizzle for a few seconds. Add the onion, garlic,
chilli and green pepper, toss once or twice and then
spread them out in the pan. Toss again and, when soft,
add the tomato and Worcestershire sauce. Season to
taste with salt and pepper.

Add the cooked asparagus and the coriander, toss a
couple of times to allow the asparagus to heat through
and serve straight away.

Note

Another garnish that goes very well with asparagus is freshly grated coconut.

Oriental or Mumbai-style coleslaw

HERE'S HOW WE MAKE COLESLAW AT CAFÉ SPICE NAMASTE, AND YOU'LL NOTICE IT'S A BIT DIFFERENT FROM THE USUAL. WE GIVE IT A KICK WITH HORSERADISH AND CHILLI, WHILE STILL RETAINING THE CRUNCH AND CREAMINESS YOU'D EXPECT. IT'S A GREAT ACCOMPANIMENT FOR MANY OF THE SPICY MEAT AND POULTRY DISHES ON OUR MENU, AND YOU CAN RING THE CHANGES BY ADDING, FOR EXAMPLE, CHOPPED HARD-BOILED EGG, PRAWNS OR SHREDDED CHICKEN – IN FACT, WHATEVER TAKES YOUR FANCY. SERVE WITH FRIED FISH OR POULTRY, BURGERS OR BARBECUED MEATS, LOBSTER OR POTATOES. THE COLESLAW GOES WITH VIRTUALLY EVERYTHING!

THIS RECIPE IS AN ACCOMPANIMENT, SO REQUIRES NO INGREDIENTS FROM THE SPICE BOX.

SERVES 4

CARROT 1, grated

CABBAGE 4–5 leaves, central stalks removed, then rolled and finely shredded

CELERIAC ½ small, grated

RED ONIONS 2 small, thinly sliced

BEETROOT 1, peeled and grated (wear rubber gloves if you don't want to stain your hands)

WHITE RADISH 1 small, grated

RED RADISH 4–5, grated

GARLIC 3 cloves, finely chopped

FRESH GREEN CHILLI 1 finger-type, finely chopped

WHOLEGRAIN ENGLISH MUSTARD 1 tablespoon

HORSERADISH SAUCE ½ tablespoon, or more to taste

HOMEMADE OR SHOP-BOUGHT MAYONNAISE 4–5 tablespoons, or as needed

FINELY CHOPPED FRESH CORIANDER 1 heaped tablespoon

DOUBLE CREAM 2 tablespoons (optional)

LIME JUICE to taste (optional)

SALT AND FRESHLY GROUND BLACK PEPPER

Combine the prepared carrot, cabbage, celeriac and onions in a bowl, and place the beetroot in a separate bowl. Cover both with cold water, add a few ice cubes and leave to soak for at least 30 minutes to crisp up. (The radishes do not need soaking – in fact, they will taint the water – so simply put them to one side. If, however, you want to reduce their smell, wash in a sieve and drain well.)

Put the garlic, chilli, mustard paste and horseradish in a large bowl and mix well. Add the mayonnaise and mix again. Stir in the coriander and cream, if using, then taste and season as you wish with salt and pepper, and lime juice if necessary (ready-made mayonnaise is already quite acidic, so you might not need the juice).

Drain the vegetables and pat dry in a clean tea towel. Tip them into a large bowl and stir gently but thoroughly until well coated, adding a bit more mayonnaise if you like. Serve immediately.

BAINGAN BHURTA

Aubergine curry

THIS DISH OF ROASTED AUBERGINE WITH TOMATO AND YOGURT IS VERY POPULAR IN BOTH PUNJABI AND MAHARASHTRIAN COOKING. IT MAKES AN EXCELLENT ACCOMPANIMENT.

SERVES 4–6 AS A SIDE DISH

SUNFLOWER OR EXTRA VIRGIN RAPESEED OIL 3 tablespoons

CUMIN SEEDS 1 heaped teaspoon

GINGER AND GARLIC PASTE (see page 199) 1 heaped teaspoon

FRESH GREEN CHILLIES 2 finger-type, chopped

ONIONS 2, chopped

WATER 200ml (⅓ pint)

GROUND TURMERIC 1 teaspoon

GROUND CORIANDER 1 teaspoon

RED CHILLI POWDER 1 teaspoon

WATER about 200ml (7fl oz)

CHOPPED TOMATOES 1 × 400g (14oz) can

THICK GREEK YOGURT 3–4 tablespoons

AUBERGINES 2–3 large, roasted (see Note below)

SALT 1 teaspoon, or to taste

CHOPPED FRESH CORIANDER 2–3 tablespoons, (optional)

Heat the oil in a flameproof casserole dish or saucepan and add the cumin seeds. As soon as they change colour, add the Ginger and Garlic Paste along with the green chillies and sauté for 2–3 minutes.

Add the onions and water, stirring to deglaze the pan, and sauté until the onions are soft and pale.

Blend the ground spices with the measured water and add to the pan. Stir and simmer for about 8–10 minutes, until the liquid has evaporated.

Add the tomatoes and yogurt and heat through, until the oil is released. Stir in more water if necessary to prevent the mixture from sticking to the pan.

Peel and chop the roasted aubergines, then add to the pan and cook for a further 10–15 minutes. Season with the salt, sprinkle with the chopped coriander, if using, and serve.

Note

Aubergines can be roasted on a barbecue, under a grill or on a gas hob. First oil the skin, place over or under the heat and turn from time to time until they are totally charred and soft. Plunge them into a large bowl of chilled water and peel off the skin. The flesh will have a delicious smoky flavour.

Purple sprouting broccoli with garlic, chilli & pomegranate

REALLY EASY TO PREPARE, THIS DISH IS A WELCOME ACCOMPANIMENT TO ANY MEAL, BUT ESPECIALLY SEAFOOD. ORDINARY GREEN BROCCOLI – OR EVEN KALE OR CAULIFLOWER – COULD BE USED WHEN PURPLE SPROUTING BROCCOLI IS NOT IN SEASON.

SERVES 4

PURPLE SPROUTING BROCCOLI
300g (10½oz)

EXTRA VIRGIN RAPESEED OIL
2 tablespoons

GARLIC 4 cloves, sliced

FRESH GREEN CHILLIES 1–2 finger-type, cut into 1cm (½in) pieces

CUMIN SEEDS 1 teaspoon

RAW SKINNED PEANUTS OR BROKEN CASHEW NUTS 2 tablespoons

ONION 1 small, diced into 1cm (½in) pieces

POMEGRANATE SEEDS from ½ pomegranate

SALT AND AND FRESHLY GROUND BLACK PEPPER

Trim the broccoli and cut any particularly thick stalks into 4 pieces (this may only be necessary if using green broccoli). Cut into 2.5cm (1in) pieces.

Heat the oil in a wok until nearly at smoking point. Add the garlic and chillies and toss a little. As soon as the garlic begins to change colour, add the cumin seeds and toss for a few seconds. When the cumin begins to darken, add the nuts and stir-fry for 30 seconds or so.

Add the onion and toss until pale, then stir in the broccoli. Cook for 1 minute, tossing regularly. When you see the broccoli wilt a little, add the pomegranate seeds, season with salt and pepper and toss well. When the broccoli is cooked to your liking but still has some crunch, transfer to a bowl and serve.

TIL PYAAZ AUR LESUNWALI HARI PHOOL GOBI

Broccoli with spring onion, fried garlic & sesame seeds

BOTH GREEN AND PURPLE SPROUTING BROCCOLI CAN BE USED FOR THIS
DISH. IT'S ALWAYS BEST TO USE WHATEVER'S IN SEASON.

SERVES 4 AS A SIDE DISH

BROCCOLI 200–250g (7–9oz)

WHITE SESAME SEEDS
1 tablespoon

CUMIN SEEDS 1 teaspoon

CORIANDER SEEDS 2 teaspoons

EXTRA VIRGIN RAPESEED OIL
2–3 tablespoons

GARLIC 5–6 cloves, cut lengthways
into 4 pieces, then thinly sliced

DRIED RED CHILLIES 1–2 large,
cut into 3–5mm (1/8–1/4in) slices

SPRING ONIONS 4–5, slit
lengthways into 4 strips, then
chopped

GRANULATED SUGAR
½–1 teaspoon

LIME JUICE from ¼ lime

WORCESTERSHIRE OR SOY SAUCE
to taste (optional)

FRESH CORIANDER a few leaves,
torn (optional)

SALT

Split the broccoli into smallish florets, keeping as much of the stalk as possible (the trimmings can be saved for soup). Blanch the florets in a pan of boiling water for just 1–2 minutes, then drain and set aside to cool. (The water can be saved for making soup.)

Set out all the other ingredients. Put the sesame seeds in a small, heavy-based frying pan and toast over a low to medium heat until just pale brown. Transfer to a mortar, then toast the cumin seeds and add them to the mortar. Finally, toast the coriander seeds and add them too. (The seeds are toasted separately because they take different amounts of time to colour.) Crush all the seeds together to the texture of breadcrumbs.

Heat the oil in a wok or large frying pan and sauté the garlic over a medium heat until pale golden. Add the red chilli and the crushed seeds and continue sautéeing, stirring continuously, until the garlic is golden. Immediately add the spring onions and cook until soft. Finally, tip in the broccoli and heat through for about 3–4 minutes, or longer if you want it less crunchy.

Stir in the sugar, some salt and the lime juice. Taste and adjust the seasoning as necessary, adding a few drops of Worcestershire sauce or soy sauce and the fresh coriander, if you wish.

KUKRA BHEENDA

Crisp fried okra

ALSO CALLED KURKURI BHINDI IN NORTHERN INDIA, THIS DISH HAS MANY FANS, NOT LEAST MY WIFE PERVIN, WHO LOVES ITS CRISP, DRY TEXTURE AND WON'T EAT IT ANY OTHER WAY. I PARTICULARLY LIKE ITS VERSATILITY BECAUSE IT CAN BE ENJOYED AS A SIDE, USED AS A GARNISH OR EVEN EATEN AS A SNACK (IT KEEPS WELL IN AN AIRTIGHT CONTAINER FOR A FEW DAYS).

I AM A FIRM BELIEVER IN WASHING OKRA, ALTHOUGH OTHERS INSIST YOU SHOULDN'T. THE KEY IS TO DRY IT THOROUGHLY BEFORE FRYING, OR IT WILL BECOME GOOEY RATHER THAN CRISP.

THE VERSION I GIVE BELOW IS DIFFERENT FROM THAT FOUND IN MOST INDIAN KITCHENS BECAUSE I HAVE SIMPLIFIED THE SPICING AND OMITTED THE MANGO POWDER, GARAM MASALA AND CHAAT MASALA THAT ARE SOMETIMES ADDED.

SERVES 4 AS A SNACK OR SIDE DISH

OKRA 250g (9oz) pods, washed and thoroughly dried

RED CHILLI POWDER 1 heaped teaspoon

GROUND CUMIN 2 teaspoons

GROUND TURMERIC 1 teaspoon

BLACK PEPPERCORNS 1 teaspoon, finely crushed

CHICKPEA (GRAM) FLOUR 3 tablespoons

RICE FLOUR 1 tablespoon (or add another tablespoon of chickpea flour)

SALT

EXTRA VIRGIN RAPESEED OIL for deep-frying

TO SERVE (optional)

LIME JUICE from ½ lime

CHOPPED FRESH CORIANDER LEAVES 1 tablespoon

Slit each okra pod in half lengthways and cut each half into 4 or 5 lengthways strips. Place on a baking tray and sprinkle with the spices, pepper and some salt. Mix well and spread out again.

Combine the 2 flours in a bowl, then sprinkle the mixture over the okra. Mix again to ensure every piece is well coated, then spread out again. Set aside to rest for 15–30 minutes. This draws the moisture out of the okra so that it forms its own batter with the coating.

Heat a 5cm (2in) depth of oil in a deep pan, until a few slices of okra dropped into the oil come to the surface. Set a colander and a tray lined with crumpled kitchen paper nearby.

Fry the okra, just a few pieces at a time, in the hot oil until crisp and golden. This will take a minute or so. Lift out with a slotted spoon and drain in the colander for 30 seconds before transferring to the lined tray to drain further.

Scoop any stray bits of batter out of the oil, then fry and drain the remaining okra as before.

If serving immediately, taste and add more salt if needed, then sprinkle with the lime juice and chopped coriander.

MALAI KOFTA PALAKWALA

Potato, nut & paneer croquettes in a spinach sauce

WHILE THIS RECIPE MAKES A LOVELY COMBINATION, THE TWO ELEMENTS CAN ALSO BE USED SEPARATELY. THE CROQUETTES, FOR EXAMPLE, CAN BE MADE IN A SMALLER SIZE AND SERVED AS DELIGHTFUL SNACKS OR CANAPÉS WITH ANY CREAM-BASED DIP. THE SPINACH SAUCE IS VERSATILE TOO, AND CAN BE COMBINED WITH MIXED VEGETABLES, SAUTÉED MUSHROOMS OR FRIED DICED PANEER.

SERVES 4

FLOURY POTATOES 2 large, roughly cubed
CORNFLOUR 2–3 tablespoons, for dusting
EXTRA VIRGIN RAPESEED OIL for frying
SALT AND FRESHLY GROUND BLACK PEPPER

FOR THE STUFFING

PANEER 50g (1¾oz), grated, or mozzarella or haloumi cheese, chopped
CHOPPED FRESH CORIANDER 1 heaped tablespoon
SULTANAS 10g (¼oz)
FRESH GREEN CHILLIES 2, chopped
RAW CASHEW NUTS, SKINNED PEANUTS AND PISTACHIOS 2–3 tablespoons, chopped and mixed
CORNFLOUR 2 tablespoons (optional)

FOR THE SAUCE

FRESH SPINACH 250g (9oz)
BUTTER 30g (1oz)
ONIONS 2, finely chopped
CUMIN SEEDS 1 teaspoon
RED CHILLI POWDER 1 tablespoon
GROUND CORIANDER 1 tablespoon
GROUND TURMERIC 1 pinch
GARLIC 6–8 cloves, crushed or ground to a paste
FRESH ROOT GINGER 5cm (2in) piece, peeled and crushed or finely chopped
SINGLE CREAM 175ml (6fl oz)
GARAM MASALA (see page 58) to taste (optional)

First make the stuffing. Combine all the ingredients in a bowl, adding a little cornflour if the mixture is too soft. Check for seasoning, then set aside.

Bring a large pan of water to the boil. When boiling, add some salt, the turmeric and the potatoes, and cook for about 8–10 minutes, until tender. Drain well, then return the potatoes to the pan and place them over a low heat, stirring with a wooden spatula from the bottom up until they look dry, slightly crushed and fluffy. Mash thoroughly, then set aside until cool enough to handle. Divide the mash into about 12 equal pieces and roll them into balls. Flatten slightly, then place an equal amount of the stuffing on each one. Wrap the potato around them and smooth into balls again.

Heat a 7.5cm (3in) depth of oil in a deep pan until hot but not smoking. Meanwhile, put the cornflour on a plate and roll each croquette in it until well coated. Shake off the excess flour, then deep-fry the croquettes, a few at a time, for about 2 minutes, until crisp and golden. Drain on kitchen paper and keep warm if you plan to eat them straight away. Alternatively, cool, then cover and store in the refrigerator for up to 3 days. They should be reheated and combined with the sauce just before serving.

To make the sauce, first blanch the spinach in boiling water for a minute or so. Drain and purée until smooth. Set aside.

Heat the butter in a pan and sauté the onions for about 5–6 minutes, until translucent but not browned. Add the cumin seeds, chilli powder, coriander and turmeric and sauté gently for another minute or so. Add the garlic and ginger and cook until fragrant.

Stir in the puréed spinach, add salt and pepper to taste and heat through for just 2 minutes so that the spinach doesn't discolour. (The spinach will bubble and splutter, so keep a lid handy to prevent splashes.)

Add the fried croquettes to the spinach mixure and stir in the cream. Taste and adjust the seasoning, then sprinkle with the Garam Masala, if using. Alternatively, place the croquettes on a platter, pour the spinach sauce over and drizzle with the cream, adding a sprinkling of Garam Masala if you wish.

Mango with coriander & coconut

UNIQUE TO BRAHMIN CUISINE IN THE KONKAN REGION OF INDIA, THIS RECIPE USUALLY CONTAINS FENUGREEK SEEDS, ASAFOETIDA AND JAGGERY, BUT I HAVE ADAPTED IT TO SUIT THIS BOOK'S EASY APPROACH. THE FLAVOUR IS DIFFERENT BUT STILL FANTASTIC. SERVE IT AS AN ACCOMPANIMENT TO CURRY, RICE, LENTILS OR FISH.

SERVES 4 AS A SIDE DISH

SLIGHTLY UNRIPE INDIAN MANGOES
2–4, depending on size

FRESHLY GRATED COCONUT from
1 coconut, or 150g (5½oz) desiccated coconut soaked in enough warm water to just cover for 30 minutes

DRIED RED CHILLIES 4–6 large

CORIANDER SEEDS 1 tablespoon

GROUND TURMERIC ½ teaspoon

EXTRA VIRGIN RAPESEED OIL
2 tablespoons

BLACK MUSTARD SEEDS 1 teaspoon

WHITE LENTILS (URAD DAAL)
2 teaspoons

CURRY LEAVES 12–25, preferably fresh, finely chopped; if using dried, soak in water for 10–12 minutes, and dry thoroughly before chopping

WATER 225ml (8fl oz)

SOFT BROWN SUGAR 1–2 tablespoons, depending on the sweetness of the mangoes

CHOPPED FRESH CORIANDER
1 tablespoon (optional)

SALT

Stone and peel the mangoes, then cut the flesh into thin slivers.

Put the coconut, chillies, coriander seeds and turmeric into a blender and whiz to a purée.

Heat the oil in a saucepan. It is hot enough when a few mustard seeds immediately crackle in it. At that point, add the rest of the seeds along with the lentils and curry leaves and sauté until the lentils are light brown and give off a lovely nutty aroma. They can burn very rapidly, so take care that this doesn't happen. Quickly add the puréed mixture and sauté for 2 minutes.

Add the mangoes and measured water and cook for about 3 minutes, until the fruit is almost tender.

Stir in the sugar and allow the mixture to bubble and thicken a bit. Add salt to taste. For extra flavour, if you wish, stir in the chopped coriander just before serving.

Notes

Indian mangoes are sour, so if using a different type, add less sugar than specified.

If using fresh coconut, you can, if you wish, finely chop a 2.5cm (1in) piece and fry it in the oil before the sauce is made. It should be set aside to drain on kitchen paper and can later be used to garnish the dish. Of course, it also flavours the oil before the rest of the sauce ingredients are cooked. Yummy!

Feta cheese salad

IN INDIA PANEER WOULD GENERALLY BE USED IN THIS SALAD, BUT I
LIKE TO MAKE IT WITH FETA BECAUSE IT HAS A SHARPNESS THAT WORKS
PARTICULARLY WELL WITH THE OTHER INGREDIENTS.

SERVES 4

FETA OR OTHER FIRM GOATS' CHEESE 200–250g
(7–9oz), cut into 1cm (½in) cubes

CUCUMBER 1 small, cored and diced

RED PEPPER 1, cored, deseeded and diced

GREEN PEPPER 1, cored, deseeded and diced

TOMATOES 3, cored and diced

WALNUT QUARTERS 100g (3½oz), toasted
(see page 56)

PINE NUTS 2 tablespoons, toasted (see page 56)

CUMIN SEEDS ½ teaspoon, toasted and crushed
(see page 56)

TORN FRESH CORIANDER LEAVES 1 tablespoon

RED ONION 1, chopped

OLIVE OR EXTRA VIRGIN RAPESEED OIL
for drizzling

SALT AND FRESHLY GROUND BLACK PEPPER

Combine all the ingredients, except the oil,
in a salad bowl, adding salt and pepper to
taste. Drizzle with the oil and toss well just
before serving.

GOBHI PAKODAY

Roasted cauliflower pakoras

OUR CHEF SANJAY RECENTLY INTRODUCED ME TO A DIFFERENT KIND OF PAKORA, WHICH (FOR THOSE WHO DON'T KNOW) IS A VEGETABLE FRITTER. HIS TECHNIQUE INVOLVED FIRST DEEP-FRYING CAULIFLOWER IN CHICKPEA BATTER AND THEN ROASTING IT IN A TANDOOR, THE TRADITIONAL INDIAN OVEN. TO MAKE IT MORE ACCESSIBLE, MY VERSION BAKES THE CAULIFLOWER IN AN ORDINARY OVEN, THEN BATTERS AND DEEP-FRIES IT. THE FINISHED PAKORAS TASTE REALLY GOOD, AND EVEN BETTER IF SERVED WITH A GOATS' CHEESE AND BEETROOT CHUTNEY SALAD.

THE SPICE BLEND I'VE USED IS BASICALLY THE MOROCCAN MIXTURE CALLED RAS EL HANOUT, TO WHICH I'VE ADDED A BIT OF FRESH GARLIC. I GIVE THE RECIPE FOR THAT TOO IN CASE YOU WISH TO MAKE YOUR OWN. IT WILL KEEP WELL IF STORED IN A STERILIZED JAR (SEE PAGE 189) COVERED WITH WARM OIL, THEN COOLED AND REFRIGERATED.

SERVES 4

CAULIFLOWER 600g (1lb 5oz), cut into large florets
EXTRA VIRGIN RAPESEED OIL for deep-frying
FETA CHEESE SALAD (see opposite) AND SIMPLE BEETROOT CHUTNEY (see page 207) to serve
SALT

FOR THE SPICE BLEND

CUMIN SEEDS 3 tablespoons
CORIANDER SEEDS 2 tablespoons
GROUND CINNAMON 1 tablespoon OR **CINNAMON STICK** 7.5cm (3in) piece
FINELY CHOPPED FRESH ROOT GINGER 2 teaspoons
BLACK PEPPERCORNS 2 teaspoons
GROUND TURMERIC 1 teaspoon
GREEN CARDAMOM PODS 10–12, lightly crushed and seeds extracted for use (save the pods for flavouring other dishes)
RED CHILLI POWDER 1½ teaspoons
SAFFRON ¼ teaspoon powdered, or a few threads

FOR THE BATTER

CHICKPEA (GRAM) FLOUR 150–200g (5½–7oz)
SALT 1 teaspoon
FRESH GREEN CHILLIES 2 hot, chopped
CHOPPED FRESH CORIANDER 2 tablespoons
LIME JUICE from ½ lime

First make the spice blend. With the exception of the chilli powder and saffron, toast all the other ingredients in a dry frying pan over a low heat until you get a lovely aroma. Transfer to a grinder, blender or mortar, add the chilli powder and saffron and whiz or crush to a powder.

Preheat the oven to 150°C/300°F/Gas Mark 2.

Meanwhile, cook the cauliflower in a large pan of boiling salted water for just 3–4 minutes. Drain well, toss with the spice blend and transfer to a baking tray. Place in the oven for 10–15 minutes, then set aside to cool.

When you're ready to cook the pakoras, combine the chickpea flour and salt in a bowl and add enough chilled water to make a batter with the consistency of double cream. Mix in the chillies, coriander and lime juice.

Heat a 5cm (2in) depth of oil in a deep pan to at least 180°C (350°F), or until a few drops of the batter float in it instantly.

Dip a cauliflower floret into the batter, lower it gently into the hot oil and fry for about 2–3 minutes, until crisp. Taste to check that the flavour and consistency are as you wish, then fry the rest.

Serve the pakoras hot with Feta Cheese Salad and Simple Beetroot Chutney.

See image overleaf

Spiced vegetables & paneer with cashew & quinoa crumble

IN THIS SIMPLE BAKED DISH, YOU CAN USE ANY SEASONAL VEGETABLES SUCH AS BROCCOLI, SQUASH, AUBERGINE – WHATEVER YOU FANCY OR HAVE TO HAND. NO FLOUR IS USED IN THE SAUCE TO THICKEN IT, BUT YOU CAN DO SO IF YOU WISH. SERVE WITH PASTA OR RICE.

SERVES 4 AS A MAIN COURSE OR 6–8 AS A SIDE DISH

CAULIFLOWER 1 small, cut into small florets, stalks chopped separately into small pieces

CARROTS 2, diced

POTATO 1, diced

ONION 1, coarsely chopped

FRESH GREEN CHILLIES 2 finger-type, coarsely chopped

GARLIC 2 cloves, roughly chopped

FRESH ROOT GINGER 5cm (2in) piece, peeled and roughly chopped, peelings reserved

EXTRA VIRGIN RAPESEED OIL 2 tablespoons

PANEER 150–200g (5½–7oz), diced

GREEN PEPPER 1 small, cored, deseeded and diced

FRESH RED CHILLI 1 small, diced

CHICKPEAS 1 × 400g (14oz) can, drained and rinsed

CHOPPED FRESH CORIANDER 2 tablespoons

TOMATO SAUCE (see page 67) to serve

SALT AND FRESHLY GROUND BLACK PEPPER

FOR THE SPICE PASTE

GROUND CUMIN 1 teaspoon

GROUND CORIANDER 2 teaspoons

GROUND TURMERIC ½ teaspoon

RED CHILLI POWDER 1 teaspoon

FOR THE CRUMBLE TOPPING

RAW CASHEW NUTS 100g (3½oz)

CUMIN SEEDS 1 teaspoon, toasted (see page 56)

CORIANDER SEEDS 1 teaspoon

QUINOA 3–4 tablespoons, uncooked

FRESH GREEN CHILLI 1, deseeded

OLIVE OIL 1 teaspoon

BUTTER 15g (½oz), at room temperature

First make the spice paste by combining all the ingredients in a small bowl with a few tablespoons of water. Cover and set aside until needed.

Cook the cauliflower florets for about 5 minutes in a pan of boiling salted water. They should be slightly firm; certainly not soft. Strain, reserving the cooking water, and immediately refresh in cold water.

Return the cooking water to the pan and cook the carrots for 3–4 minutes, again until just done. Strain, reserving the cooking water, and immediately refresh in cold water.

Return the cooking water to the pan and cook the potato for about 6–8 minutes, until tender. Strain, reserving the cooking water, and immediately refresh in cold water.

Return the cooking water to the pan and cook the cauliflower stalks with the ginger peelings for 15–20 minutes, until soft. Set the pan aside to cool.

Preheat the oven to 190°C/375°C/Gas Mark 5.

Put the onion, green chillies, garlic and ginger into a blender, add the vegetable water and its contents and purée to a smooth liquid.

Heat the oil in a deep nonstick pan or flameproof casserole dish. When hot, add the paneer and cook for 1–2 minutes, turning so that it browns nicely on all sides. Add the green pepper and the fresh red chilli and sauté for 1 minute, then add the spice paste. Cook for another 1–2 minutes, until the oil starts to be released. Pour in the puréed mixture and cook for 4–5 minutes, until gently bubbling but not spluttering.

Stir in the cooked cauliflower, carrots and potato plus the chickpeas and mix well, adding some water if the mixture seems too thick. Cover and simmer for 5–6 minutes, then taste and season. Stir in the fresh coriander and transfer to a baking dish.

To make the crumble, put the cashews, seeds, quinoa and fresh chilli into a blender and whiz to the texture of coarse breadcrumbs. Add the olive oil and softened butter and whiz again.

Sprinkle the mixture evenly over the vegetables and bake in the oven for 12–15 minutes, until the top is golden and crispy.

Serve with homemade Tomato Sauce on the side.

MÔRI DAAR

Parsee-style toor daal

THIS IS THE MOST FAMOUS DAAL OR LENTIL PREPARATION FROM THE PARSEE COMMUNITY. I BET EVERY PARSEE CHILD IN THE WORLD HAS BEEN WEANED ON THIS DAAL, AND MOST WOULD AGREE THAT THEIR MOTHER ALWAYS MADE THE BEST. MINE DID TOO, AND OUR YOUNGER SON, HORMUZD, TELLS ME THAT EVEN IF I WERE THE BEST COOK IN THE WORLD, I COULD NOT COOK THE DAAL AS WELL AS MY MOTHER. THAT'S CHILDREN FOR YOU!

TRY TO BUY OILED DAAL, IF YOU CAN FIND IT, AS THAT WORKS BEST IN THIS RECIPE. IT MUST BE WASHED WELL BEFORE USE, FIRST WITH HOT WATER AND THEN WITH TEPID WATER, UNTIL THE WATER RUNS CLEAR. IT HELPS TO RUB IT BETWEEN THE PALMS OF YOUR HANDS TO ACHIEVE THIS.

ENJOY THIS WITH STEAMED RICE, FRIED FISH AND A GOOD CHUTNEY.

SERVES 4

YELLOW LENTILS (TOOR OR TOOVAR DAAL) 250g (9oz), washed, then soaked in water overnight, or for at least a few hours

GROUND TURMERIC 1 teaspoon

BUTTER 15g (½oz), or more to taste

SUNFLOWER OR EXTRA VIRGIN RAPESEED OIL 2 tablespoons

FRESH GREEN CHILLIES 1–2 finger-type, slit lengthways into 4 strips

CUMIN SEEDS 1 tablespoon

GARLIC 2–3 cloves

CHOPPED FRESH CORIANDER 1 heaped tablespoon

SALT

Drain the daal, which should be well swollen. Place in a saucepan, add enough fresh water to cover by 5mm (¼in) and bring to the boil over a medium heat. Skim off the froth that rises to the surface, then lower the heat and add some salt and the turmeric. Skim again if necessary, then add the butter. Simmer on the lowest possible heat, covered, for 10–15 minutes, until the lentils are soft. Blend to a purée with a blender, then set aside.

Heat the oil in a frying pan. When reasonably but not very hot, add the chillies and sauté until they darken. Stir in the cumin seeds and garlic and sauté until the garlic is pale golden. At that point, turn off the heat and keep stirring the mixture until the garlic browns nicely.

Add this mixture to the daal and stir well. Taste and add salt and more butter if you wish, then stir in the coriander before serving.

LAGAN NU ISHTEW

Parsee wedding stew

PARSEES ARE NOT KNOWN FOR THEIR LOVE OF EATING VEGETABLES, WHICH IS PERHAPS WHY SO MANY COOK THEM TO DEATH – MAYBE TO CAMOUFLAGE OR DISCOLOUR THEM BEYOND RECOGNITION. MOST VEGETABLES TEND TO BE INCORPORATED INTO COOKED MEAT DISHES, BUT FOR SOME REASON, POTATOES ARE TREATED DIFFERENTLY – IN FACT, CONSIDERED AN ESSENTIAL PART OF EVERY DIET. THIS DISH DOESN'T MUCH RESEMBLE 'ISHTEW', THE LOCAL PRONUNCIATION OF 'A STEW', BEING JUST AN INTERESTING COMBINATION OF MIXED VEGETABLES SERVED AS ONE OF SEVERAL ACCOMPANIMENTS. I HAVE SIMPLIFIED THE ORIGINAL VERSION, SO ENJOY! SERVE WITH MEAT DISHES, OR WITH LENTILS AND RICE.

SERVES 4–5 AS A SIDE DISH

RED SQUASH 1 piece 10 × 10cm (4 × 4in), diced

YAM 1 piece 10 × 10cm (4 × 4in), diced

BABY POTATOES 15–20, depending on size, unpeeled if you prefer

SWEET POTATO 1, diced

CARROTS 2, diced

MINI SHALLOTS 2–3 per person, peeled

JAGGERY 5cm (2in) piece, OR MUSCOVADO SUGAR ½–1 tablespoon

CANE OR CIDER VINEGAR 3–4 tablespoons

EXTRA VIRGIN RAPESEED OIL 3 tablespoons

CUMIN SEEDS 2 teaspoons

FRESH GREEN CHILLIES 3–4 finger-type, each slit lengthways into 4 strips

FRESH ROOT GINGER 5–7.5cm (2–3in) piece, peeled and finely chopped

GARLIC 3 cloves, crushed

RED ONIONS 2, chopped

GROUND TURMERIC 1 teaspoon

RED CHILLI POWDER 1 teaspoon

TOMATOES 2–3, chopped

MINT LEAVES 15–20, chopped

CHOPPED FRESH CORIANDER 1–2 tablespoons

SALT

Put the squash, yam, potatoes, carrots and shallots in a pan of salted water with a pinch of the jaggery or sugar and a dash of the vinegar and bring to the boil. Cover and simmer until just tender. Drain and set aside, reserving the water.

Heat the oil in a saucepan, add the cumin seeds and green chillies and sauté until the seeds darken. Add the ginger and garlic and sauté until the garlic lightly colours. Add the onions and continue sautéeing for about 5 minutes, until they become pale and soft.

Combine the turmeric and chilli powder with the reserved vegetable water and whisk well. Pour into the onion mixture and cook until the liquid reduces by one-third.

Add the remaining vinegar and jaggery or sugar and the tomatoes and cook gently for 8–10 minutes, or until most of the liquid has evaporated and you are left with a glossy, aromatic sauce.

Tip the cooked vegetables into the sauce and mix well until thoroughly coated and heated through. Add salt to taste, then stir in the mint and coriander. Serve immediately.

Notes

If you wish, replace the ginger and garlic with 1½ tablespoons Ginger and Garlic Paste (see page 199).

Pickled cocktail onions can be used instead of the mini shallots, but in that case add them at the end, when the vegetables are being reheated. It's also a good idea to add the vinegar after them, just a bit at a time, until you get the right acidity.

BHUNA BHUTTA

Spiced corn on the cob

IF YOU'RE EVER IN INDIA, YOU'RE BOUND TO COME ACROSS STREET VENDORS CHARGRILLING FRESH CORN. WE INDIANS LOVE IT SPRINKLED WITH A MIXTURE OF SALT, CHILLI POWDER AND LIME JUICE. I GIVE A SLIGHTLY DIFFERENT VERSION BELOW, AND YOU CAN EVEN MAKE SOUP FROM THE COOKING LIQUID IF YOU LIKE.

SERVES 4

CORN ON THE COB 4, leaves and silks discarded

MILK 700ml (1¼ pints)

CHICKEN OR VEGETABLE STOCK 300ml (10fl oz)

FRESH ROOT GINGER 5–7.5cm (2–3in) piece, unpeeled and sliced

CLOVES 3–4, lightly crushed

CINNAMON STICK 5cm (2in) piece

DRIED RED CHILLIES 2

BLACK PEPPERCORNS 4–5, lightly crushed

BUTTER for spreading

RED CHILLI POWDER for sprinkling (optional)

SALT AND FRESHLY GROUND BLACK PEPPER

FOR THE SOUP (optional)

POTATOES 2 small, diced

CELERY 1 stick, chopped

ONION 1 small

BUTTER 15g (½oz)

VEGETABLE STOCK OR WATER as needed

CHOPPED FRESH CORIANDER OR PARSLEY LEAVES 1 tablespoon

CROUTONS (see page 15) to serve

Put the corn cobs, milk and stock in a large saucepan. Add the ginger, cloves, cinnamon, red chillies, crushed peppercorns and some salt, and top up with just enough water to cover the corn. Bring to the boil over a medium heat, then simmer for 15–20 minutes, or until tender. Set aside to cool in the liquid.

When you're ready to serve, lift the cobs out of the pan and drain thoroughly on kitchen paper. Meanwhile, heat the grill until very hot.

Place the cobs under the grill and cook until they are hot and lightly browned. Spread with butter and add a sprinkling of salt and pepper, plus a dash of red chilli powder if you like.

If you want to make the soup, strain the cooking liquid, discarding the solids, then return to the pan. Add the potatoes, celery, onion and butter and bring to the boil, adding extra stock or water if you think it's needed.

Simmer for about 12–15 minutes, until the vegetables are cooked. Purée the mixture in a blender, then taste and adjust the seasoning. Stir in the fresh coriander or parsley and serve with Croutons.

RICE, PULSES
& BREADS

ARROZ DE COCO COM GENGIBRE

Goan coconut rice with ginger

OF THE 40,000-ODD VARIETIES OF RICE GROWN GLOBALLY, INDIA GROWS ABOUT 2,000, AND THE COUNTRY'S TOTAL PRODUCTION IS ABOUT 90 MILLION TONNES. IT SEEMS ODD THAT BASMATI IS THE ONE THAT BRITISH PEOPLE MOST ASSOCIATE WITH INDIAN CUISINE, BECAUSE WE INDIANS EAT MAINLY LOCALLY GROWN RICE, MOST OF WHICH IS MORE NUTRITIOUS THAN THE USUALLY REFINED BASMATI. DON'T MISUNDERSTAND ME – THERE IS NOTHING WRONG WITH BASMATI, AND IT'S CERTAINLY THE BEST FOR MAKING PILAUS, BIRYANIS AND SUCHLIKE, BUT FOR THIS DISH I SUGGEST USING A DIFFERENT TYPE FOR A CHANGE. AMERICAN LONG-GRAIN OR A NON-STICKY RICE WOULD BE GOOD CHOICES, BUT FAILING THAT, USE BROWN UNPOLISHED BASMATI. SERVE WITH A LIGHT CURRY OR ANOTHER DISH OF YOUR CHOICE.

SERVES 4–5

CANNED COCONUT MILK 200ml (7fl oz), well shaken

DESICCATED COCONUT 100g (3½oz)

EXTRA VIRGIN RAPESEED OIL 2 tablespoons

CINNAMON STICK 5cm (2in) piece, broken in half

BLACK PEPPERCORNS 3–4

GREEN CARDAMOM PODS 2–3, lightly crushed

CLOVES 2, lightly crushed

BUTTER small knob

ONIONS 1–2 small, halved and thinly sliced

FRESH ROOT GINGER 7.5cm (3in) piece, peeled and finely chopped

GARLIC 2 cloves, finely chopped

GROUND TURMERIC 1 teaspoon

BOILING WATER 850ml (1½ pints)

LONG-GRAIN RICE 300g (10½oz), not easy-cook (see recipe introduction)

TORN OR CHOPPED FRESH CORIANDER 1–2 tablespoons

SALT

Warm the coconut milk in a pan until you see wisps of steam rising. Stir in the coconut and set aside to soak for 30 minutes. Drain through a sieve set over a bowl, reserving the liquid.

Preheat the oven to 150°C/300°F/Gas Mark 2.

Heat the oil in a large flameproof casserole dish. When hot, add the cinnamon, peppercorns, cardamoms and cloves. As soon as the cloves swell, add the butter and onions. Sauté until the onions lightly brown. Add the ginger and garlic and sauté until the garlic colours slightly.

Stir in the turmeric and sauté for 1 minute, then add the drained coconut. Sauté for another few minutes, until you get a lovely toasted aroma. Pour in the measured boiling water and reserved coconut milk, add salt to taste and bring to the boil.

Tip in the rice, stir lightly and bring it up to the boil. Lower the heat to medium and cook for 5–6 minutes, stirring occasionally with a spatula to ensure the rice doesn't stick. Continue cooking for about 4–6 minutes, until the water is nearly absorbed. Scrape down the sides of the dish to neaten, then level the surface. Cover and put on the middle shelf of the oven for 10 minutes. Turn off the heat and leave in the oven for about another 15 minutes. (It can actually be kept in there for up to an hour if left untouched.)

When ready, stir gently to release the heat and allow the rice to expand. Stir in the fresh coriander and serve immediately.

ARROZ REFOGADO COM CHOURIÇO

Baked rice with hot sausage

THE WORD 'REFOGADO' REFERS TO THE ONION AND TOMATO SAUCE THAT IS THE BASIS OF MANY PORTUGUESE DISHES. IN THE PAST, IT WOULD HAVE BEEN COMBINED WITH RICE AND STOCK AND COOKED SLOWLY IN A WOOD-BURNING OVEN. HERE WE TREAT IT MORE LIKE A RISOTTO, FEEDING THE MIXTURE WITH LIQUID AS IT COOKS ON THE HOB, THEN TRANSFERRING IT TO THE OVEN TO FINISH. FOR THIS REASON, I SUGGEST USING A SHORT-GRAIN RISOTTO OR PAELLA RICE.

INCLUDING CHORIZO IN THE DISH ADDS GREAT FLAVOUR, BUT ANY SPICY SAUSAGE CAN BE USED. LOOK OUT FOR SMOKED PIRI-PIRI FLAVOUR, WHICH WORKS VERY WELL. EAT THIS ON ITS OWN, OR SERVE WITH ANY LIGHTLY SAUCED MEAT, FISH, POULTRY OR VEGETABLE DISH.

SERVES 5–6

OLIVE OIL 4–5 tablespoons

CLOVES 4–5, lightly crushed

BLACK PEPPERCORNS 5–6

CHORIZO 250–300g (9–10½oz) piece, skinned and chopped

ONIONS 2, chopped

GARLIC 4 cloves, chopped

GROUND TURMERIC ½ teaspoon

FRESH GREEN CHILLIES 3, each slit lengthways into 4 strips

DRIED RED CHILLIES 2 large, deseeded and broken up

RISOTTO OR PAELLA RICE 300–400g (10½–14oz), such as Arborio, Bahia, Balilla, Bomba, Calaspara, Carnaroli or Senia)

HOT CHICKEN OR VEGETABLE STOCK 1.1 litres (just under 2 pints)

GREEN PEPPERS 1, cored, deseeded and chopped

PLUM TOMATOES 2–3, chopped

TORN OR CHOPPED FRESH CORIANDER, PARSLEY OR MINT 1–2 tablespoons

SALT

FOR THE GARNISH

HARD-BOILED EGGS 5–6 (1 per person), kept unshelled in cold water until needed

UNPEELED PRAWNS 2–3 per person, sautéed to a good colour (optional)

LIME JUICE a dash

Heat the oil in a flameproof casserole dish over a medium–low heat. When hot, sauté the cloves and peppercorns for 2–3 minutes. Once the cloves swell, add the chorizo and sauté until some of its fat is released. Stir in the onions and garlic and continue to sauté until the onions are soft, then add the turmeric and both types of chilli. By now the kitchen should be filled with a wonderful aroma.

Once the onions are slightly browned, add the rice and mix well. Sauté for a few minutes, then add half the stock and stir over a low–medium heat until the liquid has been absorbed. Set aside 100ml (3½fl oz) of the remaining stock, then add the rest to the rice a ladleful at a time, allowing each addition to be absorbed before adding the next. The texture should be soft and quite liquid.

Meanwhile, preheat the oven to 140°C/275°F/Gas Mark 1.

Taste the rice and season very lightly with salt. Stir in the green peppers, then add the tomatoes and reserved stock. Scrape down the sides of the dish to neaten, then level the surface. Cover and put on the middle shelf of the oven for 10 minutes. Turn off the heat and leave there for about another 15 minutes. (It can actually be kept in there for up to an hour if left untouched.) When ready, stir in the chopped herbs.

To serve, shell and quarter the eggs, then arrange them on top of the rice with the prawns, if using, and a dash of lime juice.

DAHI MA MURGHI NI BIRYANI

Chicken biryani

THE ULTIMATE ONE-POT DISH, A BIRYANI IS A MIXTURE OF RICE, SPICES AND MEAT. HOWEVER, NO TRUE PARSEE WOULD EAT IT WITHOUT POTATOES, SO I'VE INCLUDED SOME BELOW. THE DISH TASTES FANTASTIC WHEN FRESHLY MADE, BUT IS PERHAPS EVEN BETTER WHEN REHEATED AND EATEN THE NEXT DAY.

SERVES 4–6

CHICKEN 1 × 1.3kg (3lb) bird, jointed into 8–12 pieces

POTATOES 2–3, cut into chunks

WATER 3 litres (5¼ pints)

BAY LEAVES 2–3

BASMATI RICE 400g (14oz)

SAFFRON THREADS a generous pinch

FRESH MINT LEAVES 20–25, torn

FRESH CORIANDER 6–8 sprigs, chopped

BUTTER a generous knob

SALT

FOR THE MARINADE

ONIONS 500–600g (1lb 2oz–1lb 5oz), sliced as thinly as possible

EXTRA VIRGIN RAPESEED OIL 200ml (7fl oz), for frying

THICK GREEK YOGURT 250ml (9fl oz)

RED CHILLI POWDER 1 heaped teaspoon

GROUND CUMIN 1 heaped teaspoon

GROUND CORIANDER 1 tablespoon

GINGER AND GARLIC PASTE (see page 199) 1½ tablespoons

GARAM MASALA (see page 58) 1 teaspoon

LIME JUICE from ½ lime

FRESH GREEN CHILLIES 2–3 large finger-type, sliced lengthways into 4 strips

CHOPPED OR WHOLE PLUM TOMATOES 1 × 400g (14oz) can

SALT about 1 teaspoon

TO SERVE

MIXED RAITA (see page 194)

DAAL such as my Parsee-style Toor Daal (see page 151)

First make the marinade. Put the onions into a bowl and rub them gently under running cold water. Drain well in a colander, then dry in a salad spinner or with kitchen paper.

Heat the oil in a deep pan. When hot, fry the onions in 3 separate batches until pale golden. Using a slotted spoon, transfer them to a colander, where they will continue to brown in their own heat. The oil can be reused another time if cooled and strained.

Put all but 2 tablespoons of the fried onions into a blender, add the remaining marinade ingredients and whiz to a purée. You might need to do this in batches so that the machine can create a smooth paste and the motor doesn't overheat. Transfer the mixture to a large flameproof casserole dish.

Trim any excess skin from the chicken pieces, then place the meat in the marinade. Cover with a tight-fitting lid and set aside in the refrigerator for at least 1 hour.

Preheat the oven to 180°C/350°F/Gas Mark 4. Transfer the casserole dish to the oven and cook for about 1 hour, until the chicken is tender.

Meanwhile, cook the potatoes in a pan of boiling salted water for about 8–10 minutes, until tender. Drain and set aside.

Put the measured water into a large saucepan with the bay leaves and some salt and bring to the boil. Add the rice and boil for roughly 6 minutes, until al dente. Drain well, reserving the water to make soup if you wish. Fork through the rice to loosen the grains.

Heat the saffron threads in a warm small frying pan over a gentle heat until they are crisp. Add 2–3 tablespoons of water and set aside to rest for 10 minutes.

Pour the saffron and its liquid over the rice while still in the colander and mix lightly to partially colour the grains.

When the chicken is ready, the sauce might look too thin or a bit oily, but don't worry about that. Heat it, uncovered, for a few minutes to reduce it if you wish, but a generous amount of sauce is needed to finish the dish. Taste and adjust the salt if necessary, then add the fresh mint and coriander. Transfer the chicken to a plate and pour the sauce into a jug. Lower the oven temperature to 150°C/300°F/Gas Mark 2.

Melt the butter in a large saucepan. Return some of the sauce to the empty casserole dish and cover with one-third of the rice. Arrange the chicken pieces and a few chunks of potato on top, then cover with another third of the rice. Pour over some more sauce, dot with the remaining potatoes and cover with the remaining rice. Press down gently. Drizzle the remaining sauce over the rice, sprinkle with the reserved onions and cover tightly.

Place on the middle shelf of the oven for up to 40 minutes to heat through fully. If the ingredients have become cold during the process of putting the dish together, they might need longer to heat through. In this case, lower the temperature to 120°C/250°F/Gas Mark ½ and continue heating until completely hot.

Serve the biryani with Mixed Raita or a daal, allowing people to help themselves straight from the dish if you like.

See image overleaf

ALOO GOBHI KI TAHIRI

Potato & cauliflower pilau

I LEARNT TO MAKE THIS RECIPE BACK IN 1974, WHEN I WAS AT CATERING COLLEGE, AND IT HAS BEEN ONE OF MY FAVOURITE RICE DISHES EVER SINCE. INEVITABLY, I HAVE TWEAKED IT A BIT, BUT I LOVE ITS VERSATILITY: IT GOES WELL WITH MOST ACCOMPANIMENTS, IN ADDITION TO CURRIES OR SIMPLY PLAIN YOGURT.

SERVES 3–4 AS A MAIN COURSE

SUNFLOWER OIL 3–4 tablespoons

CLOVES 6–8

CINNAMON STICK 5mm (¼in) piece

BAY LEAVES 2–3

GROUND CUMIN ¾ teaspoon

POTATOES 200g (7oz), cubed

BASMATI RICE 500g (1lb 2oz), washed and drained

CAULIFLOWER 200g (7oz) florets, stalks thinly sliced

GROUND TURMERIC 1½ teapoons

RED CHILLI POWDER 1 teaspoon

FINELY CHOPPED FRESH ROOT GINGER 1 tablespoon

GARAM MASALA (see page 58) ½ teaspoon

HOT WATER OR STOCK 1 litre (1¾ pints)

SALT

SPICY MANGO CHUTNEY to serve

Preheat the oven to 140°C/275°F/ Gas Mark 1.

Heat the oil in a flameproof casserole dish and add the cloves, cinnamon stick and bay leaves. Fry for about 1 minute, until the cloves are well swollen and the bay leaves colour a bit. Stir in the cumin and fry for about 30 seconds, then add the potatoes and sauté for 1–2 minutes, until the edges are lightly browned.

Add the rice and cauliflower and sauté for 2–3 minutes, stirring often so that the rice doesn't stick on the bottom.

Mix in the turmeric, chilli powder and ginger, followed by a sprinkling of salt. Pour in the measured hot water or stock. Stir gently, cover with a lid and cook over a medium heat for 5–6 minutes, until the liquid is nearly absorbed. Scrape down the sides of the dish and place on the middle shelf of the oven for 10–12 minutes. Switch off the heat and leave the dish inside the oven for another 10–15 minutes.

Sprinkle the Garam Masala over the cooked rice, mix gently and serve with spicy mango chutney.

GOSHT KA PULAV

Meat pilau

THERE HAS ALWAYS BEEN CONTROVERSY ABOUT THE DIFFERENCE BETWEEN A PILAU WITH VEGETABLES, POULTRY, SEAFOOD OR MEAT AND A BIRYANI CONTAINING SIMILAR INGREDIENTS. I BELIEVE THERE IS NO CLEAR-CUT ANSWER. THE ONLY DIFFERENCE I CAN DISCERN IS THAT A PILAU IS A ONE-POT DISH – EVERYTHING, INCLUDING THE MEAT, IS COOKED TOGETHER – WHILE A BIRYANI IS LAYERED WITH SEMI-COOKED INGREDIENTS.
THE RECIPE BELOW REMAINS FAITHFUL TO THE TRADITIONAL ONE WITH PERSIAN ROOTS, BUT HAS BEEN TWEAKED TO SUIT MODERN TASTES BY INCLUDING LESS FAT (MY GREAT GRANDMOTHER'S VERSION WAS A HEART ATTACK ON A PLATE!).

SERVES 6

BONELESS SHOULDER OF LAMB 500g (1lb 2oz), diced

GHEE 60g (2¼oz)

BASMATI RICE 1kg (2lb 4oz), washed and drained

SALT 20g (¾oz)

ONIONS 3, finely sliced

MACE BLADES 2–3

CUMIN SEEDS ½ teaspoon

THICK GREEK YOGURT 500ml (18fl oz)

SAFFRON THREADS a pinch

LIME JUICE from 1 lime

FLAKED ALMONDS 125g (4½oz)

SULTANAS 125g (4½oz)

FOR THE MASALA

GHEE 150g (5½oz)

BAY LEAVES 3–4

CINNAMON STICK 2 × 5cm (2in) pieces

GREEN CARDAMOM PODS 4–5, lightly crushed

CLOVES 4–5

DRIED RED CHILLIES 3–4 whole

Place the lamb in a flameproof casserole dish, add just enough water to cover it, then bring to the boil. Lower the heat, cover and simmer for 30–40 minutes, until most of the water has evaporated and the meat is tender. Drain off and reserve any remaining liquid, then set the pan aside.

Fill a large saucepan with water (about 2 litres/3½ pints), add a knob of the ghee and bring to the boil. Add the rice and salt and bring back to the boil, then simmer for 6–7 minutes, until al dente. Drain in a colander.

Preheat the oven to 160°C/325°F/Gas Mark 3.

To make the masala, melt the ghee in a frying pan and fry all the masala ingredients until lightly browned and fragrant. Transfer the masala to a plate and set aside.

Melt 150g (5½oz) of the ghee in the frying pan and sauté the onions for 10–12 minutes over a medium heat, stirring often, until brown. Transfer a few spoonfuls of the onions to a plate and set aside for garnish.

Put the mace and cumin seeds into a mortar and pound until powdered. Add to the onions, along with the fried masala mixture, and continue frying until the onions are nice and dark.

Stir the yogurt into the boiled lamb.

Heat the saffron threads in a warm small frying pan over a gentle heat until crisp, then transfer to a small bowl. Add the lime juice and allow to infuse for 10–15 minutes. Sprinkle this mixture over the boiled rice in the colander and mix gently.

Add the almonds and sultanas to the onion mixture and fry for a minute or so, until golden. Tip in the lamb mixture and stir well.

Alternate layers of lamb and rice in a large flameproof casserole dish, finishing with a rice layer. Pour over the reserved lamb stock, cover and place on the middle shelf of the oven for up to 1 hour, or until heated through.

Serve with the reserved onions sprinkled on top.

CHANNA PAALAK SUKHA

Chickpeas with spinach

IN INDIA, THESE TWO DISHES ARE PROBABLY COOKED IN A HUNDRED DIFFERENT WAYS, SO FEEL FREE
TO BE BOLD AND ADD OTHER INGREDIENTS TO THE BASIC MIXTURES IF YOU LIKE.

SERVES 4–6

BUTTER 30g (1oz)
GARLIC 4 cloves, finely crushed
CUMIN SEEDS 1 heaped teaspoon
DRIED RED CHILLIES 2, broken in half and deseeded
FRESH GREEN CHILLIES 2 finger-type, cut into lengthways strips
ONIONS 2 small, finely chopped
CHICKPEAS 2 × 400g (14oz) cans, drained
FRESH SPINACH 150–200g (5–7oz), thinly shredded
SALT AND FRESHLY GROUND BLACK PEPPER

Melt the butter in a flameproof casserole dish over a medium heat, then fry the garlic, cumin seeds and chillies for 1–2 minutes, until the garlic is light brown. Take care that the butter doesn't burn. Add the onions and sauté until they are soft and translucent.

Stir in the chickpeas and spinach and cook until fully heated through. The spinach will release enough liquid to make the mixture moist. Season to taste and serve.

KHICHDI

Rice & lentil pilau

SERVES 4–5

EXTRA VIRGIN RAPESEED OIL
1 tablespoon
GREEN CARDAMOM PODS 3,
lightly crushed
CLOVES 2
BAY LEAF 1
SHALLOTS 2, finely chopped
GARLIC 1 or 2 cloves, chopped
BOILING WATER OR STOCK
750–900ml (1⅓–1½ pints)
BASMATI RICE 350g (12oz), washed and drained
PINK LENTILS (MASOOR DAAL) OR SPLIT MUNG BEANS (MUNG DAAL) 100–150g (3½–5oz), soaked in water for 1–2 hours and drained
BUTTER 30g (1oz), at room temperature
SALT AND FRESHLY GROUND BLACK PEPPER

Preheat the oven to 140°C/250°F/Gas Mark 1, arranging the shelves so that your lidded cooking pot will fit on the middle one.

Heat the oil in a large flameproof casserole dish over a medium heat. When hot, add the cardamom pods, cloves and bay leaf and sauté for about 1 minute, until the cloves swell a bit.

Add the shallots and garlic and cook gently for 2–3 minutes, without colouring, stirring occasionally. Pour in the measured boiling water or stock, add a little salt and mix well. When it returns to the boil, add the rice and lentils and cook for 5–6 minutes, stirring regularly. (This method is not traditional – the sequence of steps would be different in India – but it's the best for using with the types of rice and lentils available elsewhere.)

Once most of the water has been absorbed, cover the casserole dish and place in the oven for 10 minutes. Turn off the heat and leave in the oven for about another 10 minutes. (It can actually be kept in there for up to an hour if left untouched.)

When ready, season the mixture with some pepper. Fold in the butter, stirring until it has melted and the pilau is creamy.

Remove the whole spices if you wish, and serve the pilau with a kadhi (see page 196) or a curry, or even eat on its own with some thick yogurt blended with chopped mint and coriander, and perhaps a green chilli.

Egg & vegetable fried rice with ginger

INDIA HAS QUITE A LARGE ETHNIC CHINESE POPULATION THAT MIGRATED SEVERAL HUNDRED YEARS FROM THE REGION OF HAKKA, WITH A FEW FROM SICHUAN AND HUNAN. SINCE THAT TIME, THEIR CUISINE HAS TAKEN ON CERTAIN INDIAN QUALITIES AND FLAVOURS, SO IT NOW INCLUDES MORE GINGER, GARLIC, GREEN CHILLIES AND FRESH CORIANDER THAN PREVIOUSLY. FRIED RICE IS PROBABLY THEIR BEST-KNOWN CONTRIBUTION TO INDIAN CUISINE. THIS RECIPE IS AN ACCOMPANIMENT, SO REQUIRES NO INGREDIENTS FROM THE SPICE BOX.

SERVES 4–5

EXTRA VIRGIN RAPESEED OIL 2–3 tablespoons

EGGS 2, well beaten

SPRING ONIONS 3, diagonally sliced

FRESH ROOT GINGER 5cm (2in) piece, peeled and finely chopped

GREEN PEPPER 1 small, cored, deseeded and cut lengthways into fine strips

MIXED VEGETABLES OF YOUR CHOICE about 150g (5½oz) total weight, blanched and diced, or use a mixture of uncooked shredded carrot, sliced fine beans, diced mushrooms and peas

BOILED RICE 500g (1lb 2oz), well drained and refrigerated after cooling

SOY SAUCE to taste (add carefully; the dark type is very salty)

SALT AND FRESHLY GROUND BLACK PEPPER

Heat the oil in a wok until it reaches smoking point. Add the eggs and mix with a spoon, breaking them up as you do so.

Add the spring onions, ginger and green pepper and stir-fry for 1 minute over a high heat. Mix in the mixed vegetables along with some salt and pepper, and sauté for 1–2 minutes, stirring and tossing from time to time.

Tip in the chilled rice and toss or stir gently to combine. Once the rice is heated through, add a dash or so of soy sauce. Taste, adding more salt and pepper if necessary, then serve.

Mushroom & egg fried rice

FRIED RICE IS VERY POPULAR IN INDIA, AND CHINESE HAWKERS STAND ON CITY STREET CORNERS SELLING VARIOUS FRESHLY PREPARED TYPES. THIS RECIPE IS AN ACCOMPANIMENT SO REQUIRES NO INGREDIENTS FROM THE SPICE BOX.

SERVES 4

EXTRA VIRGIN RAPESEED OIL 2 tablespoons

EGGS 2, beaten

CARROT 1 small, finely chopped

MIXED MUSHROOMS 100g (3½oz), sliced

SPRING ONIONS 3, finely sliced on the diagonal

COLD BOILED RICE 500g (1lb 2oz) (see above)

SALT AND FRESHLY GROUND BLACK PEPPER

Place a wok over a high heat and, when hot, add the oil. Heat until smoking, then pour in the eggs and break up with a spatula as they cook.

Add the carrot, mushrooms and spring onions, tossing the mixture constantly for about 2–3 minutes, until the vegetables are cooked.

As soon as the liquid dries and the oil escapes again, stir in some salt and pepper. (I enjoy the flavour of sautéed pepper, but you can season at the very end if you wish.) Now mix in the rice and toss for about 2–3 minutes, until heated through. Taste and adjust the seasoning as necessary, then serve.

CHAPATTI

Plain chapattis

AS WITH SO MANY INDIAN FOODS, MAKING CHAPATTIS SUCCESSFULLY IS NOT JUST A MATTER OF USING THE RIGHT INGREDIENTS – IT DEPENDS ON EXPERIENCE AND HOW WELL YOU UNDERSTAND THE DOUGH YOU ARE PREPARING. IT MIGHT NEED A BIT MORE OR LESS OF EACH ITEM, BUT HAVE A GO AND YOU WILL SOON GET IT RIGHT! THIS RECIPE IS AN ACCOMPANIMENT, SO REQUIRES NO INGREDIENTS FROM THE SPICE BOX.

MAKES 10–12

WHOLEMEAL FLOUR 250g (9oz), plus extra for dusting

SALT 1 teaspoon

EXTRA VIRGIN RAPESEED OIL 1 tablespoon, warmed

MELTED GHEE OR EXTRA VIRGIN RAPESEED OIL 1–2 tablespoons, for spreading (optional)

Sift the flour and salt into a large bowl. Make a well in the centre and pour in the warm oil. Add just a little water and mix together, adding more water a bit at a time and kneading between additions until a dough forms. Continue kneading for 3–4 minutes, until the dough comes away cleanly from the bowl and feels firm but not hard. Cover and set aside in a warm place for 1–2 hours. (The dough will not change much in size or texture, but resting it reduces the elasticity of its gluten.)

Place the dough on a floured work surface and divide into 12 equal pieces that can be rolled into balls about 2.5cm (1in) in diameter. (The number and size can be adjusted as you wish to make bigger or smaller chapattis.)

Heat a flat griddle until hot. Meanwhile, put the melted ghee or oil, if using, in a small bowl and place a teaspoon or pastry brush alongside.

Flatten a ball of dough with your palm or fingers, then use a rolling pin to roll it into a circle about 2mm ($^1/_{16}$ in) in diameter. Don't worry if the shape isn't perfectly round – it takes years of experience to achieve that and sometimes it eludes even top chefs. The best women cooks, however, manage to get a 1mm ($^1/_{32}$ in) thickness without batting an eyelid.

Dust any excess flour off the chapatti and place it on the griddle for about 30 seconds until speckled brown. If the pan is too hot, the chapatti will brown instantly, so watch out for that. Flip the chapatti over, brush with ghee or oil, if using, and flip again after another 30 seconds. It should be cooked through but not have any burn marks.

When done, fold the chapatti in half and place in a lidded container lined with a clean tea towel or kitchen paper. The cloth will absorb the steam and prevent it from softening the chapatti.

Wipe the griddle with kitchen paper and cook the remainder of the chapattis in the same way.

NAAN

Naan

THE WORD NAAN MEANS 'BREAD', SO THE BRITISH HABIT OF REFERRING TO 'NAAN BREAD' IS THE EQUIVALENT OF SAYING 'BREAD BREAD', WHICH I FIND VERY ODD. IT MUST BE SAID THAT NAANS ARE NOT THE EASIEST THINGS TO MAKE AT HOME, BUT A NUMBER OF MY FRIENDS HAVE HAD SUCCESS WITH THIS RECIPE. ENJOY WITH CURRIES, DIPS OR JUST AS AN INDULGENT SNACK.

MAKES 4–6

THICK BIO YOGURT 100ml (3½fl oz), at room temperature

MILK 150ml (5fl oz), at room temperature

FAST-ACTION DRIED YEAST ½ teaspoon

WHITE SUGAR ½ teaspoon

FINE SALT ½ teaspoon

STONEGROUND PLAIN WHITE FLOUR 500g (1lb 2oz), plus extra for dusting

EXTRA VIRGIN RAPESEED OIL 3 tablespoons, plus extra for oiling

BUTTER 20g (¾oz)

MIXED SEEDS (**CUMIN**, NIGELLA, POPPY) about 1–2 tablespoons (optional)

SEA SALT FLAKES to garnish

Combine the yogurt, milk, yeast, sugar and fine salt in a bowl and mix together.

Sift the flour into a separate large bowl and make a well in the centre. Pour in the yogurt mixture and 2 tablespoons of the oil and mix to form a soft dough. Knead for a minute or so, just until it stops looking ragged. Cover with a damp tea towel and set aside in a warm place for 10 minutes.

Transfer the dough to a lightly floured work surface and knead for another minute. Return it to the bowl, cover again and leave to rise in a warm place for 1–2 hours, or until doubled in size.

Punch the dough to knock out the air, then place on a lightly oiled work surface. Divide it into 4–6 equal pieces and roll them into balls. Cover with a damp tea towel and leave to rise again for about 30–45 minutes, depending on room temperature.

Place a large dry frying pan over a medium heat. Meanwhile, use your fingers or a rolling pin to flatten a ball into a circle about 1cm (½in) thick. Transfer it to the hot frying pan and cover tightly with a lid. Cook the naan for 3–4 minutes, until the underside is mottled golden brown and puffed up. Flip it over and cook the other side in the same way.

While the naan is cooking, melt the butter and mix it with the remaining tablespoon of rapeseed oil. As soon as the naan is cooked, brush it generously on one side with the melted butter mixture and sprinkle with some sea salt and the seeds, if using. Prepare and cook the remaining dough in the same way.

Let the naans sit for a couple of minutes, then tear up and eat.

Note

The **mixed seeds** can be kneaded into the basic dough if you wish.

BARBECUES, FLAVOURINGS & ACCOMPANIMENTS

LEELI CHUTNEY MA SALMON

Fillet of salmon in fresh green chutney

SALMON IS A POPULAR FISH ON THE SUBCONTINENT, AND IT IS MOST LIKELY TO BE SERVED WITH A VERSION OF THE CHUTNEY GIVEN BELOW. THE NAME 'GREEN CHUTNEY' ALLUDES TO THE FACT THAT IT INCLUDES LOTS OF FRESH GREEN INGREDIENTS. IT IS EXTREMELY VERSATILE AND MAKES AN IDEAL ACCOMPANIMENT TO SNACKS, CHARGRILLED FOODS AND TANDOORI DISHES. IT IS ALSO AN EXCELLENT MARINADE.

SERVES 4

SALMON FILLET 500–600g (1–1lb 5oz), scaled and pin-boned

LIME JUICE from ½ lime

GROUND TURMERIC ½ teaspoon

EXTRA VIRGIN RAPESEED OIL for mixing, and oiling (optional)

SALT

FOR THE FRESH GREEN CHUTNEY

CHOPPED FRESH CORIANDER 4 tablespoons, leaves and stems, plus extra to garnish

FRESH MINT LEAVES 30–40, plus extra to garnish

FRESH GREEN CHILLIES 4–5, coarsely chopped

GARLIC 4–6 cloves, coarsely chopped

FRESH ROOT GINGER 5cm (2in) piece, peeled and coarsely chopped

WHITE SUGAR 1 teaspoon

SALT 1–2 teaspoons

LIME JUICE from ½ lime

RED ONION SLICES to garnish (optional)

NAAN (see page 173) to serve

Put all the chutney ingredients in a blender and whiz to a smooth purée, adding a little water if necessary to help the blades combine the ingredients. The chutney needs to be as thick as possible, so add the water just a bit at a time. (If it does become too thin, add a tablespoon of roasted skinned nuts to the chutney and whiz together in a blender.)

Cut the salmon into 4cm (1½in) squares. Place in a shallow bowl and sprinkle with the lime juice, turmeric and some salt. Cover and leave to marinate in the refrigerator for at least 30–40 minutes.

Heat a grill or prepare a barbecue until very hot. Meanwhile, combine a tablespoon or so of the chutney with a little oil and spread the mixture over the salmon pieces so that they are totally coated. (The oil will help to stop the fish from sticking to the rack.)

If grilling the salmon, place the pieces skin-side up on a well-greased or nonstick baking tray and grill for about 5 minutes, until the skin is well browned. Turn and cook the other side for about 3 minutes. It is better to have the fish slightly undercooked than overcooked, so keep an eye on it. If you wish to give it an attractive glaze, briefly grill the skin side again at the end.

If barbecueing the fish, thread the pieces on to metal or presoaked bamboo skewers, keeping the skin on the underside so that it will be directly over the heat source. Oil the rack thoroughly and place the skewers on them skin-side down. Cook for about 5 minutes, until the skin is well browned, then turn and cook the other side for about 3 minutes. It is better to have the fish slightly undercooked than overcooked, so keep an eye on it. Lift off with a fish slice to avoid breaking.

Garnish with extra fresh coriander and mint leaves, and red onion slices if you wish, and serve with Naan.

BATTAKH TIKKA DHUANAAR

Smoked duck tikka

TIKKA IS THE PERSIAN WORD FOR 'CUBE', SO TIKKA DISHES ARE MADE FROM ANY CUBED MEAT (OR FISH) AND COMBINED WITH THE MARINADE OF YOUR CHOICE. IN THIS RECIPE, HOWEVER, THE MARINADE IS A HOT ONE OF SYRIAN CHRISTIAN ORIGIN, AND GOES BEST WITH DUCK, SO DON'T BE TEMPTED TO TRY IT WITH OTHER THINGS. DUCK BREAST IS THE BEST OPTION, BUT DUCK LEGS, SLOWLY ROASTED UNTIL THE MEAT IS FALLING OFF THE BONE, ARE A GOOD ALTERNATIVE. BOTH BREAST AND LEG MEAT BENEFIT FROM BEING MARINATED OVERNIGHT, SO BUILD THIS INTO YOUR PREPARATION TIME. SERVE WITH A SALAD AND GOOD BREAD.

SERVES 4–5

DUCK BREAST MEAT 500–625g
(1–1lb 6oz) – about 2–3 breasts

EXTRA VIRGIN RAPESEED OIL
1 teaspoon

FOR THE MARINADE

TAMARIND PULP 2 tablespoons
(take care if using tamarind paste, as some preparations are very strong)

GINGER AND GARLIC PASTE (see page 199) 1 tablespoon

FRESHLY CRUSHED BLACK PEPPER
1 teaspoon

RED CHILLI POWDER 1 heaped tablespoon

GROUND TURMERIC 1 teaspoon

CUMIN SEEDS 1 teaspoon

THICK GREEK YOGURT 3 tablespoons

LIME JUICE from ½ lime

TOMATO PURÉE 1 tablespoon

ENGLISH MUSTARD PASTE 1 tablespoon

FRESH GREEN CHILLIES 2 finger-type, coarsely chopped

EXTRA VIRGIN RAPESEED OIL
2 tablespoons

SALT

FOR THE SMOKING MIXTURE

CLOVES 2

GREEN CARDAMOM PODS 2,
lightly crushed

CINNAMON STICK 5cm (2in) piece

Trim some of the skin from around the edge of each breast, but leave a decent covering on top, as it will keep the meat moist. Cut into 2.5cm (1in) cubes and place in a bowl. (If the breast is large, you should get 6–8 pieces; if small, the yield will be 4–6 pieces.)

Place all the marinade ingredients in a blender and whiz to a purée. Taste and adjust the seasoning as necessary. Tip into the duck bowl and mix well. Transfer to a lidded plastic container and refrigerate overnight, or for at least 2–3 hours.

Place 3–4 pieces of charcoal on a barbecue and heat until red and glowing. Meanwhile, finely crush the ingredients for the smoking mixture in a mortar.

Place an old small pan or metal bowl inside a larger flameproof casserole dish. Arrange the marinated duck pieces around the old container so that they don't actually touch it. Carefully place the glowing charcoal in the old container, sprinkle the crushed spices on top and pour over the teaspoon of oil. Cover tightly with a lid and allow the smoke to infuse the duck for 5–10 minutes. Take care that the oil doesn't burn, as this will taint the flavour. When done to your liking, transfer the duck to a plate and leave to cool. Cover and chill before cooking.

Preheat the oven or grill to its highest temperature. Transfer the duck pieces to a baking tray, skin-side up, and cook on the top shelf for about 4 minutes, until the skin is nicely browned. Turn and cook for a further 4–5 minutes. This will give you medium-cooked meat, so cook for less time if you want it medium–rare.

Set aside to rest for 4–5 minutes, then serve warm.

JHINGA ZAFRANI

Grilled saffron prawns with carrot & coconut salad

TRADITIONALLY, THIS DISH IS MADE IN A TANDOOR OVEN, BUT THOSE ARE FEW AND FAR BETWEEN IN BRITISH HOMES. NOT TO WORRY – THESE PRAWNS CAN BE COOKED IN CONVENTIONAL WAYS TOO, AND THESE ARE GIVEN BELOW. THE SAFFRON MUST BE TOASTED AND SOAKED BEFORE USE, SO BUILD TIME FOR THIS INTO YOUR PREPARATION.

SERVES 3 AS A STARTER OR LIGHT LUNCH

LARGE RAW TIGER PRAWNS 12, peeled but heads left on and deveined

FRESH ROOT GINGER 2.5cm (1in) piece, peeled and finely chopped, then crushed in a mortar

RED CHILLI POWDER, preferably Kashmiri, ½ teaspoon

LIME OR LEMON JUICE from ½ lime or lemon

GROUND WHITE OR BLACK PEPPER ¼ teaspoon

SALT

BUTTER to serve

FOR THE MARINADE

SAFFRON THREADS a pinch

WARM MILK 1 tablespoon

THICK GREEK YOGURT 100ml (3½fl oz)

GROUND CARDAMOM ½ teaspoon

GROUND MACE ½ teaspoon

FRESH GREEN CHILLI 1 small, very finely chopped

VEGETABLE OIL 1 tablespoon

FOR THE SALAD

SUNFLOWER OIL ½ tablespoon

BLACK MUSTARD SEEDS ½ teaspoon

CURRY LEAVES 6, preferably fresh; if using dried, soak in water for 10–12 minutes, and dry thoroughly before adding

FRESH ROOT GINGER 2cm (¾in) piece, peeled and grated

CARROTS 2 large, grated

FRESHLY GRATED COCONUT 4 tablespoons

MINT LEAVES 4 or 5, shredded

LIME JUICE from ½ lime

Rinse the prawns and drain well. Combine the ginger paste, chilli powder, juice, pepper and some salt in a bowl and mix well. Add the prawns and toss lightly to coat. Cover and refrigerate for at least 30 minutes.

Meanwhile, start the marinade. Heat the saffron threads in a warm small frying pan over a gentle heat until crisp, then transfer to a small bowl. Cover with the warm milk and leave to infuse for 15–20 minutes. Put the yogurt and remaining marinade ingredients in a bowl. Add the saffron and its liquid and whisk to form a smooth paste. Add the prawns to the marinade and stir to coat, then cover and chill for at least 2 hours.

Make the salad just before barbecuing. Heat the oil in a large frying pan over a medium heat. Add the mustard seeds and curry leaves and sauté until they release their aroma. Add the ginger and stir for a few seconds, then take off the heat and set aside to cool. Put the carrots and coconut in a serving bowl and add the cooked ginger mixture. Stir in the mint leaves. Squeeze in the lime juice and season with salt.

Light a barbecue, heat the oven to 240°C/475°F/Gas Mark 9 or heat a grill to high. Thread the prawns on to metal or presoaked bamboo skewers, pushing the tip through the head and tail of each one. Suspend the skewers above the barbecue rack or over an oven tray (to prevent sticking) and cook for about 6–7 minutes, until the tail part becomes dark and the meat changes colour. Take care that the prawns don't overcook and become rubbery; test by slitting one open to see if the meat is opaque. Brush with butter and serve with the salad.

See images overleaf

TANDOORI MALAI BATAER

Quail tandoori

WHEN I WAS GROWING UP IN RAJASTHAN, IT WAS NORMAL TO BUY LIVE WILD QUAIL, GROUSE AND PARTRIDGE IN THE LOCAL MARKETS, AND THE HABIT CONTINUES TO THIS DAY. OFTEN THE BIRDS WOULD BE TAKEN HOME AND FATTENED UP BEFORE BEING PREPARED FOR THE TABLE, AND THIS QUIET TIME ALLOWED THE STRESSED MUSCLES TO RELAX, MAKING THE FLESH MORE TENDER. MOST OF THE TIME THE BIRDS ENDED UP IN A HOT RED MASALA, THEN WERE EITHER QUICKLY GRILLED OR SLOWLY STEWED FOR HOURS. PRESENT-DAY FARMED BIRDS ARE PLUMP AND READY TO EAT, WHICH ALLOWS THE USE OF MORE DELICATE MARINADES, LIKE THE ONE GIVEN BELOW. IT IS RICH AND CREAMY WITH JUST A HINT OF SPICE.

SEVERAL ITEMS IN THE INGREDIENTS LIST NEED TO BE MARINATED AND/OR RESTED BEFORE USE, SO DO ALLOW FOR THIS IN YOUR PREPARATION TIME.

SERVES 4 AS A MAIN COURSE OR 6 AS A STARTER

WHOLE BONELESS QUAILS 8, about 100g (3½oz) each
SALT AND FRESHLY GROUND BLACK PEPPER

FOR THE MARINADE

GREEN CARDAMOM PODS 6, lightly crushed
MACE 3–4 blades, broken into pieces
SKINNED ALMONDS 100g (3½oz)
GINGER AND GARLIC PASTE (see page 199) 1 tablespoon
FRESH GREEN CHILLIES 1–2, coarsely chopped
THICK GREEK YOGURT 150–200ml (5–7fl oz)
EXTRA VIRGIN RAPESEED OIL 2–3 tablespoons
MATURE CHEDDAR CHEESE 100g (3½oz), grated
DOUBLE CREAM 125ml (4fl oz)

TO SERVE

GREEN SALAD
LIME HALVES
NAAN (see page 173)

Preheat the oven to 150°C/300°F/Gas Mark 2.

Skin the quails, trim off any gristle or sinew and chop each bird into 4 pieces. Place in a dish, rub with salt and pepper, then cover and chill until the marinade is ready.

Put the cardamom pods and mace on a baking tray. Place in the hot oven, switch off the heat and leave inside for 30 minutes. Set aside to cool and crisp up.

Meanwhile, put the almonds in a bowl, cover with warm water and leave to soften for 10–15 minutes. Drain, reserving the soaking water, and pat dry with kitchen paper.

Put the cardamom and mace in a blender along with the almonds, Ginger and Garlic Paste, green chillies, yogurt, oil, cheese and some of the reserved almond water. Purée to a fine paste, then blend in the cream.

Drain any water out of the quail dish, then add the marinade to the meat a bit at a time, until every piece is well coated. Cover and chill for up to 8 hours, but no less than 2. Any leftover marinade can be saved for another recipe – simply store in an airtight container in the refrigerator for up to 3 days. Alternatively, use it to marinate some chicken legs along with the quail meat.

When you're ready to start cooking, heat the grill until medium hot. Thread the meat on to metal or presoaked bamboo skewers, or place on a rack with a drip tray underneath, and grill for about 4–5 minutes, until well coloured on one side. Turn and cook the other side for about 4–5 minutes, until the meat is cooked through (check by piercing a thin knife into the meat near the bone. If the juices run red, cook for a few more minutes and then try again).

Serve with a green salad, lime halves to squeeze over and some warm Naan.

Note

For an excellent rice accompaniment to this dish, mix piping-hot boiled rice with nuts and sultanas that have been lightly fried in butter, then blend in a beaten egg and season.

HIRAN SHEEK KAVAAB

Venison kebabs

THE IDEA OF COOKING MEAT ON SKEWERS IS PERSIAN IN ORIGIN, AND DATES BACK MANY CENTURIES. GENERALLY, LAMB OR MUTTON IS FAVOURED FOR KEBABS, BUT THIS RECIPE USING MINCED VENISON IS ONE MY FATHER OFTEN MADE AFTER HIS HUNTING TRIPS. AS VENISON IS VERY LEAN, IT'S GOOD TO ADD SOME KIDNEY FAT TO BRING OUT THE BEST FLAVOUR AND TEXTURE, BUT THE CHOICE IS YOURS.

MAKES 8–10 KEBABS

VENISON SHOULDER MEAT
500g (1lb 2oz), chopped into
small pieces

FRESH CORIANDER 20g (¾oz),
leaves and stems

FRESH MINT 20g (¾oz), leaves
and stems

FRESH ROOT GINGER 2.5cm (1in)
piece, peeled and coarsely chopped

GARLIC 6–8 cloves, peeled

FRESH GREEN CHILLI 1 large,
coarsely chopped

GARAM MASALA (see page 58)
1 teaspoon

GROUND CUMIN 1 teaspoon

GROUND CORIANDER 1 teaspoon

GROUND TURMERIC ½ teaspoon

RED CHILLI POWDER ½ teaspoon

LIME JUICE 1 teaspoon

SALT

TO SERVE

FRESH GREEN CHUTNEY
(see page 176)

ONION-BASED SALAD

Place the meat in a bowl and add the fresh herbs, ginger, garlic and green chilli. Pass the mixture through a mincer fitted with a medium blade. Add the ground spices, lime juice and some salt and knead well. Take a small ball of the meat mixture, flatten it into a patty and fry for a few minutes. Taste and adjust the seasoning of the uncooked mixture accordingly. Cover the bowl and chill until needed. The meat mixture can be made a day in advance if you wish, but keep it chilled and well covered.

Light a barbecue and leave it to get very hot before you start the next step.

Set out 8–12 thick metal skewers. Take a 5cm (2in) piece of the meat mixture and roll it into a smooth ball. Press it on to the middle of a skewer and squeeze it around with your hand. Moisten your hand with a little oil or water and gently press the meat again to form it into a sausage shape about 2.5cm (1in) in diameter. This takes a bit of practice. Rest the skewer over a small baking tray so that air and heat can circulate all around meat. Repeat this process with the rest of the meat.

Place the tray over the barbecue and cook the kebabs for about 8–10 minutes, turning often, until the meat is cooked through but still moist.

Serve with Fresh Green Chutney and an onion-based salad. Alternatively, roll inside a chapatti or a warmed flour tortilla filled with salad and sliced onion (see page 86).

Note

The meat mixture can be shaped into burgers if you prefer.

LEHSUN AUR LAAL MIRICH KA MURG

Garlic & red chilli chicken

HERE IS A DELIGHTFULLY EASY DISH THAT PACKS A LOT OF FLAVOUR, SO IT'S
IDEAL FOR A BARBECUE.

SERVES 4–6

CHICKEN LEGS 6 whole, 3 cut into drumstick
and thigh – alternatively, divide all into
drumstick and thigh, then cut each piece
in half
LIME JUICE from 1 lime
SALT AND FRESHLY GROUND BLACK PEPPER

FOR THE MARINADE
THICK GREEK YOGURT 4–5 tablespoons
GARLIC 8–9 cloves, finely crushed
RED CHILLI POWDER 2 heaped teaspoons
GROUND CUMIN 1 teaspoon
SEA SALT 1 heaped teaspoon
EXTRA VIRGIN RAPESEED OIL 2 tablespoons

TO SERVE
CHICKPEAS WITH SPINACH (see page 168)
BREAD, RICE OR BOILED POTATOES

Make 1 or 2 slashes in each chicken
piece. Combine the marinade ingredients
in a bowl and mix well. Add the chicken
and work the marinade into it. Cover and
chill overnight, or for at least 2–3 hours.

Preheat the oven to 230°C/450°F/
Gas Mark 8 or light a barbecue.

Transfer the marinated chicken to a
flameproof casserole dish, cover tightly
with a lid and place on the hob over a
medium heat for 5–6 minutes without
opening. Take off the lid and stir well,
then cover again and cook for another
8–10 minutes.

If oven-cooking the meat, place the dish
in the oven for a further 15–20 minutes.
After this time, check to see if the chicken
is cooked by piercing a thin knife into a
drumstick at the thickest point. If the juices
run red, cook for a few more minutes and
then try again. When done, arrange the
chicken skin-side up and place under a
hot grill to give it a good colour.

If barbecuing the meat, transfer it piece
by piece, skin-side down, to the barbecue
rack and cook, turning once or twice, for
10–12 minutes or until cooked through.

Season the browned chicken with salt
and pepper to taste, then squeeze the
lime juice over it.

Serve with Chickpeas with Spinach plus
some bread, rice or boiled potatoes. The
meat juices can be mixed into the rice or
potatoes just before serving.

See image overleaf

CHOSISE ANI DUKRACHEM BURGER

Pork & chorizo burger with cumin-flavoured onion relish

TAKE MY TIP AND CHOOSE GOOD ORGANIC PORK FOR THIS RECIPE. AS PATRON OF THE LOP PIG SOCIETY, I NATURALLY PROMOTE THE BRITISH LOP, WHICH PRODUCES AMAZING MEAT AND DESERVES TO BE MORE WIDELY KNOWN. TRY TO GET IT FRESHLY MINCED BY YOUR BUTCHER, OR DO IT YOURSELF WITH A FOOD PROCESSOR OR SHARP KNIFE. PAIRED WITH LIGHTLY SMOKED, PIRI-PIRI CHORIZO, IT'S A WINNING COMBINATION.

MAKES 6–8 BURGERS AND 200G (7OZ) RELISH

LEAN MINCED PORK 750g (1lb 10oz)

CHORIZO SAUSAGES 200–250g (7–9oz) Portuguese piri-piri type, skinned and finely chopped

FRESH GREEN CHILLIES 2, finely chopped

FRESH CORIANDER STEMS 10–12, finely chopped

BREAD 5 slices, crusts removed

EXTRA VIRGIN RAPESEED OIL 1 tablespoon

CINNAMON STICK 5cm (2in) piece

ONION 1, very finely chopped

FRESH ROOT GINGER 5–7.5cm (2–3in) piece, peeled and very finely chopped

GARLIC 3–4 cloves, very finely chopped

GROUND TURMERIC 1 teaspoon

GROUND CUMIN 1 tablespoon

GROUND CORIANDER 1 heaped tablespoon

SALT AND FRESHLY GROUND BLACK PEPPER

FOR THE ONION RELISH

BUTTER 15g (½oz), at room temperature

CUMIN SEEDS 1 heaped teaspoon

CINNAMON STICK 7.5cm (3in) piece

MUSCOVADO SUGAR 3–4 heaped tablespoons

CHOPPED FRESH ROOT GINGER 1 tablespoon

DRIED RED CHILLIES 2, deseeded and broken into pieces

RED CHILLI POWDER 1 heaped teaspoon

RED ONIONS 2, quartered and sliced

TO SERVE

SPLIT TOASTED BUNS

SALAD LEAVES

FRIED EGGS (optional)

POTATO WEDGES (optional)

First make the relish. Put the butter on a board, sprinkle with the cumin seeds and chop them together. Transfer to a saucepan and heat until the butter foams, then add the cinnamon stick, sugar and ginger and stir until the sugar dissolves.

Add the dried red chillies and chilli powder, then mix in the onions a little at a time, breaking the slices into their separate layers as you do so. Add a little salt, cover the pan and simmer for 1–2 minutes. Remove the lid and simmer for another 8–10 minutes, until the onions are soft and the butter is rich and syrupy.

The chutney can be made in advance if you wish, and it's easy to double the quantities so that you have some for future use. (It goes well with many other things, such as goats' cheese tarts.) Simply cool and store in a sterilized jar (see Note below).

To make the burgers, put the pork, chorizo, green chillies and fresh coriander in a bowl or food processor and mix well.

Soak the bread in a little water until thoroughly wet, then place in a sieve and press with a spatula to squeeze out all the moisture. Add the bread to the meat mixture and mix well.

Heat the oil in a large frying pan and sauté the cinnamon stick until slightly browned and aromatic. Add the onion, ginger, garlic and half a teacupful of water, and sauté until the onion is soft and translucent. Stir in the ground spices and cook for a further 2–3 minutes. Strain the mixture, reserving the oil for use in other recipes or when barbecuing.

Remove the cinnamon and finely crush about 1cm (½in) of it in a mortar. (If you wish, you can rinse the remainder of the stick and store it in a sealed container for future use.) Add the crushed cinnamon to the meat mixture.

Once the onion mixture has cooled for about 30 minutes, stir it into the meat mixture. Continue mixing vigorously for a few minutes so that everything is well combined. Take a small knob of the mixture, flatten it into a patty and fry or griddle it until cooked. Taste and then season the uncooked mixture as much as you think necessary. (The chorizo is already salty, so you might need to add only pepper.)

Light a barbecue or heat a grill until very hot. Meanwhile, divide the mixture into 6 or 8 equal pieces and roll them into very soft, smooth balls. Flatten them into patties about 1.5cm (½in) thick.

Barbecue each side for 3–4 minutes, or grill on one side for 5–6 minutes, then flip over and repeat on the other side. The burgers must remain juicy even if you cook them well. If you like them less well cooked, reduce the cooking time accordingly.

Serve each burger in a toasted bun with salad leaves, and with a fried egg and potato wedges as accompaniments if you wish. Offer the onion relish alongside.

See image overleaf

Notes

To sterilize glass jars and lids or bottles, wash them well in very hot water. Allow the lids to air-dry, but place the actual jars or bottles in a microwave and heat on high for 1–2 minutes.

For a change, you can put some Stilton inside each one before cooking it.

Yogurt

INDIAN CUISINE WOULD BE UNTHINKABLE WITHOUT THE FERMENTED MILK PRODUCT CALLED YOGURT. IT PLAYS NUMEROUS ROLES, BUT IS MOST COMMONLY USED AS A MARINADE, DIP, ACCOMPANIMENT, DRINK OR DESSERT. IN INDIA WE TEND TO USE SET CURD, WHICH WE MAKE AT HOME USING LIVE BACTERIA. IT IS FANTASTIC FOR TENDERIZING MEAT, AND IS ALSO USED IN THE SOURDOUGH PROCESS FOR MAKING NAAN. YOGURT IS RUNNIER THAN CURD, BUT STILL WORKS WELL AS LONG AS IT CONTAINS LIVE BACTERIA. IN THE RECIPES GIVEN IN THIS BOOK I TEND TO SPECIFY THICK GREEK YOGURT, WHICH IS ACTIVE AND HAS AN APPEALING CREAMY TEXTURE.

DAHI PUDINA SAUCE

Minted yogurt sauce

THERE ARE SEVERAL MINT-BASED SAUCES IN INDIA, BUT MINTED YOGURT IS PROBABLY THE MOST POPULAR, AS IT CAN BE USED WITH MOST TYPES OF SNACKS AS WELL AS KEBABS. PLEASE USE REGULAR MINT RATHER THAN SPEARMINT OR PEPPERMINT, AS THOSE COMPLETELY ALTER THE FLAVOUR.

SERVES 10–12 AS A DIP

THICK GREEK YOGURT 200ml (7fl oz)
FRESH MINT 25–30 leaves, chopped
LIME JUICE 1 teaspoon
CUMIN SEEDS ½ teaspoon, toasted and finely crushed (see page 56)
WHITE SUGAR 1 teaspoon
SALT

Put all the ingredients into a blender and whiz until the yogurt is smooth and the mint almost puréed. Taste and adjust the seasoning if necessary.

TANDOORI MASALA

Easy tandoori marinade

TANDOORI MARINADES TEND TO BE COMPLICATED, BUT THIS SIMPLIFIED VERSION IS QUICK TO PUT TOGETHER AND IDEAL FOR FISH, POULTRY, VEGETABLES, PANEER AND SO FORTH. IN AN IDEAL WORLD THE MARINATING SHOULD BE DONE OVERNIGHT OR EVEN LONGER, BUT 3–4 HOURS IS AN ABSOLUTE MINIMUM. IT IS BEST TO SKEWER THE MARINATED ITEMS AND SUSPEND THEM JUST ABOVE THE GRILL RACK SO THAT THEY COOK AND COLOUR EVENLY AND DON'T STICK.

MAKES ENOUGH TO MARINATE 1KG (2LB 4OZ)

THICK GREEK YOGURT 250ml (9fl oz)
GROUND TURMERIC 1 teaspoon
RED CHILLI POWDER 1½ teaspoons
GROUND CUMIN 2 teaspoons
GROUND CORIANDER 2 teaspoons
GARAM MASALA (see page 58)
¾ teaspoon
GINGER AND GARLIC PASTE (see page 199) 2 tablespoons
LIME JUICE from ½ lime
TOMATO PURÉE 1 tablespoon
EXTRA VIRGIN RAPESEED OIL
4 tablespoons
SALT

Put all the ingredients into a bowl or blender and whisk or whiz until smooth. Taste and adjust the seasoning. If possible, transfer to an airtight container and refrigerate overnight before use.

Put the food to be marinated into a shallow dish and pour just enough marinade over it to coat all sides. Any left over can be stored in an airtight container in the refrigerator, where it will keep for a few days if unopened.

Mixed raita

A RAITA IS SIMPLY A YOGURT-BASED ACCOMPANIMENT, IDEALLY SERVED WITH PILAU AND BIRYANI DISHES, BUT ALSO WITH FRIED AND GRILLED FOODS. SOMETIMES IT IS SIMPLY MIXED INTO COLD BOILED RICE AND EATEN AS A LIGHT MEAL. THE INGREDIENTS LISTED BELOW CAN BE ADDED TO AS YOU WISH, SO FEEL FREE TO INCLUDE ROASTED CHOPPED PEANUTS OR CASHEW NUTS, DICED BOILED POTATO, DEEP-FRIED OKRA OR ANYTHING ELSE THAT TAKES YOUR FANCY. (ANYTHING DEEP-FRIED SHOULD BE ADDED AT THE LAST MINUTE SO THAT IT REMAINS CRISP.)

SERVES 4

THICK GREEK YOGURT 200ml (7fl oz)

RED ONION 1 small, finely chopped

CUCUMBER 7.5–10cm (3–4in) piece, finely diced or grated

TOMATO 1, deseeded and finely chopped

FRESH GREEN CHILLI 1 finger-type, finely chopped

FRESH MINT 8–10 leaves, finely chopped

RED CHILLI POWDER ½ teaspoon

CUMIN SEEDS 1 teaspoon, toasted and finely crushed (see page 56)

LIME JUICE to taste

SALT

CHOPPED FRESH CORIANDER 1 tablespoon to garnish (optional)

Place the yogurt in a deep bowl and whisk well. Add all the ingredients, except the lime juice and salt, and mix them in thoroughly. Taste and season with salt and a little lime juice.

Transfer to a bowl and garnish with the coriander, if you like.

KADHI

Easy yogurt curry

QUICK TO MAKE AND LIGHT ON THE STOMACH, KADHIS ARE STAPLE DISHES THROUGHOUT INDIA – GREAT FOR FEEDING A HUNGRY FAMILY, BUT ALSO SUITABLE FOR THOSE RECOVERING FROM ILLNESS. IN THE GUJARATI COMMUNITY THEY ARE AN ESSENTIAL PART OF A THALI MEAL, WHICH CONSISTS OF SEVERAL SMALL DISHES.

SERVE WITH RICE AND PAPADS (POPPADUMS) OR WHATEVER YOU WISH.

SERVES 4–6

THICK GREEK YOGURT 250ml (9fl oz)

WATER 400ml (14fl oz)

CHICKPEA (GRAM) FLOUR
2 tablespoons

EXTRA VIRGIN RAPESEED OIL
2–3 tablespoons

CUMIN SEEDS 1 teaspoon

FRESH ROOT GINGER 5cm (2in) piece,
peeled and finely chopped

CURRY LEAVES 10–12, preferably
fresh, finely shredded; if dried, soak
in water for 10–12 minutes, and dry
thoroughly before shredding

FRESH GREEN CHILLIES 2 finger-type,
chopped

ONION 1, chopped

GROUND TURMERIC ½ teaspoon

CHOPPED FRESH CORIANDER
1 tablespoon

SALT

Put the yogurt, measured water and flour into a bowl and beat well, then set aside.

Heat the oil in a deep saucepan. When hot, add the cumin seeds, ginger, curry leaves and chillies and sauté until the seeds darken. Add the onion and cook over a medium heat until pale and soft.

Mix the turmeric with a little water to make a paste, then pour this into the onion mixture. Sauté for about 30 seconds, until the aroma changes.

Beat the yogurt again and pour it into the pan, stirring well and scraping up any bits sticking on the bottom. The mixture will thicken slightly, but add a little water if thicker than you want. Add salt to taste, then serve immediately.

Notes

This kadhi can also be used as a poaching liquid for vegetables or white fish. Some people even drink it as a soup, adding more seasoning or chopped vegetables according to taste.

To vary the flavour, try adding cracked black mustard seeds, asafoetida or fresh coriander.

MASALEDAR DAHI

Spiced yogurt for chaats

CHAAT MEANS 'LICK', AND HAS COME TO BE THE NAME USED FOR THE FINGER-LICKING SNACKS SOLD ON THE STREETS OF INDIA. YOU WILL FIND THAT VENDORS OFTEN POUR THIN SPICED YOGURT OVER THEM, AND THIS CAN BE FURTHER TOPPED WITH SOMETHING CRISP, SUCH AS CRUMBLED POORIS OR PLAIN FRIED TORTILLAS, FOR ADDED TEXTURE.

USE THE MIXTURE BELOW FOR STIRRING INTO VEGETABLE SALADS, FOR USING AS A DIP WITH KEBABS OR SNACKS OR AS A BASE FOR ADDING ROASTED NUTS. IT CAN ALSO BE MIXED INTO COLD BOILED RICE ALONG WITH SOME DICED TOMATO AND EATEN AS A SNACK OR LIGHT MEAL.

SERVES 6–8

THICK GREEK YOGURT 250ml (9fl oz)

RED CHILLI POWDER 1 heaped teaspoon

CUMIN SEEDS 1 teaspoon, toasted and finely crushed (see page 56)

FRESHLY GROUND WHITE PEPPER ¼ teaspoon

FRESH GREEN CHILLI 1 finger-type, finely chopped

CHOPPED FRESH CORIANDER 2 teaspoons

CHOPPED FRESH MINT 1 heaped teaspoon

WHITE SUGAR 1 teaspoon

YUZU OR MANGO POWDER (AAMCHUR) to taste (optional)

BLACK ROCK SALT OR HIMALAYAN PINK SALT

Pour the yogurt into a bowl and beat in all the spices, herbs and sugar. Mix in a little water to make it of pouring consistency, then add the yuzu (take care, as it is very strong) or mango powder, if using, and salt to taste.

Flavour enhancers

MOST KITCHEN CUPBOARDS ARE FULL OF FLAVOUR ENHANCERS – SALT, SUGAR, SAUCES AND MANY OTHER THINGS – THAT WE OFTEN THROW IN AT THE VERY END OF THE COOKING PROCESS TO BRING A LITTLE WOW INTO OUR FOOD. HERE ARE A FEW ENHANCERS THAT WE'VE COME UP WITH AT CAFÉ SPICE NAMASTE, AND THEY WILL CERTAINLY ADD ZING TO WHATEVER YOU'RE MAKING.

Shrimp & tamarind curry enhancer

ALL THE INGREDIENTS BELOW ARE READILY AVAILABLE IN MANY SUPERMARKETS. WHEN COMBINED, THEY PACK A SUPERB PUNCH AND LIFT PLAIN RICE OR CURRY TO NEW HEIGHTS.

MAKES 500G (1LB 2OZ)

FRESH GREEN CHILLIES 2–3, coarsely chopped

PINK SHALLOTS 3–4, coarsely chopped

GARLIC 4–5 cloves, coarsely chopped

FRESH ROOT GINGER 7.5cm (3in) piece, peeled and coarsely chopped

GALANGAL 7.5cm (3in) piece, peeled and coarsely chopped

LEMON GRASS 3–4 stems, finely chopped

TAMARIND PULP 4–5 tablespoons, or to taste (some tamarind products can be very strong)

CORIANDER SEEDS 1 tablespoon, crushed

SHRIMP PASTE 2 teaspoons

LIME JUICE 1 tablespoon

EXTRA VIRGIN RAPESEED OIL 100ml (3½fl oz)

SALT

Put all the ingredients, except the oil, into a blender and whiz to a fine paste. Season to taste with salt.

Heat the oil in a saucepan over a low heat. Add the paste and cook, stirring slowly, for a few minutes, gradually increasing the heat, until the oil separates from the paste (you will see it form a puddle). Set aside to cool.

When cold, transfer to an airtight container, seal securely and refrigerate until needed. This will keep for up to 2–3 months.

Use this sparingly, tasting as you add it, because the mixture may be quite strong.

ADRAK AUR LEHSUM MASALA

Ginger & garlic paste

THIS IS A VERY USEFUL PASTE, AS GARLIC AND GINGER ARE SO OFTEN USED IN INDIAN RECIPES. THE IMPORTANT THING IS TO WORK WITH EQUAL WEIGHTS OF GINGER AND GARLIC, WHATEVER AMOUNT YOU WANT TO MAKE. THOSE LISTED BELOW ARE JUST EXAMPLES. THE LARGER YOUR BLENDER, THE MORE YOU WILL NEED IN ORDER FOR THE BLADES TO PROCESS IT EFFICIENTLY. THIS BASIC RECIPE REQUIRES NO INGREDIENTS FROM THE SPICE BOX.

MAKES 250G (8OZ)

GARLIC 115g (4oz), roughly chopped

FRESH ROOT GINGER 115g (4oz), peeled and roughly chopped

OIL (ANY EXCEPT OLIVE OIL) about 2 tablespoons, plus extra for preserving

Put the garlic and ginger into a blender, add the oil and a dash of water and whiz to a purée. If too thick, add more water and a little more oil until you get a smooth consistency.

Transfer the paste to a container, cover with a layer of oil to preserve, seal tightly and store in the refrigerator for up to 3 months. Use as needed, always using a dry spoon and keeping the rim of the container clean. If the paste begins to dry out, pour some oil over the top before resealing.

HARA DHANIA, LAAL MIRICH AUR JEERA MASKA

Coriander, red chilli & cumin butter

ALTHOUGH FLAVOURED BUTTERS ARE NOT A TRADITIONAL PART OF INDIAN CUISINE, WE FIND THEM VERY USEFUL AS A MEANS OF ADDING FLAVOUR AND RICHNESS TO DISHES. TO USE, CUT OFF SLICES TO FLAVOUR ROAST POTATOES, CARROTS, PARSNIPS AND CHICKEN.

MAKES 250G (9OZ)

CORIANDER SEEDS 1 teaspoon

CUMIN SEEDS ¾ teaspoon

DRIED RED CHILLI FLAKES 1 teaspoon

BLACK PEPPERCORNS 6–8, crushed

BUTTER 1 × 250g (9oz) pack, at room temperature

Place all the seeds and spices in a small, heavy-based frying pan and toast over a medium heat until darkened and aromatic. Set aside to cool.

Put the butter on a chopping board and sprinkle with the toasted ingredients. Using a large knife, chop them into each other until the seasonings are very finely chopped.

Place an A4 sheet of baking parchment or clingfilm on a work surface with a long side nearest to you. Place 3–4 tablespoons of the butter on it in a row about 5cm (2in) from the near edge. Fold the parchment or film over it, then roll into a sausage shape. Twist the ends tightly to seal and place on a tray. Make as many more rolls as you can, then freeze.

Fresh raspberry, mustard, lime & cumin butter

WE SERVE A RICHER VERSION OF THIS BUTTER WITH OUR OSTRICH STEAKS AT THE RESTAURANT, BUT THE SIMPLIFIED INGREDIENTS BELOW WILL GIVE YOU SOMETHING EQUALLY DELICIOUS. KEEP IT IN YOUR FREEZER SO THAT YOU HAVE A LAST-MINUTE ENHANCER AS AND WHEN NEEDED. TO USE, CUT OFF SLICES TO PLACE ON GRILLED STEAKS, FISH OR CHICKEN, OR DOT OVER A BAKED DISH OR PIE. AS THE BUTTER MELTS, IT RELEASES A WONDERFUL FLAVOUR.

MAKES 250G (9OZ)

FRESH RASPBERRIES 150g (5½oz)

CUMIN SEEDS ¾ teaspoon

SALTED BUTTER 1 × 250g (9oz) pack, at room temperature

ENGLISH MUSTARD PASTE 1 tablespoon

FINELY GRATED LIME ZEST AND JUICE from ½ lime

Put the raspberries in a saucepan over a low heat and cook slowly, stirring often, for about 15–20 minutes, until well pulped and reduced by two-thirds. Set aside to cool.

Meanwhile, toast the cumin seeds in a small, heavy-based frying pan over a medium heat until aromatic, then crush them as finely as possible in a mortar.

Put the butter into a bowl, add the cumin and beat well with a wooden spoon. Beat in the mustard, then the lime zest and juice a bit at a time. Finally, gradually incorporate the raspberry coulis.

Place an A4 sheet of baking parchment or clingfilm on a work surface with a long side nearest to you. Place 3–4 tablespoons of the butter on it in a row about 5cm (2in) from the near edge. Fold the parchment or film over it, then roll into a sausage shape. Twist the ends tightly to seal and place on a tray. Make as many more rolls as you can, then freeze.

Worcestershire-style seasoning sauce

IN GOA THERE IS A VERY POPULAR CONDIMENT CALLED BANCAL SAUCE, WHICH IS SIMILAR TO WORCESTERSHIRE SAUCE. HERE IS MY WHISKY-LACED VERSION OF THAT FAMOUS AND VERY USEFUL FLAVOURING.

MAKES 700–750ML (1 ¼–1 ⅓ PINTS)

MALTED WHISKY 500ml (18fl oz)

FRESH ROOT GINGER 7.5cm (3in) piece, peeled and roughly chopped

GARLIC 2 cloves, roughly chopped

RED CHILLI POWDER 1–2 teaspoons

SOFT BROWN SUGAR 2 tablespoons

MALT VINEGAR 3 tablespoons

FRESH GREEN CHILLIES 2, chopped

TOMATO KETCHUP 150ml (5fl oz)

TAMARIND PULP 3 tablespoons, or to taste

EXTRA VIRGIN RAPESEED OIL 3 tablespoons

GROUND WHITE PEPPER 1 teaspoon

SALT

Put all the ingredients into a blender and whiz until smooth. Strain, pour into a sterilized bottle (see page 189) and seal tightly. Use as desired. Store in the refrigerator for 6–8 months.

CHUTT PUTTA CHAAT MASALA

All-fries spice dust

A GREAT MIXTURE FOR SPRINKLING ON FRIED PRODUCTS, FROM CHIPS TO PAKORAS, FRITTERS TO OMELETTES. IT'S ALSO GOOD ON BOILED EGGS AND FOR SEASONING BUTTER.

MAKES 95G (3 ⅓ OZ)

RED CHILLI POWDER 1 tablespoon

FINE SEA SALT 3 tablespoons

CUMIN SEEDS 1 tablespoon, toasted and finely ground (see page 56)

YUZU OR MANGO POWDER (AAMCHUR) 1 tablespoon

GROUND WHITE PEPPER 1 teaspoon

Put all the ingredients in a container and seal tightly, then shake well to combine. Use as desired. Store in a dark, cool and dry place for up to 3 months.

Note

We sometimes add ground dried mint to the basic mixture for a different flavour.

BHUJAN MASALA

Rub for grilling

MOST WHITE MEAT SUITS THIS FRESH RUB, AND THE OIL CONTENT ALLOWS IT TO KEEP WELL FOR SOME
TIME. IT IS BEST APPLIED TO FISH OR CHICKEN BEFORE ROASTING OR GRILLING.

**MAKES ENOUGH FOR COATING
UP TO 1KG (2LB 4OZ)**

EXTRA VIRGIN RAPESEED OIL 150ml (5floz)
DRIED RED CHILLIES 4–5
LIME JUICE from 1 lime
GROUND TURMERIC ½ teaspoon
FRESH CORIANDER 10–12 sprigs
FRESH MINT 20–25 sprigs
FRESH ROOT GINGER 5cm (2in) piece, peeled
and roughly chopped
GROUND CUMIN 1 teaspoon

Put all the ingredients into a blender and whiz to a paste.
Transfer to a sterilized airtight jar (see page 189) and
refrigerate for up to 6–8 months until needed.

Note

The rub also makes an ideal chicken tikka marinade if you adjust
the ingredients. First massage in 1 teaspoon ground turmeric per
1kg (2lb 4oz) of meat. Beat 150ml (5fl oz) thick Greek yogurt into
the basic rub and add salt to taste. Use to marinate the chicken.

Rub for pork or chicken

PERFECT FOR RUBBING INTO A LOIN OR SHOULDER OF PORK OR A WHOLE CHICKEN BEFORE ROASTING,
THIS MIXTURE CAN ALSO BE USED WHEN GRILLING SMALLER PIECES OF MEAT.

**MAKES ENOUGH FOR COATING
2–2.5KG (4LB 8OZ–5LB 8OZ)**

CINNAMON STICK 7.5cm (3in) piece
GREEN CARDAMOM PODS 6, lightly crushed
DRIED RED CHILLIES 6–8
EXTRA VIRGIN RAPESEED OIL 150ml (5fl oz)
SHALLOTS 4, chopped
GARLIC 6–8 cloves
FRESH ROOT GINGER 2 × 5cm (2in) pieces, peeled
TAMARIND PASTE 4 tablespoons, or to taste
HONEY 4–6 tablespoons
GROUND CORIANDER 1 tablespoon
GROUND CUMIN 1 heaped teaspoon
CURRY LEAVES 18–20, preferably fresh; if using
dried, soak in water for 10–12 minutes, and dry
thoroughly before adding

Put the cinnamon stick, cardamom pods and chillies in a
dry, heavy-based pan and toast over a gentle heat until
aromatic. Set aside to cool.

Meanwhile, heat the oil in another pan and sauté the
shallots for about 6–8 minutes, until soft. Set aside to cool.

Place all the remaining ingredients, plus the cooled spices
and shallots, in a blender and whiz to a purée. Transfer to
a sterilized airtight jar (see page 189) and refrigerate until
needed. This will keep for up to 6 months.

Note

Adding some light soy sauce to the basic rub gives it a lovely
flavour and also colours it slightly.

SINGDANA AUR KAJU CHUTNEY

Peanut, cashew & walnut pesto

THIS SPICY NUT CHUTNEY IS VERY POPULAR IN MAHARASHTRA, WHERE IT HAS A VARIETY OF USES. TRY IT AS A SIMPLE ACCOMPANIMENT TO CURRY, USE IT ON PASTA OR RICE, IN SALADS AND SANDWICHES, ADD IT TO SAUCES ... THE POSSIBILITIES ARE ENORMOUS, SO EXPERIMENT TO FIND THE WAYS YOU LIKE IT BEST.

MAKES 500G (1LB 2OZ)

SKINNED AND ROASTED PEANUTS 100g (3½oz)
CASHEW NUTS 50g (1¾oz), broken into pieces
WALNUTS 50g (1¾oz), broken into pieces
SESAME SEEDS 50g (1¾oz), toasted and cooled (see page 56)
CUMIN SEEDS 1 tablespoon, toasted and cooled (see page 56)
EXTRA VIRGIN RAPESEED OIL 250–300ml (9–10fl oz)
FRESH CORIANDER 10–12 sprigs, coarsely chopped
FRESH GREEN CHILLIES 3, coarsely chopped
GARLIC 4–5 cloves, coarsely chopped
LIME JUICE from 1 lime
WHITE SUGAR 1 teaspoon

Put all the ingredients into a blender and whiz to a smooth paste – you might need to scrape the sides of the blender several times and add a bit more oil to get the texture you want. Taste and adjust the seasoning.

Transfer to a sterilized airtight jar (see page 189) and refrigerate until needed. This will keep for up to 1 month.

Mustard, garlic & chilli mayonnaise

MAYONNAISE-BASED SAUCES ARE GREAT ACCOMPANIMENTS TO MANY FOODS. THE INGREDIENTS LISTED BELOW CAN BE COMBINED IN AMOUNTS THAT SUIT YOUR PALATE, SO I HAVE NOT GIVEN SPECIFIC QUANTITIES.
THIS BASIC RECIPE REQUIRES NO INGREDIENTS FROM THE SPICE BOX.

MAKES AS MUCH AS YOU LIKE

HOMEMADE OR SHOP-BOUGHT MAYONNAISE
GARLIC
FRESH GREEN CHILLI
PREPARED ENGLISH MUSTARD
FRESH CORIANDER STEMS
LIME JUICE

Put the mayonnaise into a bowl. Chop all the other ingredients very finely and beat them into the mayo a little at a time, tasting as you go, until you are happy with the flavour. Use the mayo as it is, or purée in a blender if you want a smoother texture.

PIRI-PIRI MASALA

Piri-piri masala

MADE FROM A SMALL AFRICAN CHILLI CALLED PIRI-PIRI, WHICH WAS INTRODUCED FROM SOUTH AMERICA, THIS SAUCE STARTED OUT AS A MARINADE FOR CHARGRILLED CHICKEN IN MOZAMBIQUE AND ANGOLA. PORTUGUESE COLONISTS TOOK IT BACK TO PORTUGAL, AND ALSO INTRODUCED IT TO GOA, WHERE IT IS NOW AN INDISPENSIBLE CLASSIC. IT WORKS WELL WITH SEAFOOD AND WHITE MEATS, BUT IS RARELY USED WITH RED MEATS. INEVITABLY, THE SAUCE HAS ACQUIRED SOME INDIAN NOTES, THE MAIN ONE BEING PALM VINEGAR.

MAKES ENOUGH FOR COATING 3–4KG (6LB 8OZ–8LB 13OZ)

DRIED RED CHILLIES 100g (3½oz) of 2 or 3 varieties

FRESH ROOT GINGER 3 × 5cm (2in) pieces, unpeeled and coarsely chopped

GARLIC 12 cloves, coarsely chopped

CORIANDER SEEDS 1½ tablespoons

CUMIN SEEDS 2 teaspoons

CINNAMON STICK 2 × 5cm (2in) pieces

BLACK PEPPERCORNS 6–8

EXTRA VIRGIN RAPESEED OIL 200ml (7fl oz), plus extra for covering

PALM OR CIDER VINEGAR 250–350ml (9–12fl oz)

Break the chillies into pieces and place in a large jar with all the remaining ingredients. Seal tightly and leave overnight, or for at least 3–4 hours, shaking now and then.

Pour the mixture into a blender and whiz to a smooth paste, adding a little more vinegar if it's very thick.

Transfer the paste to a sterilized Kilner jar or a screwtop jar that has a plastic-lined lid (see page 189) and pour a spoonful or more of oil over the surface before sealing tightly. The paste will keep indefinitely if refrigerated. If it does become a bit dry-looking, add a little vinegar and oil to revive it from time to time, taking care to wipe the rim clean and dry before resealing.

CHUKUNDER CHUTNEY

Simple beetroot chutney

THE WORD 'CHUTNEY' CAN BE A SOURCE OF CONFUSION. MANY PEOPLE THINK IT APPLIES TO COOKED MIXTURES GENERALLY CONTAINING SUGAR, SUCH AS MANGO CHUTNEY. IN INDIA, THOUGH, CHUTNEY CAN ALSO BE UNCOOKED. IT TENDS TO CONTAIN FRESH HERBS AND SPICES, WHICH ARE SIMPLY POUNDED TOGETHER AND USED AS A DIP OR SAUCE, SOMEWHAT LIKE ITALIAN PESTO.

MAKES 250G (9OZ)

BEETROOT 2, peeled and soaked in iced water for 15 minutes, then drained

BUTTER 15g (½oz)

RED CHILLI POWDER 1 teaspoon

GREEN CARDAMOM PODS 2 lightly crushed and seeds extracted

CLOVES 2

CINNAMON STICK 2.5cm (1in) piece

WHITE SUGAR 3–4 tablespoons

LIME JUICE from ½ lime

Wearing thin rubber gloves (or a couple of plastic bags) if you want to avoid staining your hands, grate the chilled beetroot.

Melt the butter in a saucepan, then add the beetroot and spices and sauté for 10–12 minutes, until much of the liquid evaporates. Stir in the sugar and cook until it forms a thin syrup. Squeeze in the lime juice, then set aside to cool before serving.

Any leftovers can be stored in a sterilized screwtop jar (see page 189) in the refrigerator for up to 3 months. If you want to make the chutney for future use, add some citric acid crystals or pectin to preserve it for longer (use the amount specified by the manufacturer).

DESSERTS & DRINKS

ZAFRANI CRÈME BRÛLÉE

Saffron & cardamom crème brûlée

HERE WE HAVE AN INTERNATIONALLY POPULAR DESSERT, THE ADDITION OF SAFFRON AND CARDAMOM GIVING IT MY OWN PARTICULAR STAMP. FOR AN EVEN MORE SOPHISTICATED VERSION, SOAK THE SUGAR IN NEUTRAL ALCOHOL, SUCH AS VODKA, BEFORE FLAMING IT.

SERVES 4

CREAMY MILK 250ml (9fl oz), preferably non-homogenized

FRESH ROOT GINGER 40g (1½oz) piece, unpeeled and coarsely chopped

GREEN CARDAMOM PODS 4–5, lightly crushed

DOUBLE CREAM 450ml (16fl oz)

VANILLA EXTRACT a few drops

EGG YOLKS 6

CASTER SUGAR about 150g (5½oz)

POWDERED SAFFRON a good pinch, or according to taste

Preheat the oven to to 150°C/300°F/Gas Mark 2 and set out 4 × 150ml (5fl oz) ramekins.

Put the milk, ginger and cardamom pods into a heavy-based saucepan and bring gently to the boil. Lower the heat and simmer until the milk has reduced by about three-quarters to 100ml (3½fl oz). Keep scraping down the sides of the pan during this reduction to prevent wastage and burning.

Allow to cool slightly, then transfer to a blender and whiz to a purée. Pass the mixture through a sieve, using the back of a spoon to press all the milk into a bowl. Discard the solids, or use them to make tea.

Return the milk to the pan, add the cream and bring to a simmer over a medium heat.

Add the vanilla extract. Stir well and slowly return the mixture to a simmer.

Meanwhile, put the egg yolks and 115g (4oz) of the caster sugar into a bowl and whisk together until frothy. Add the cream mixture and beat well. Return the mixture to the pan and stir over a gentle heat for 1–2 minutes, until the sugar has dissolved. If you want to make this in advance, at this point the mixture can be cooled, then covered and chilled for up to 24 hours.

Add the saffron a bit at a time, until the mixture has the colour you want (we like it to be quite deep).

Pour the mixture into the ramekins. Place in a deep baking tray and pour in enough hot water to come halfway up the sides of the dishes. Place in the oven and cook for about 30–35 minutes, until firm but still with a slight wobble in the centre. Set aside to cool, then cover in clingfilm and store in the refrigerator until needed.

When you're ready to serve, preheat the grill on its highest setting, or get out a kitchen blowtorch. Sprinkle half the remaining caster sugar over the cream mixture in the dishes. Heat under the grill or with the blowtorch until a thin layer of caramel forms. Sprinkle the rest of the sugar over the caramel and grill or blowtorch again to form a thick crunchy layer.

Serve immediately, or within 2–3 hours, so that the brûlée topping is still crisp.

BHAPA DAHI

Sweetened steamed yogurt

A TRADITIONAL PARSEE DISH, SWEETENED YOGURT IS SERVED ON FESTIVE OCCASIONS BEFORE THE MEAL, ALONG WITH ROSE AND NUTMEG-FLAVOURED VERMICELLI. THE USUAL PRACTICE IS TO SET IT IN PART-BAKED EARTHEN POTS, WHICH ARE THEN THROWN AWAY. HERE I GIVE A SIMPLIFIED (BUT STILL VERY SWEET) VERSION OF THE DESSERT, USING READY-MADE THICK YOGURT AND SHOP-BOUGHT CONDENSED MILK. BENGALI PURISTS WILL BE HORRIFIED!

SERVES 5–6

SAFFRON THREADS a pinch
THICK GREEK YOGURT 250ml (9fl oz)
CONDENSED MILK 300g (10½oz) canned
MILK 50ml (2fl oz)
GROUND CARDAMOM ¼ teaspoon, or to taste
PISTACHIOS 2 tablespoons, crushed or chopped
FRESH ROSE PETALS AND/OR FLAKES OF SILVER OR GOLD LEAF a few, to decorate

Preheat the oven to 160°C/325°F/Gas Mark 3.

Heat the saffron threads in a warm small frying pan over a gentle heat until crisp, then transfer to a small bowl.

Put the yogurt, condensed milk and milk into a bowl and whisk until frothy. Add the cardamom and pistachios, crumble in the saffron and beat well.

Pour the mixture into a heatproof glass bowl or a baking dish and place in a roasting tray. Put the tray on the middle shelf of the oven and pour in enough boiling water to come 1cm (½in) up the sides of the bowl or dish. Bake for 25–30 minutes, then insert a skewer to see if it is set – it should come out clean and dry. If not, give it a few more minutes. Transfer the bowl or dish to a work surface and leave to cool before covering and refrigerating.

To serve, decorate with the rose petals and/or silver or gold leaf.

See image overleaf (left)

PISTA ILAICHI DAHI

Cardamom pistachio junket

THE WORD DAHI REFERS TO CURD THAT IS SET BY COMBINING IT WITH RENNET OR BIO YOGURT. THE FORMER IS EASIER AND FASTER TO USE, BUT IT MEANS YOU HAVE TO WORK FAST TOO. FOR THIS REASON, SET OUT ALL THE NECESSARY EQUIPMENT AND PREPARE ALL THE INGREDIENTS IN ADVANCE. FOR EXTRA CREAMINESS, THE CURD CAN BE WHISKED BEFORE SERVING, OR STRAINED THROUGH A PIECE OF FINE MUSLIN.

SERVES 4–6

SAFFRON THREADS a pinch

CREAMY MILK 500ml (18fl oz), preferably non-homogenized, plus 1 extra tablespoon

SUGAR 1 tablespoon, preferably golden, but any will do

GREEN CARDAMOM PODS 2–3, lightly crushed

FRESH ROOT GINGER 5cm (½in) piece, peeled and crushed

FINELY GRATED LIME ZEST from ½ lime

SULTANAS 2 tablespoons

COARSELY CHOPPED PISTACHIOS 1 tablespoon, plus 1 teaspoon finely chopped

UNSKINNED ALMONDS 15–20, chopped, plus 6–8, finely chopped

RENNET 8–10 drops OR BIO YOGURT 1 tablespoon

WARMED HONEY for drizzling

Heat the saffron threads in a warm small frying pan over a gentle heat until crisp, then transfer to a small bowl. Warm the tablespoon of milk, pour it over the saffron and leave to infuse for 15–20 minutes.

Put the remaining milk in a saucepan along with the sugar, cardamom pods, ginger and lime zest and bring to the boil over a medium heat, stirring constantly to prevent sticking. Lower the heat and simmer for 5 minutes. Strain into a jug or bowl, add the saffron mixture and stir well.

Once the milk has settled, strain it into a clean bowl in which you wish to set it, discarding the solids. Add the sultanas, coarsely chopped pistachios and chopped almonds.

For the important step of adding the rennet, the milk needs to be at body temperature, 37°C (98.6°F), so test it with a thermometer. When it reaches that point, add the rennet and beat well. Clean the sides of the bowl with kitchen paper, then allow to sit for 6–8 minutes. When it has set, cover and transfer to the refrigerator.

If using live yogurt instead of rennet, mix it into the body-temperature milk, cover with a clean cloth and leave to rest in a warm place until set. This will take much longer (a few hours, or overnight) than it does with rennet. Transfer to the refrigerator once it has set.

Serve cold, sprinkled with the finely chopped nuts and a drizzle of some gently warmed honey. (The warming can be done by placing the bottle or jar in a bowl of hot water for a minute or so.)

See image overleaf (right)

Spiced fruit trifle

IN INDIA, TRIFLE IS ONE OF THE MOST ENDURING LEGACIES OF BRITISH INFLUENCE. ALTHOUGH OFTEN REGARDED AS A SUMMER DESSERT, IT CAN BE ENJOYED AT ANY TIME OF YEAR, MAKING USE OF WHATEVER SEASONAL FRUIT IS AVAILABLE. HERE I HAVE USED SUMMERY FRUITS, AND ALSO INCLUDED A RECIPE FOR MAKING YOUR OWN SPONGE, BUT IF PRESSED FOR TIME, YOU CAN SIMPLY BUY A READY-MADE SWISS ROLL.

SERVES 4–6

FRESH STRAWBERRIES 150–200g (5½–7oz), hulled, plus a handful of whole strawberries to decorate

ICING SUGAR for sprinkling (optional)

FRESHLY GROUND BLACK PEPPER for sprinkling (optional)

BLUEBERRIES 100g (3½oz), fresh or frozen

RASPBERRIES 100g (3½oz), fresh or frozen

GELATINE LEAVES 6 (about 10g/¼oz)

READY-MADE CUSTARD 1.2 litres (2 pints)

DOUBLE CREAM 1 litre (1¾ pints), whipped

FOR THE SPICED FRUIT SYRUP

GREEN CARDAMOM PODS 3, lightly crushed and seeds extracted for use (save the pods for flavouring other dishes)

CINNAMON STICK 5cm (2in) piece

CLOVES 2–3

BLACK PEPPERCORNS 3–4

WATER 600ml (20fl oz)

LIME 1, cut into small pieces and pips removed

WHITE SUGAR 250g (9oz)

FOR THE SWISS ROLL

LARGE EGGS 3

GOLDEN CASTER SUGAR 70g (2½oz)

SELF-RAISING FLOUR 70g (2½oz), sifted

GROUND CINNAMON OR VANILLA EXTRACT a little, to taste

ICING SUGAR for sprinkling

STRAWBERRY JAM for spreading

First make the syrup. Put all the spices in a mortar and crush coarsely. Transfer to a saucepan, add the measured water and lime and bring to the boil. Simmer for 10 minutes or so, until the spices are well infused in the liquid. Stir in the sugar, bring back to the boil, then simmer for a further 10 minutes, until the sugar has dissolved. Set aside to cool slightly, then strain into a bowl. The solids can be discarded or reused, as you wish.

If making your own Swiss roll, preheat the oven to 200°C/400°F/Gas Mark 6 and line a Swiss roll tin or shallow baking tray with greaseproof paper or baking parchment.

Break the eggs into a clean heatproof bowl and, using an electric whisk, gradually beat in the caster sugar and continue whisking until the mixture is light and foamy, cream in colour, and forms a visible trail behind the whisk. (This is easier to do, and produces a frothier result, if you place the bowl over a pan of simmering water.)

Transfer to a work surface lined with a tea towel (to prevent slipping) and gently fold in the flour a tablespoon at a time. When you have a smooth batter, mix in the cinnamon or vanilla. Pour into the prepared tin and bake for 8–10 minutes, until the sponge feels springy to the touch. Allow to cool for about 5 minutes, then turn out on to a sheet of baking parchment sprinkled with a little icing sugar. Peel off the top layer of paper and spread a generous layer of the jam over the sponge.

Using the paper to help you, roll up the sponge as tightly as possible. Set aside until cool and firm, refrigerating it if you wish.

Quarter or thickly slice the strawberries. Place in a bowl and sprinkle with a little icing sugar and black pepper, if you wish. Put the blueberries and raspberries in a saucepan, add the spiced syrup and bring to a gentle boil. Cook for a few minutes, until the fruits are soft, then whiz the mixture to a purée. Strain through a sieve, discarding any solids. Set aside until needed.

To make the jelly, soak the gelatine in a little cold water for about 10 minutes. Meanwhile, measure 500ml (18fl oz) of the syrup into a saucepan and heat gently. Squeeze the gelatine dry, then add to the syrup, stirring until completely dissolved. Depending on the look you want for your trifle, you can either set the jelly in a shallow tin, then chop it and spread it over the top, or allow to cool a bit, then pour it over the trifle. Note that it will not be a crystal clear jelly because it contains puréed fruits.

To assemble the trifle, slice the Swiss roll and arrange it on the bottom and sides of a 3.4-litre (6-pint) serving bowl. Add the strawberries, including any juice they have released, spooning it over the sponge. Now add the jelly, followed by the custard and whipped cream. Garnish with the whole strawberries.

See image overleaf

DOODH MAEWA NO RAWO

Semolina pudding

WHY SEMOLINA PUDDING IS SUCH AN INTEGRAL PART OF PARSEE CELEBRATIONS I DO NOT KNOW, BUT MOST OCCASIONS ARE UNTHINKABLE WITHOUT IT. FOR EXAMPLE, MUMS MAKE IT FIRST THING IN THE MORNING FOR A BIRTHDAY OR WEDDING, BUT IT IS ALSO SERVED AS PART OF OR AFTER MEALS. TRY IT AND YOU'LL PERHAPS UNDERSTAND WHY WE LOVE IT SO MUCH.

SERVES 4–5

MILK 500ml (18fl oz)

EVAPORATED MILK 1 × 400ml (14fl oz) can

SUNFLOWER OIL 50ml (2fl oz)

BUTTER 125g (4½oz)

FINE SEMOLINA 100g (3½oz)

WHITE SUGAR 100–150g (3½–5½oz), or to taste

WATER 100–150ml (3½–5fl oz)

GROUND CARDAMOM ¼ teaspoon, or to taste

VANILLA EXTRACT a few drops

ROSEWATER 1–2 teaspoons

FRESH ROSE PETALS 5–6, to decorate (optional)

FOR THE DECORATION

GHEE OR OIL 1–2 tablespoons

SKINNED PISTACHIOS 15–20

UNSKINNED ALMONDS 8–10, diagonally sliced about 2mm (1/16 in) thick

SUNFLOWER SEEDS 2 teaspoons OR BROKEN CASHEW NUTS 8–10, toasted (see page 56)

GREEN OR GOLDEN SULTANAS 20–30

First prepare the decoration. Heat the ghee or oil in a pan until medium–hot, then add the remaining ingredients and stir from side to side, until the cashews, if using, become pale brown. (Nuts burn easily, so take care.)

Tip the mixture into a sieve and toss a few times to release the heat. Transfer to a plate lined with kitchen paper and leave to cool. (I always prepare more than necessary because I can't resist having a nibble.)

Pour the 2 milks into a saucepan and bring to the boil. Set aside to cool.

Put the oil and butter into a saucepan over a medium heat. When the butter is fully melted and starts to bubble, add the semolina, stirring regularly to prevent it sticking and burning. As soon as it becomes a nice ivory colour, take the pan off the heat for 30 seconds or so, still stirring gently.

Carefully pour in the cooled milk, stirring constantly until free of lumps, then return to the heat.

Add the sugar and measured water, heat, stirring for about 6–8 minutes, until the sugar has dissolved, taking care that the thickened mixture doesn't stick and burn on the bottom. Taste to check if the semolina is cooked, and adjust the consistency with more milk or water, or even single cream if you wish. The semolina should be of a pouring consistency, but will become 3 or 4 times thicker as it cools.

Once you think it's ready, beat in the cardamom, then stir in the vanilla and rosewater. Taste and adjust as necessary.

Transfer the semolina to a serving dish and sprinkle with the fried nuts and sultanas.

Enjoy cold or at room temperature, scattered with a few fresh rose petals if you wish.

KAELI CHEM PARATHA

Banana parathas

PARATHAS ARE TRADITIONAL LAYERED OR FILLED FLATBREADS MADE BY NUMEROUS INDIAN COMMUNITIES. THIS ONE IS INFLUENCED BY PARSEE AND MAHARASHTRAN COOKING, AND IS A DELICIOUS TREAT AT ANY TIME OF DAY.

MAKES 8

BANANAS 3, quite soft

POTATO 1 large, boiled

FRESH GREEN CHILLIES 1–2, very finely chopped

FRESH ROOT GINGER 5cm (2in) piece, peeled and very finely chopped

CUMIN SEEDS ½ teaspoon, coarsely crushed

GROUND CARDAMOM ¼ teaspoon, or to taste

FRESH CORIANDER a few sprigs, finely chopped

SOFT BROWN SUGAR 1 teaspoon

SALT

SWEET CHUTNEY to serve

FOR THE PARATHAS

WHOLEMEAL FLOUR 250g (9oz), plus extra for dusting

SALT 1 teaspoon

EXTRA VIRGIN RAPESEED OIL 1 tablespoon, warmed

MELTED GHEE OR OIL for brushing

To make the paratha dough, sift the flour and salt into a large bowl. Make a well in the centre and pour in the warm oil. Add just a little water and mix together, adding more water a bit at a time and kneading between additions until a dough forms. Continue kneading for 2–3 minutes, until the dough comes away cleanly from the bowl and feels firm but not hard. Cover with another bowl, domed-side up, and set aside in a warm place for 1–2 hours, until the dough develops a soft texture.

Meanwhile, peel the bananas and put them into a bowl, add the remaining ingredients and mash to form a soft dough. Taste and adjust the seasoning if necessary.

Divide the banana mixture into 8 equal pieces and roll into balls. Set aside.

Place the paratha dough on a floured work surface and divide into 8 equal pieces. Roll them into balls.

Flatten a ball of dough with your palm or fingers, then use a rolling pin to roll it into a circle about 15cm (6in) in diameter. Don't worry if the shape isn't perfectly round – it takes years of experience to achieve that and sometimes it eludes even top chefs.

Place a ball of stuffing on the paratha and dampen the edges of the paratha with water. Roll out another ball of dough and place it over the stuffing. Press down to flatten them together and seal the edges.

Heat a flat griddle until hot. Meanwhile, put the melted ghee or oil in a small bowl and place a pastry brush alongside.

Brush the stuffed paratha with melted ghee or oil and place it on the griddle for about 3 minutes, until the underside is speckled brown. If the pan is too hot, the paratha will brown instantly, so let it cool down a bit before continuing. Flip the paratha over, brush with ghee or oil and cook for another 30–40 seconds. It should be glossy and cooked through.

Transfer to a lidded container lined with a clean tea towel or kitchen paper. The cloth will absorb the steam and prevent it from softening the paratha.

Cook the remainder of the parathas in the same way and keep warm.

Serve cut into pieces with a sweet chutney for dipping.

Spiced pecan pie

THE GOOEY SWEETNESS OF THE FILLING IN THIS PIE IS A WONDERFUL TREAT, SO I LIKE TO MAKE THE PASTRY WITH UNSWEETENED SHORTCRUST, AS THERE IS ALREADY ENOUGH SUGAR TO SATISFY THE SWEETEST TOOTH.

SERVES 8 PEOPLE OR 6 GREEDY PEOPLE

BUTTER 125g (4½oz)

GOLDEN SYRUP 100g (3½oz)

MUSCOVADO OR SOFT BROWN SUGAR 100g (3½oz)

EGGS 3

PECAN HALVES 300g (10½oz)

GROUND CINNAMON
¼ teaspoon, or to taste

VANILLA ICE CREAM OR FRESH CREAM to serve (optional)

FOR THE PASTRY

PLAIN FLOUR 185g (6½oz), plus extra for dusting

SALTED BUTTER 90g (3¼oz), chopped

CLOVES 2 small, finely crushed

CHILLED WATER
3–4 tablespoons

First make the pastry. Sift the flour into a large bowl, add the butter and rub it in with your fingers until the mixture resembles coarse breadcrumbs. Stir in the ground cloves.

Using a spatula, mix in the measured water a bit at a time until a dough forms. Bring it together with your hands, wrap in clingfilm and refrigerate for 15–20 minutes. Meanwhile, preheat the oven to 180°C/350°F/Gas Mark 4.

Lightly flour a work surface and roll out the pastry so that it's large enough to line a 23cm (9in) tart tin and overhang the sides by about 2cm (¾in).

Crumple a sheet of greaseproof paper and use it to line the pastry case. Fill with baking beans, uncooked rice or chickpeas. Reduce the oven temperature to 150°C/300°F/Gas Mark 2 and bake for 8–10 minutes. Set aside to cool slightly, then remove the paper and beans.

Increase the oven temperature to 180°C/350°F/Gas Mark 4.

To make the filling, put the butter, syrup and sugar in a saucepan and heat gently until the sugar dissolves.

Beat the eggs in a bowl until light and frothy. Gradually pour in the warm sugar mixture, folding it together with a spatula as you do so.

Chop half the pecans and stir them into the egg mixture along with the cinnamon. Pour into the baked pastry case and arrange the remaining pecan halves on top. Bake in the centre of the oven for 12–15 minutes, until bubbling and golden. Set aside to cool and firm up.

Trim off the excess pastry, then remove the pie from the tin and serve with vanilla ice cream or fresh cream, if you wish.

BOLO REI

King's cake

AS THE NAME SUGGESTS, THIS CAKE IS FIT FOR A KING, AND DATES FROM A TIME WHEN PISTACHIOS WERE QUITE RARE AND EXPENSIVE, SO ENJOYED ONLY BY THE ELITE. YOU MIGHT LIKE TO KNOW THAT THE CAKE MIXTURE CAN ALSO BE USED TO MAKE BISCUITS. EITHER WAY, I SUGGEST YOU TUCK IN AT TEATIME AND YOU WILL FEEL PRETTY SPECIAL TOO!

SERVES 16–20

BUTTER 375g (13oz), at room temperature

CASTER SUGAR 375g (13oz)

EGGS 5, plus 4 extra yolks

PLAIN FLOUR 250g (9oz)

BAKING POWDER 1 teaspoon

SALT ½ teaspoon

FINE SEMOLINA 125g (4½oz)

GROUND ALMONDS 300g (10½oz)

GROUND PISTACHIOS 300g (10½oz)

GREEN CARDAMOM PODS 10–12, lightly crushed and seeds extracted and finely ground for use (save the pods for flavouring other dishes)

VANILLA EXTRACT 1 teaspoon

FOR THE TOPPING

WHITE CHOCOLATE 250g (9oz), broken into pieces or chopped

GROUND PISTACHIOS 50g (1¾oz)

Preheat the oven to 160°C/325°F/Gas Mark 3. Line a 24 × 20cm (9½ × 8in) rectangular cake tin with greaseproof paper.

Put the butter and sugar into a bowl and beat together until smooth and creamy. Mix in the eggs and yolks, but don't beat them in.

Sift in the flour, baking powder and salt and stir well to combine. Mix in the semolina, ground nuts and ground cardamom seeds, then add vanilla.

Pour the batter into the prepared tin and bake for 10 minutes, then lower the temperature to 140°C/275°F/Gas Mark 1 and bake for a further 40–50 minutes, until a skewer inserted in the middle comes out clean.

Set aside to cool in the tin. The cake is crumbly and delicate, so carefully turn it out, peel off the paper and place on a rack.

To make the topping, melt the chocolate in a heatproof bowl set over a pan of simmering water. Take off the heat and mix in the ground pistachios, then pour over the cake. Allow to set, then cut into small squares and present in mini paper cases.

FOODNA NI CHAI

Mint & lemon grass tea

PARSEES SIMPLY LOVE THIS TEA AND IT'S THE PERFECT PALATE-CLEANSING ACCOMPANIMENT TO THE SPICY DISHES IN THIS BOOK. THE MINT COMES FROM OUR PERSIAN HERITAGE, BUT THE LEMON GRASS WAS PROBABLY INTRODUCED FROM INDIA AT A TIME WHEN TEA LEAVES WERE NOT COMMONLY AVAILABLE AND PEOPLE INSTEAD DRANK HOT WATER FLAVOURED WITH THINGS SUCH AS FRESH ROOT GINGER OR LIME. THIS RECIPE DOES INCLUDE TEA LEAVES, AND WHILE YOU CAN USE WHATEVER TYPE YOU LIKE, ORANGE PEKOE – ESPECIALLY THE GOLDEN VARIETY – PRODUCES A WONDERFUL COLOUR.

THREE DIFFERENT WAYS OF MAKING THIS TEA ARE GIVEN BELOW. INDIANS TEND TO DRINK IT WITH HOT MILK BECAUSE WE LIKE IT TO REMAIN HOT FOR AS LONG AS POSSIBLE, BUT IT'S ALSO A HABIT FROM THE DAYS WHEN MILK NEEDED TO BE BOILED TO PREVENT IT CURDLING.

MAKES 4 LARGE CUPS

WATER 1 litre (1¾ pints)
FRESH MINT 1 sprig, leaves torn
LEMON GRASS 1 stem, chopped
TEA LEAVES 3–4 teaspoons
HOT OR COLD MILK to serve

METHOD 1

Put the measured water into a saucepan with the mint and lemon grass and bring to the boil. Put the tea leaves into a teapot and pour the boiling water over them. Cover and infuse for 2–3 minutes, then serve with hot or cold milk, as you wish.

METHOD 2

Put the water into a saucepan with the mint, lemon grass and tea leaves. Bring to the boil, then pour into a teapot and strain into individual cups. Serve with hot or cold milk, as you wish.

METHOD 3

Put the water into a saucepan with the mint and lemon grass and bring to the boil. Add the tea leaves and return to the boil. Add milk to taste and again return to the boil. Take off the heat, cover with a lid and leave to settle for 2–3 minutes. Pour and serve.

ADRAKI ANAAR SHURBUT

Spring chilli blossom

MY FELLOW INDIANS LOVE BRIGHT COLOURS, SO SHERBET DRINKS ARE MADE IN ALL SORTS OF 'VIOLENT' SHADES. THE CONCOCTION BELOW WAS CREATED BY MY SON JAMSHEED, WHO IS BECOMING QUITE EXPERT AT MIXING DRINKS.

**MAKES 1 LARGE OR
2 SMALL DRINKS**

DRIED RED CHILLI, preferably Kashmiri,
1–2 pieces
CHOPPED FRESH ROOT GINGER
1 tablespoon
CINNAMON STICK 1
VANILLA EXTRACT 1 teaspoon (optional)
ORANGE ZEST from 1 orange, thinly sliced
POMEGRANATE JUICE 200ml (7fl oz)
COX'S APPLE JUICE 4 tablespoons
ICE CUBES AND CRUSHED ICE
GRENADINE 2 teaspoons

Put the chilli, ginger, cinnamon, vanilla, if using, and orange zest in a pan and toast over a low heat until lightly browned.

Put the pomegranate and apple juices into a cocktail shaker or large screwtop jar, along with the toasted spice mixture and some ice cubes. Shake for 20 seconds, then strain into a large glass or 2 small glasses half-filled with crushed ice.

Drizzle with the grenadine and serve straight away.

Note

The spices left in the strainer can be reused for flavouring a neutral spirit, such as vodka.

Indian summer

HERE IS A DELIGHTFUL NON-ALCOHOLIC SUMMER COCKTAIL PACKED WITH FLAVOURS FROM THE EAST. AS WITH THE PREVIOUS RECIPE, THE SPICES LEFT IN THE STRAINER CAN BE REUSED FOR FLAVOURING SOMETHING ELSE.

**MAKES 1 LARGE OR
2 SMALL DRINKS**

CINNAMON STICKS 2–3

ELDERFLOWER CORDIAL 3 tablespoons

SOFT BROWN SUGAR ½ tablespoon

CHOPPED FRESH ROOT GINGER 1 tablespoon

FRESH MINT 6–8 leaves and stems, plus 1–2 sprigs to decorate

CRUSHED ICE

MANGO JUICE 90ml (3½fl oz)

POMEGRANATE JUICE 2 tablespoons

SODA WATER 2 tablespoons

GRENADINE OR BERRY SYRUP 1 tablespoon

Toast the cinnamon in a pan over a low heat for about 2 minutes, until aromatic. Drizzle with 1 teaspoon of the elderflower cordial, then sprinkle a little of the sugar over the top. Heat for about 20 seconds, then add half the ginger and all the mint stems. Stir briefly and heat for 1 minute, before turning off the heat.

Put the mint leaves into a 350ml (12fl oz) glass or divide between 2 small glasses and mix in the remaining sugar and ginger. Add enough crushed ice to half-fill the glass or glasses, then add the spice mixture from the pan and stir well.

Pour in the mango and pomegranate juices, followed by the soda water. Top up the glass or glasses with crushed ice and drizzle the grenadine or berry syrup over the top. Decorate with the mint sprig or sprigs and serve straight away.

Twisted Pimm's cocktail

AS EVERYONE KNOWS, PIMM'S IS A CLASSIC SUMMER DRINK IN BRITAIN, SO I
HAVE DEVISED MY OWN SPICED VERSION TO MAKE IT THAT BIT DIFFERENT.
IF YOU WANT TO MAKE IT EVEN MORE INTERESTING, ADD A FEW SLICES OF
NECTARINE AND A LITTLE CHOPPED LEMON GRASS. AS A FINAL FLOURISH, ADD
A LEMON GRASS SWIZZLE STICK.

MAKES 1 LARGE OR 2 SMALL DRINKS

CINNAMON STICK 1

GREEN CARDAMOM PODS 2

CLOVES 5

CHOPPED FRESH ROOT GINGER 2 tablespoons

FRESH MINT 1 long sprig, leaves torn and
stem crushed, plus 1–2 sprigs to decorate

PIMM'S NO.1 50ml (2fl oz)

SOFT BROWN SUGAR 1½ teaspoons

LEMON 1

ORANGE 1

CRUSHED ICE

LEMONADE 500ml (18fl oz)

ROSE SYRUP 1 tablespoon (rosehip syrup
may be used instead, but the flavour will
be different)

Put the cinnamon stick, cardamom pods
and cloves in a pan over a low heat and
toast for 20 seconds. Add the ginger and
crushed mint stem and stir for about
2 minutes.

Turn off the heat, add the Pimm's and
the sugar to the pan and give it a light
stir until the sugar has dissolved.

Cut 4–5 semicircular slices of the lemon
and orange and place in a 225–300ml
(8–10fl oz) glass along with the torn mint
leaves, or divide between 2 small glasses.
Use a swizzle stick or the handle of a
wooden spoon to press down lightly on
the fruit and leaves to release some of
their juices.

Add a handful of crushed ice to the glass
or a smaller amount to the small glasses
and lightly stir it around, then pour in
the spiced Pimm's mixture. Add enough
crushed ice to fill the glass or glasses
about three-quarters full. Top up with
the lemonade, leaving a little room for
the garnish. Stir lightly, making sure to
incorporate all the fruit at the bottom.

Drizzle the rose syrup over the ice.
Decorate with the mint sprig or sprigs,
and grate a little lemon and orange zest
over the top.

Cocorumba

ALTHOUGH INDIA IS THE WORLD'S LARGEST PRODUCER OF SUGAR CANE, IT IS NOT WIDELY KNOWN THAT IT ALSO PRODUCES THE MOST RUM. THAT'S BECAUSE IT'S ALL CONSUMED WITHIN THE COUNTRY. RECENTLY, HOWEVER, INDIA'S FAVOURITE BRAND, OLD MONK, HAS BECOME AVAILABLE IN SOME DUTY-FREE OUTLETS.

MAKES 1 LARGE OR 2 SMALL DRINKS

CLOVES 6–7

CHOPPED FRESH ROOT GINGER 2 tablespoons

CINNAMON STICKS 2–3

FRESH MINT 10 leaves, with stems, plus 1–2 sprigs to garnish

FINELY GRATED ORANGE ZEST from 1 orange

RUM, PREFERABLY APPLETON ESTATE 2–3 tablespoons

SOFT BROWN SUGAR ½ tablespoon

ELDERFLOWER CORDIAL 3 tablespoons

COCONUT WATER WITH BITS 250ml (9fl oz)

ICE CUBES 5–6

CRUSHED ICE

FINELY GRATED LEMON ZEST from 1 lemon

ROSE SYRUP 1 teaspoon (rosehip syrup may be used instead, but the flavour will be different)

Put the cloves, ginger, cinnamon sticks, mint stems and three-quarters of the orange zest into a pan over a low heat and toast lightly. Add the rum, immediately turn off the heat and stir for about 20 seconds.

Put the sugar into a cocktail shaker or screwtop jar and add the mint leaves, elderflower cordial and coconut water. Add the ice cubes and shake lightly, then swirl for 10–15 seconds, as you don't want to break up the ingredients too much.

Take a 350ml (12fl oz) glass or 2 small glasses and half-fill with crushed ice. Pour in the spiced rum mixture and stir with a spoon, then add your shaker ingredients, including the ice cubes. Top up the glass with crushed ice.

Garnish with the lemon zest and the remaining orange zest plus the mint sprig or sprigs. Drizzle the rose syrup over the top and serve straight away.

CHAAS

Buttermilk

COME SUMMERTIME, WHEN THE HEAT RISES, INDIANS LOVE TO COOL DOWN BY DRINKING BUTTERMILK. THE BASIC RECIPE BELOW IS VERY SIMPLE, BUT YOU CAN ENLIVEN IT WITH FRESH MINT LEAVES AND CRUSHED FRESH ROOT GINGER, OR EVEN ADD A LITTLE GARLIC AND GREEN CHILLI ALONG WITH FRESH CORIANDER AND MINT.

SERVES 3–4

THICK GREEK YOGURT 200ml (7fl oz)
WATER 500ml (18fl oz)
CUMIN SEEDS ¼ teaspoon, toasted and ground (see page 56)
SALT a pinch
ICE CUBES (optional)

Put the yogurt and measured water into a bowl and beat thoroughly until completely smooth.

Add the cumin and salt, mix well and pour into glasses, adding ice cubes if you wish.

MASALA CHAAS

Spiced buttermilk

HERE A SPICE MIXTURE CALLED A VAGHAAR OR TADKA IS ADDED TO THE BASIC BUTTERMILK RECIPE TO MAKE AN UNUSUAL AND REFRESHING DRINK. TO RING THE CHANGES, TRY ADDING SOME FINELY SHREDDED FRESH CORIANDER AND CURRY LEAVES AT THE SAME TIME AS THE MUSTARD SEEDS.

SERVES 3–4

EXTRA VIRGIN RAPESEED OIL 2 teapoons
BLACK MUSTARD SEEDS ¼ teaspoon
CUMIN SEEDS ¼ teaspoon
BUTTERMILK 1 quantity (see recipe above)
SALT

Heat the oil in a small frying pan. Add the mustard seeds and immediately cover with a lid while they crackle and pop. When the noise stops, lower the heat, add the cumin seeds and sauté until brown.

Pour the buttermilk into a jug and quickly stir in the spice mixture. Add salt to taste.

Index

Acknowledgements

I owe a huge debt of gratitude to my assistant, Nitin Kapoor, who has worked tirelessly to keep me and this book on track. He carefully typed up all my recipes from messy scrawls – a necessity, as the computer and I are not the best of friends and I can't be trusted to save things correctly. He then pushed me to work through the edited manuscript when my restaurant day was over, leaving me reminders and sending me text messages before he himself went to bed. Without him, this book would never have seen the light of day, so thank you, Nitin.

Thanks also to my son, Mr Jamsheed Todiwala, who created all the recipes in the drinks section with me.

In addition, I want to thank my wife Pervin, who has provided unwavering support through all of my endeavours. She too has had a big hand in getting this book to materialize and I will be forever grateful.

TRIFLE BOWL KINDLY SUPPLIED BY WILLIAM YEOWARD (WWW.WILLIAMYEOWARDCRYSTAL.COM).

SPICE BOX EXPERTLY CRAFTED BY PETER WILLIAMS.